5 STEPS TO A 5™
AP Human Geography
2020

ELITE STUDENT EDITION

5 STEPS TO A 5™

AP Human Geography

2020

Carol Ann Gillespie, PhD

New York Chicago San Francisco Athens London Madrid
Mexico City Milan New Delhi Singapore Sydney Toronto

1 2 3 4 5 6 7 8 9   LHS   24 23 22 21 20 19   (Cross-Platform Prep Course only)
1 2 3 4 5 6 7 8 9   LHS   24 23 22 21 20 19   (Elite Student Edition)

ISBN   978-1-260-45577-9   (Cross-Platform Prep Course only)
MHID   1-260-45577-7

e-ISBN   978-1-260-45578-6   (Cross-Platform Prep Course only)
e-MHID   1-260-45578-5

ISBN   978-1-260-45579-3   (Elite Student Edition)
MHID   1-260-45579-3

e-ISBN   978-1-260-45580-9   (Elite Student Edition)
e-MHID   1-260-45580-7

The series editor was Grace Freedson, and the project editor was Del Franz.
Series design by Jane Tenenbaum.

McGraw-Hill Education products are available at special quantity discounts to use as premiums and sales promotions or for use in corporate training programs. To contact a representative, please visit the Contact Us pages at www.mhprofessional.com.

CONTENTS

ELITE STUDENT EDITION

5 Minutes to a 5

PREFACE

Welcome to the wonderful adventure of Advanced Placement (AP) Human Geography! AP Human Geography is the study of the world and its inhabitants in spatial terms. In your AP class, you have examined the world's cultures, economic and urban systems, political organization, and other aspects of human geography. It may seem to be a daunting task to review all those models, important concepts, and systems, but don't despair! This review guide will give you a chance to undertake a solid review of AP Human Geography, as well as train you in valuable test-taking strategies.

This study guide will help you plan your review strategy for the AP Human Geography exam. Various review plans are outlined so you can choose the one that best meets your needs. Test-taking skills are also taught in this guide so you can approach the AP Human Geography exam with confidence! Turn to the Introduction to learn about the 5-step study program and how it can help you to organize your exam preparation.

ACKNOWLEDGMENTS

I would like to thank some of the wonderful people I have worked with and learned from during the past several years of the Advanced Placement Human Geography readings and appreciate your support and encouragement: Barbara Hildebrant, David Lanegran, John Trites, Debbie Lange, Judy Ware, Paul Gray, Kelly Swanson, Don Peterson, Hank Bullamore, Dan Berry, Jon Moore, Sarah Bednarz, Catherine Lockwood, Mike Sublett, Max Lu, and many other friends and colleagues from the past readings. I also owe a huge debt of gratitude to Del Franz, my editor, for his patience and apt guidance throughout the production process. Last, I especially thank my husband, Mike and my sons, Josh, Dave, and Kevin for their encouragement and support.

ABOUT THE AUTHOR

CAROL ANN GILLESPIE teaches Advanced Placement Human Geography and is the author of several books on geography. She has served as a reader, leader, and question writer for Advanced Placement Human Geography since the inaugural reading in 2001. The mother of three grown sons and grandmother of two granddaughters, she and her husband make their home in Cranberry Township, Pennsylvania. Dr. Gillespie spends most of her free time writing, cycling, and hiking in West Virginia.

INTRODUCTION: THE 5-STEP PROGRAM

This book is organized as a 5-step program to prepare you for success on the AP Human Geography exam. These steps will provide you with essential skills and test-taking strategies and give you practice so you can score the perfect 5. Here are the 5 steps.

STEP 1: Set Up Your Study Program

In this step you will read a brief overview of the AP Human Geography exam. This includes an outline of topics and the approximate percentage of the exam that will test knowledge of each topic. You will learn:

- Background information about the AP exam
- Reasons for taking the exam
- What to bring to the exam
- Additional tips to prepare for the exam
- How to select the exam preparation plan that's right for you
- Calendars for three suggested plans

STEP 2: Determine Your Test Readiness

In this step, you will take a diagnostic exam in AP Human Geography. This full-length practice AP Human Geography exam will show you what you're up against and give you an idea of how prepared you are before beginning your study program. Use the diagnostic test to help you identify weak areas in which you will need to focus your review.

- Go through the diagnostic exam step-by-step and question-by-question to build your confidence level.
- Review the correct answers and explanations so that you see what you do and do not understand.
- Customize your study program based on your level of test readiness and the areas you most need to review.

STEP 3: Develop Strategies for Success

In this step, you will learn strategies that will help you do your best on the exam. These strategies show you:

- How to read multiple-choice questions
- How to answer multiple-choice questions, including how to improve your chances of guessing correctly when you don't know an answer
- How to answer free-response questions

Included are frequently-asked questions and advice taken from my experience as a reader of the AP Human Geography exam.

STEP 4: Review the Knowledge You Need to Score High

In this step, you will review the material you need to know for the exam. This review section comprises most of this book. It contains major content areas, key concepts and models, vocabulary lists, and review questions. The material is organized by major themes covered in the AP Human Geography course. Each unit will serve to refresh your memory of the key terms, concepts, and facts relating to the main theme covered.

STEP 5: Build Your Test-Taking Confidence

In Step 5, you will finish preparing for the exam by taking two full-length practice exams modeled after the actual Advanced Placement Human Geography examination. Each test is followed by a section that explains the correct answers for each question so you learn from any mistakes and understand the answers you have missed. The questions in these practice exams are not questions from previous AP exams; however, they are modeled after the questions that are typically asked in an actual exam.

- Use the strategies provided in Chapters 4 and 5 of this guide for the multiple-choice questions and the free-response questions.
- Read the explanations provided for each question and make sure you understand the strategy and reasoning behind each answer.

Finally, at the back of this guide, you'll find helpful resources to aid your preparation. Use these resources to review and improve your knowledge and understanding of AP Human Geography topics. These resources include:

- Glossary
- Key Geographic Models and Their Creators
- Recommended Reading
- Useful Websites

The Graphics Used in this Book

Icons

To emphasize particularly important ideas, strategies, and tips, we've used several icons throughout this book. An icon in the margin will alert you that you should pay special attention to the accompanying text. The three icons you'll find in this book are:

 The Key Idea icon points out a very important concept or fact that you should not pass over.

 The Strategy icon calls your attention to a problem-solving or test-taking strategy that we recommend you try.

 The Tip icon indicates a tip that you might find useful.

Boldface Type

We have boldfaced key terms when they are introduced and explained in the text of the review chapters. Use the key terms list at the beginning of Chapters 6 through 12 to review and check your knowledge; then, if there's a term you don't know, look for the term in boldface in the chapter text to find the definition and get the explanation you'll need. Words that are boldfaced in the text also appear in the Glossary located in the Appendixes of the book. The Glossary contains definitions of key geographic terms and concepts.

5 STEPS TO A 5™

AP Human Geography

2020

STEP 1

Set Up Your Study Program

CHAPTER 1

What You Need to Know About the AP Human Geography Exam

IN THIS CHAPTER

Summary: Learn background information on the AP Human Geography program, the AP Human Geography exam, and how the exam is scored. Learn about the two types of test questions, the topics tested, and test-taking tips.

Key Ideas

✪ Many colleges and universities award credit for exam scores of 3 and above; others give credit only for exam scores of 4 or 5.

✪ Multiple-choice questions reflect content areas based on the seven major themes of AP Human Geography.

✪ Free-response essay questions require synthesis and application of two or more topics from the seven major themes of AP Human Geography.

The Basics

What Is the Advanced Placement Program?

In 1955 the College Board introduced the Advanced Placement program to give high school students the opportunity to earn college credit while still in high school. The AP program now serves over 2.4 million enterprising high school students. Thirty-seven different AP courses are now offered with AP exams administered every May. The first AP Human Geography exam was given in 2001, and the number of students successfully taking this exam has exponentially expanded. The AP exam is offered in many subjects in social studies besides human geography, including European history, world history, US history, US government and politics, comparative government, microeconomics, macroeconomics, and psychology.

Who Writes and Scores the AP Human Geography Exam?

The AP Human Geography exam is written by high school, college, and university instructors who actually teach introductory-level human geography in their schools. A committee called the Test Development Committee meets to select and refine exam questions. The questions are finally field-tested before they are included on the AP Human Geography exam. Multiple-choice questions on the AP Human Geography exam are scored electronically; the free-response questions are scored by a group of high school, college, and university instructors, who meet in a central location in June following the May administration of the exam. Each reader, as these instructors are called, is carefully checked and evaluated during the entire scoring process (called a reading) to ensure accuracy and consistency of scoring. In this way, each AP Human Geography test-taker is guaranteed a fair exam scoring process.

About the AP Human Geography Exam

What Should You Study for the AP Human Geography Exam?

The exam tests your knowledge of the seven major themes of human geography— (1) geographical concepts and skills, (2) population, (3) culture, (4) the political organization of space, (5) agricultural and rural land use, (6) industrialization and economic development, and (7) cities and urban development. This guide will help you review the main ideas, models, terms, and concepts you will need to know to score well on the exam.

What Kind of Questions Will You Be Asked on the AP Human Geography Exam?

The exam consists of two sections—multiple-choice and free-response questions (FRQs). There are 75 multiple-choice questions in Section I of the exam and three free-response questions in Section II of the exam. Each of these two sections accounts for half of your exam grade. You should expect to interpret maps, graphs, charts, photographs, and tables on both sections of the exam.

How Long Do You Have to Answer the Questions?

The exam is two hours and 15 minutes long and is timed. You will be given 60 minutes to answer the 75 multiple-choice questions in Section I and 75 minutes to answer the three free-response questions in Section II. There will be a 5-minute break between exam sections. In Chapters 4 and 5 of this book, you'll find some tips on how to pace yourself on both sections so you have enough time to attempt all the questions.

What Should You Study for the Exam?

The test questions will be divided among the different topics in the following percentages:

Geography: Its Nature and Perspectives	5–10 percent
Population	13–17 percent
Cultural Patterns and Processes	13–17 percent
Political Organization of Space	13–17 percent
Agriculture and Rural Land Use	13–17 percent
Industrialization and Economic Development	13–17 percent
Cities and Urban Land Use	13–17 percent

How Is the Exam Scored?

Multiple-Choice Section

There are 75 multiple-choice questions on the first section of the exam. Your score is based on the total number of multiple-choice questions you answer correctly. That means that you should definitely take a guess and try not to leave any answers blank! Your goal is to get as many correct answers as possible. There is no longer any penalty for guessing as was the case in previous years. Try to get at least 50 of the 75 multiple-choice answers correct—that will help give you a score of 4 or 5 on the exam.

Free-Response Questions

The three free-response essay questions on the exam will be worth from 6 to 12 points each. You will not know how many points each question is worth, however. Your goal is to *read very carefully* each word in each sentence of the questions and answer the questions completely and in detail. When the essays are scored, the readers will look for specific concepts, explanations, and descriptions in your answer. If you do not give the correct information, you will not receive points. If you give the correct information in excellent detail, you will receive the maximum points allowed for that part of the essay question. A "somewhat correct but not quite complete" response will earn you a smaller number of points. The reader grading your exam will add up your points. The total points you earned on all three essays need to add up to at least 60 percent of the total available points for you to earn a 4 or a 5 on the overall exam.

What Does Your Exam Score Mean?

The results of both the multiple-choice section and the free-response section are combined and the total raw score is converted to a composite score from 1 to 5 on the Advanced Placement 5-point scale below. When you receive your exam score in early July, it will be a number from 1 to 5. These scores mean:

- 5–Extremely well qualified
- 4–Well qualified
- 3–Qualified
- 2–Possibly qualified
- 1–No recommendation

How Do You Get Credit at a College for a Good Score?

Check with the admissions offices of the colleges and universities you are interested in attending and ask for their policy regarding awarding of credit for the AP Human Geography exam. Most colleges also post this information on their Websites. The chances are very good that a score of 4 or 5 will provide either introductory geography or general education credit and save you the time and expense of taking those credits at a much higher cost! Your freshman year will be very busy, and you will want to save your time for classes that are in your major course of study. If you earned a score of 3 on the exam, do not despair! Many schools also give credit for a 3, so be sure and check! Even if you don't earn credit, the experience of doing college-level work while still in high school is very valuable. It helps freshman students adjust more quickly to the increased rigors of a heavier college course load.

How Do You Register for the Exam?

Your high school will register you and administer the exam. Check with your AP Human Geography teacher or guidance counselor to make sure you are registered to take it in May.

If you are being homeschooled, you will need to find a local high school that is willing to proctor the exam for you. Your parents will need to contact the local school guidance counselor or principal and make the necessary arrangements. Do this early—preferably in January, so you do not miss the sign-up deadline in March. The high school does *not* have to actually teach AP Human Geography in order to allow you to take the exam there. Anyone who administers *any* AP exam at the school can proctor it for you!

What Is the Cost to Take the Exam?

The current cost of the AP exam is $94 and $124 for exams administered outside the United States and Canada. The fee usually increases a little each year. Pay the fee when you register to take the exam.

What Should You Bring to the Exam?

You should bring the following items:

1. Number-two pencils—several sharp ones to fill in the multiple-choice bubbles on the score sheet. No mechanical pencils are allowed.
2. An eraser.
3. Pens (blue or black ink only) for the free-response essay section. Ballpoint pens do not smear like pencils. Do not use gel pens, as they smear.
4. Bring a watch so you can plan your exam time in case there is no wall clock in the exam room. No beeper alarms are permitted, however!
5. Bring a government-issued or school ID and your social security number for exam entrance and registration purposes.
6. Bring a warm garment such as sweatshirt or sweater in case the exam room is chilly.

These items **cannot** be brought to the exam:

1. Cell phones, iPhones, smartwatches, laptops, tablet computers, Bluetooth devices, portable listening or recording devices, cameras, or any electronic device (unless approved for exam-taking purposes).
2. Books, highlighters, rulers, correction fluid, or any other office supplies.
3. Calculators.
4. Portable music players and devices.
5. Timers or other devices that beep.
6. Food or drinks, including bottled water.

When Will You Get Your Score?

You will need a College Board account to get your AP exam score. Go to https://cbaccount.collegeboard.org/iamweb/smartRegister?appId=287&DURL=https://apscore.collegeboard.org/scores/view-your-scores?appId=287&DURL=https://apscore.collegeboard.org/scores/view-your-scores to create your personal account to access your scores online and also to send them to colleges. This account is free so do it now!

Additional Resources to Prepare for Exam

The College Board has provided extra online resources for you to help you prepare for the AP exam! Go to https://apstudent.collegeboard.org/apcourse/ap-human-geography/exam-practice to find resources such as: sample questions and responses, exam practice tips, and scoring guidelines for past free-response questions (FRQs).

How Can You Get in Touch with the Advanced Placement Program?

If you would like additional information on AP Human Geography or want to register for the exam, contact:

College Board intends all communication to come via their website:
Phone: 888-225-5427
International callers: 212-632-1780
Fax: 610-290-8979
Email: apstudents@info.collegeboard.org
Web: https://apstudent.collegeboard.org/home

CHAPTER 2

How to Plan Your Time

IN THIS CHAPTER

Summary: Your review for the AP Human Geography exam depends on your study habits and how much time you have to review before the exam.

Key Idea

✪ Choose the study plan that is best suited to your needs!

Three Approaches to Preparing for the AP Human Geography Exam

The type of exam-review program you choose to use is up to you. No one knows you better than you! Think about how you study, how much time you have to review for the exam, and what you like and dislike doing. Look over the following three study plans and find the one that will suit your study habits and time frame best. Don't hesitate to adapt any of these plans specifically to your needs.

You're a full-school-year prep student if:

1. You really love human geography.
2. You plan to major in geography in college.
3. You like to get things done and never put off doing your work.
4. You make an outline, a to-do list, or a schedule to plan your work.
5. You must be prepared for this exam—it is imperative!
6. You totally agree that "If you fail to plan, you plan to fail!"

If this is you, choose **Plan A!**
You're a one-semester prep student if:

1. Human geography is kind of interesting to you.
2. Most of the time you plan your work in advance.
3. You like to know what to expect, but don't get too shook up by surprises.
4. You are never late for appointments.
5. You want to do well on the test but feel that starting to review too early wouldn't help you much. At the same time, you don't like to leave things to the last minute.

If this fits you, consider **Plan B.**
You're a six-week prep student if:

1. Human geography interests you a bit.
2. You thrive on tight deadlines.
3. You work well under pressure.
4. You feel adequately prepared already for the exam.
5. You don't mind surprises and don't feel a lot of pressure to do well on the test.
6. This planning approach has worked for you well in the past.

If this planning approach describes you, consider **Plan C.**

Check out the following calendars for plans A, B, and C. One of these plans will fit your time frame and learning style. Once you choose a review plan, commit to it and follow through!

Plan A: You Have a Year to Review

Check off the activities as you complete them.

SEPTEMBER–OCTOBER
— Decide which review plan you need.
— Read Chapter 1 of this book.
— Check out the diagnostic test in Chapter 3 to get a feel for what is expected of you on the AP Human Geography exam.
— Go to the College Board's AP website. Check it out and become informed.
— Begin to study the Step 4 section of this guide.
— Read some of the books on the suggested reading list in the back of this guide.
— Familiarize yourself with this book as a resource to prepare for the exam.

NOVEMBER
— Read Chapter 5 of this guide to begin to prepare for the free-response questions on the AP Human Geography exam.
— Keep reading the books on the suggested reading list at the back of this guide.
— Read and study the human geography review sections of this book that match the subjects you are studying in your AP class.
— Learn and review maps and locations using the review games and activities on the websites in the list at the back of this guide.

DECEMBER
— Review the human geography sections in this guide that match what you have already covered in class.
— Keep reading the suggested books on the reading list for valuable background information for the exam.
— Keep practicing map interpretation skills using the websites listed at the back of this guide.

JANUARY
— Choose two essay questions at the end of each chapter in your AP Human Geography textbook that you have covered so far this year. Close your book and give yourself 20 minutes to write accurate and thorough short essays to answer the questions.
— Join a study group of fellow students to review for the AP exam (or start such a group yourself!).
— Keep reading books and magazines about the world and human geography.

— Study the sections in this guide that correspond to the material you are currently covering in class.
— Spend an hour or two each week practicing map interpretation and review games and activities.

FEBRUARY–MARCH
— Write essays for the free-response questions from the diagnostic test in Chapter 3.
— Continue reviewing content from Chapters 6 through 12 in this book.
— Read Chapter 4 on the multiple-choice section.
— Take the multiple-choice section in the diagnostic test.
— Review the list of models and their creators at the back of this guide.

APRIL
— Take Practice Test 1 (Step 5) in the first week of April.
— Evaluate your strengths and weaknesses. What topics are you unclear about? What don't you really understand?
— Go back and study the chapters with topics you didn't completely understand to improve your knowledge.
— Review the key terms for Chapters 6 through12 in this guide to review key concepts, theories, and content.
— Scan the Glossary at the back of this guide. Make sure you understand and can use each term correctly.

FIRST TWO WEEKS OF MAY—YOU'RE ALMOST THERE!
— List concepts, theories, and terms you are unsure of and ask your teacher to explain them.
— Take Practice Test 2 (Step 5).
— How did you do? Where is there room for improvement? What concepts are still unclear?
— Review concepts, etc. in your book and in this guide that are still unclear to you.
— On the day before the exam, stop reviewing and do something fun! Of course, go to bed early and try to get a good night's sleep.
— Walk into the examination room with a confident smile on your face! You *will* do well! You had a plan, and you followed it.

Plan B: You Have One Semester to Review

Check off the activities as you complete them.

JANUARY–FEBRUARY

— Read Chapters 1, 4, and 5 of this guide very carefully.
— Take the diagnostic test.
— Read and study the parts of this review guide that relate to material you have already covered in class.
— Read one or two books from the suggested reading list at the back of this guide.
— Go to at least one of the websites suggested for map review in this guide. Spend an hour or two each week playing map interpretation and review games and activities.

MARCH

— Review the human geography content sections in this guide that cover the material you have already studied in class.
— Ask your fellow students to form a study group with you to review for the exam. Meet weekly or at least twice a month.
— In your study group, practice writing essays to respond to the free-response questions on the AP Human Geography exam.

APRIL

— Take Practice Test 1 (Step 5) during the first week of April.
— Evaluate your strengths and weaknesses. What do you know well? What was unclear?

— Study the concepts and content areas in which you need more knowledge.
— Review the key terms in each chapter of this guide to review.

FIRST TWO WEEKS OF MAY—YOU'RE PRACTICALLY DONE!

— Ask your teacher for explanations of any concepts or models that you are still unclear on.
— Review the concepts, vocabulary, models, etc., in your book and in this guide that are still unclear to you.
— Take Practice Test 2 (Step 5).
— Score your answers and find where you made mistakes. Evaluate your strengths and weaknesses. What topics are you unclear about? What don't you really understand?
— On the day before the exam, stop reviewing and do something fun! Of course, go to bed early and try to get a good night's sleep.
— Walk into the examination room with a confident smile on your face! You *will* do well! You had a plan, and you followed it.

Plan C: You Have Six Weeks to Review

Check off the activities as you complete them.

APRIL

— Read Chapters 1, 4, and 5 of this guide.

— Take the diagnostic test (Chapter 3).

— Review areas you are weak in.

— Read *all* the human geography review chapters in this guide (Chapters 6 through 12).

— Take Practice Test 1 (Step 5).

— Score your exam and analyze your mistakes.

— Form a weekly review group with your friends.

— Review the Glossary and make sure you understand all the terms.

MAY

— Complete Practice Test 2 (Step 5).

— Score your exam and analyze your mistakes.

— Read any remaining human geography review chapters in this guide that you have not covered.

— Review Step 3 (Chapters 4 and 5) regarding strategies for multiple-choice and free-response essay questions.

— Go to at least one of the websites suggested for map review in this guide. Spend an hour or two each week playing map interpretation and review games and activities.

— On the day before the exam, stop reviewing and do something fun! Go to bed early!

— Walk into the examination room with a confident smile on your face! You *will* do well! You had a plan, and you followed it.

STEP 2

Determine Your Test Readiness

CHAPTER 3 Take a Diagnostic Exam

CHAPTER 3

Take a Diagnostic Exam

IN THIS CHAPTER

Summary: This chapter contains a diagnostic exam that is very similar to the actual AP Human Geography exam you will take in May. Taking this diagnostic exam now will let you know what you're up against and help you identify the areas of human geography that you need to concentrate on during your review.

Key Ideas

✪ Discover the level of difficulty you will need to study for in the actual exam.
✪ Answer questions that correspond to the seven major themes of AP Human Geography.
✪ Review the answers for the diagnostic exam questions.
✪ Determine areas you need to review.
✪ Select the concepts you need to review in depth and put them on a list for further study.

How to Take the Diagnostic Exam

Give yourself exactly 60 minutes to complete the 75 multiple-choice questions of Section I and 75 minutes to write the three free-response essays of Section II. Set a timer so that the timing is exact and you don't have to keep looking at a clock. Try to re-create the conditions of the actual exam as much as possible. Set aside a block of time when you won't be interrupted. Be sure to also choose a quiet place where you'll be free from distractions and interruptions; go to the library or some other place outside your house if you need to.

Taking the diagnostic exam is a good time to begin practicing pacing yourself. For Section I, you have less than a minute to complete each question. Work quickly but carefully; if you don't know an answer, eliminate answer choices you know are incorrect, guess among those remaining, and move on. You can mark the ones you want to come back to if you have more time. For Section II, give yourself 20 minutes to complete each question, which will leave 5 minutes for you to look each question over and make corrections and changes at the end. Be sure to read Step 3, which contains complete strategies and tips for both the multiple-choice questions (Chapter 4) and the free-response questions (Chapter 5). Only if you understand and practice the best test-taking strategies can you get the highest score you are capable of.

After you have completed both sections of this diagnostic exam, check your answers. Review the explanations for both sections and make sure you jot down the concepts and terms that you missed or did not really remember. Then, whichever plan you chose in Chapter 2, make sure you include time to review the concepts and terms on your list.

Diagnostic Test

ANSWER SHEET FOR SECTION I

1 (A) (B) (C) (D) (E)	26 (A) (B) (C) (D) (E)	51 (A) (B) (C) (D) (E)
2 (A) (B) (C) (D) (E)	27 (A) (B) (C) (D) (E)	52 (A) (B) (C) (D) (E)
3 (A) (B) (C) (D) (E)	28 (A) (B) (C) (D) (E)	53 (A) (B) (C) (D) (E)
4 (A) (B) (C) (D) (E)	29 (A) (B) (C) (D) (E)	54 (A) (B) (C) (D) (E)
5 (A) (B) (C) (D) (E)	30 (A) (B) (C) (D) (E)	55 (A) (B) (C) (D) (E)
6 (A) (B) (C) (D) (E)	31 (A) (B) (C) (D) (E)	56 (A) (B) (C) (D) (E)
7 (A) (B) (C) (D) (E)	32 (A) (B) (C) (D) (E)	57 (A) (B) (C) (D) (E)
8 (A) (B) (C) (D) (E)	33 (A) (B) (C) (D) (E)	58 (A) (B) (C) (D) (E)
9 (A) (B) (C) (D) (E)	34 (A) (B) (C) (D) (E)	59 (A) (B) (C) (D) (E)
10 (A) (B) (C) (D) (E)	35 (A) (B) (C) (D) (E)	60 (A) (B) (C) (D) (E)
11 (A) (B) (C) (D) (E)	36 (A) (B) (C) (D) (E)	61 (A) (B) (C) (D) (E)
12 (A) (B) (C) (D) (E)	37 (A) (B) (C) (D) (E)	62 (A) (B) (C) (D) (E)
13 (A) (B) (C) (D) (E)	38 (A) (B) (C) (D) (E)	63 (A) (B) (C) (D) (E)
14 (A) (B) (C) (D) (E)	39 (A) (B) (C) (D) (E)	64 (A) (B) (C) (D) (E)
15 (A) (B) (C) (D) (E)	40 (A) (B) (C) (D) (E)	65 (A) (B) (C) (D) (E)
16 (A) (B) (C) (D) (E)	41 (A) (B) (C) (D) (E)	66 (A) (B) (C) (D) (E)
17 (A) (B) (C) (D) (E)	42 (A) (B) (C) (D) (E)	67 (A) (B) (C) (D) (E)
18 (A) (B) (C) (D) (E)	43 (A) (B) (C) (D) (E)	68 (A) (B) (C) (D) (E)
19 (A) (B) (C) (D) (E)	44 (A) (B) (C) (D) (E)	69 (A) (B) (C) (D) (E)
20 (A) (B) (C) (D) (E)	45 (A) (B) (C) (D) (E)	70 (A) (B) (C) (D) (E)
21 (A) (B) (C) (D) (E)	46 (A) (B) (C) (D) (E)	71 (A) (B) (C) (D) (E)
22 (A) (B) (C) (D) (E)	47 (A) (B) (C) (D) (E)	72 (A) (B) (C) (D) (E)
23 (A) (B) (C) (D) (E)	48 (A) (B) (C) (D) (E)	73 (A) (B) (C) (D) (E)
24 (A) (B) (C) (D) (E)	49 (A) (B) (C) (D) (E)	74 (A) (B) (C) (D) (E)
25 (A) (B) (C) (D) (E)	50 (A) (B) (C) (D) (E)	75 (A) (B) (C) (D) (E)

Section I: Multiple-Choice Questions

Time: 60 Minutes

Section I Comprises 50 Percent of Total AP Score

Directions: Each of the following questions is followed by five answer choices. Choose the one answer choice that best answers the question or completes the statement.

1. Human geography is defined as the study of

   (A) human interactions with the physical environment.
   (B) human interactions with the cultural environment.
   (C) human interactions with the physical and cultural environments.
   (D) human interactions within the natural landscape.
   (E) human interactions within the physical landscape.

2. Cities developed 4000 to 6000 years ago to provide a center for all of the following functions EXCEPT

   (A) religion.
   (B) trade.
   (C) protection.
   (D) production.
   (E) scientific study.

3. Which one of the following individuals is engaged in a secondary economic activity?

   (A) A computer programmer
   (B) A city clerk
   (C) The CEO of General Motors
   (D) An aspirin production worker
   (E) A farmer

4. Which of the following best describes the likely impact of a large, young, single migrant population on its destination country?

   (A) An increase in the aging population
   (B) An increase in births
   (C) A general increase in death rates
   (D) A decline in the carrying capacity of the host country
   (E) An excess of deaths over births

5. All of the following factors directly influence the birth rate of a country EXCEPT

   (A) government population policies.
   (B) the customs and family size expectations of its residents.
   (C) the age composition of its population.
   (D) government economic policies.
   (E) the sex composition of its inhabitants.

6. "Singapore is located on an island at the north-western end of the Straits of Malacca adjacent to the Malay Peninsula." This statement is a description of Singapore's

   (A) site.
   (B) situation.
   (C) absolute location.
   (D) function.
   (E) geological history.

7. Which one of the following is not usually a reason why people move from rural areas to urban areas?

   (A) Jobs
   (B) Better healthcare
   (C) Schools
   (D) Safer environment
   (E) Cultural and social reasons

8. The demographic transition model

   (A) assumes high birth and death rates will gradually be replaced by low rates over time.
   (B) traces changes in fertility and mortality associated with agricultural progress.
   (C) consists of six stages.
   (D) was developed by Thomas Malthus.
   (E) traces the relationship between population growth and social development.

9. The belief that our physical environment is the chief factor influencing human thoughts, behaviors, and actions is called

   (A) environmental perception.
   (B) possibilism.
   (C) environmental determinism.
   (D) environmentalism.
   (E) a culture system.

10. The country with the largest territory is

    (A) United States.
    (B) Brazil.
    (C) China.
    (D) Australia.
    (E) Russia.

11. Population pressure on an agricultural land is typically expressed as the

    (A) crude density.
    (B) arithmetic density.
    (C) physiological density.
    (D) rate of natural increase.
    (E) population density.

12. Land in the CBD of a city is more expensive because it

    (A) has maximum interaction potential.
    (B) is more attractive.
    (C) has a better sense of place.
    (D) provides a better quality of life.
    (E) encompasses a larger area.

13. A political state whose territory is the same as the area occupied by people sharing a common heritage and value system is best described as a

    (A) state.
    (B) country.
    (C) nation.
    (D) political state.
    (E) nation-state.

14. Most scientists agree that the Egyptian pyramids and the Mayan temple pyramids were most likely caused by the process of

    (A) relocation diffusion.
    (B) stimulus diffusion.
    (C) contagious diffusion.
    (D) hierarchical diffusion.
    (E) independent invention.

15. The movement of people from Nigeria, Cameroon, Togo, and Gabon to the Americas in the sixteenth, seventeenth, and eighteenth centuries is an example of

    (A) chain migration.
    (B) circular migration.
    (C) cluster migration.
    (D) forced migration.
    (E) voluntary migration.

16. A piece of land surrounded by a foreign territory would be viewed by the foreign territory as

    (A) an enclave.
    (B) an exclave.
    (C) a colony.
    (D) an edge city.
    (E) a unitary state.

17. The carrying capacity of land

    (A) directly correlates with conditions of life there.
    (B) is high in many Sub-Saharan African countries.
    (C) is the number of people a piece of land can support in a sustainable fashion.
    (D) is related to social development.
    (E) is high in traditional slash-and-burn societies.

18. The Indus Valley, Egypt, West Africa, and Mesopotamia are a few examples of

    (A) culture basins.
    (B) cultural convergences.
    (C) culture hearths.
    (D) culture complexes.
    (E) cultural divergence.

19. The most rapidly growing minority group in the United States is

    (A) Asian.
    (B) Hispanic.
    (C) Native American.
    (D) Black or African American.
    (E) European.

20. Using the rank-size rule, if Wood County's largest city has 200,000 residents, how many people live in Wood County's fourth-largest city?

    (A) 75,000
    (B) 100,000
    (C) 50,000
    (D) 25,000
    (E) 10,000

21. The Earth's surface as modified by humans is called

    (A) folk culture.
    (B) the carrying capacity.
    (C) environmental determinism.
    (D) the cultural landscape.
    (E) the physical environment.

22. Which of the following statements correctly describes migrants today?

    (A) They represent an accurate cross-section of their home country.
    (B) They represent an accurate cross-section of their destination country.
    (C) They include an equal number of males and females.
    (D) They include an equal representation from each age group.
    (E) They are usually young singles.

23. Which one of the following statements does NOT correctly describe global urbanization?

    (A) The percentage of people living in cities is growing.
    (B) Cities are growing in size.
    (C) Most of the world's population will soon live in cities.
    (D) Most urban growth will occur in LDCs.
    (E) Severe environmental destruction is inevitable due to urban growth.

24. An economy in which goods and services are usually produced for internal consumption only is called a

    (A) free market economy.
    (B) commercial economy.
    (C) planned economy.
    (D) command economy.
    (E) subsistence economy.

25. Which one of the following does NOT correctly associate a religion with its place of worship?

    (A) Shinto—shrines
    (B) Islam—mosques
    (C) Buddhism—pyramids
    (D) Judaism—temples
    (E) Christians—churches

26. Population pyramids visually depict

    (A) a population's age and economic composition.
    (B) a country's dependency ratio.
    (C) the ethnic composition of a population.
    (D) a country's population density.
    (E) the carrying capacity and overcrowding in a country.

27. The French language, how to weave a basket, and the belief in ancestral spirits are all examples of

    (A) mentifacts.
    (B) artifacts.
    (C) culture hearths.
    (D) culture traits.
    (E) dialects.

28. The practice of judging other cultures against the standards of one's own culture is called

    (A) ethnicity.
    (B) assimilation.
    (C) ethnocentrism.
    (D) acculturation.
    (E) egocentrism.

29. Renewable fuels derived from biological materials that can be recycled are called

    (A) renewable resources.
    (B) fossil fuels.
    (C) agricultural fuels.
    (D) biofuels.
    (E) farm products.

30. Since 1860, death rates in Europe have declined due to all the following factors EXCEPT

    (A) improved sanitation.
    (B) cleaner water supplies.
    (C) epidemics becoming less frequent and far-reaching.
    (D) a lack of warfare.
    (E) improved nutrition and increased food supply.

31. All of the following factors play a role in the economic actions of humans EXCEPT

    (A) physical environment.
    (B) linguistic background.
    (C) political decisions.
    (D) technological development.
    (E) market conditions.

Use this figure to answer question 37.

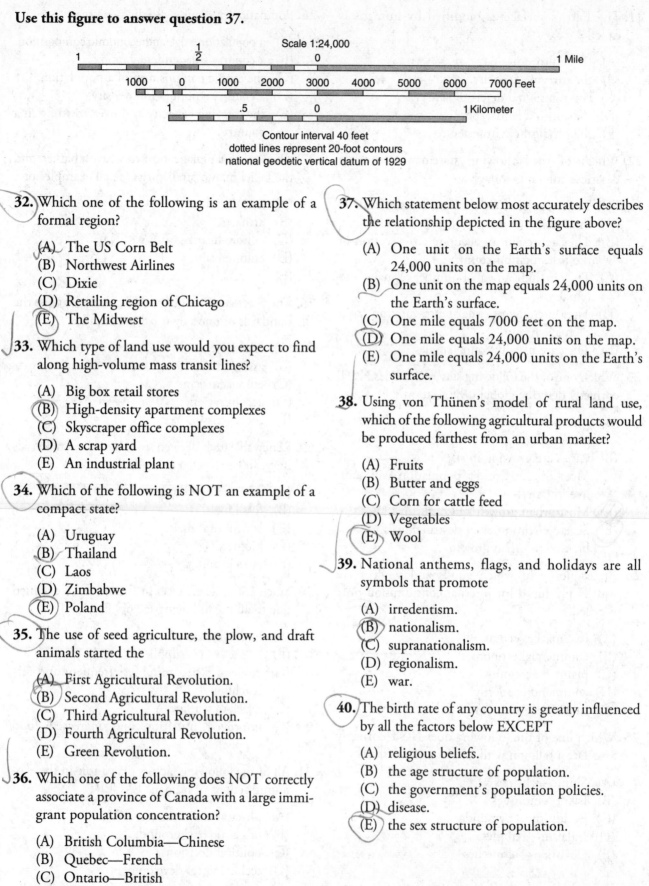

Scale 1:24,000

Contour interval 40 feet
dotted lines represent 20-foot contours
national geodetic vertical datum of 1929

32. Which one of the following is an example of a formal region?

(A) The US Corn Belt
(B) Northwest Airlines
(C) Dixie
(D) Retailing region of Chicago
(E) The Midwest

33. Which type of land use would you expect to find along high-volume mass transit lines?

(A) Big box retail stores
(B) High-density apartment complexes
(C) Skyscraper office complexes
(D) A scrap yard
(E) An industrial plant

34. Which of the following is NOT an example of a compact state?

(A) Uruguay
(B) Thailand
(C) Laos
(D) Zimbabwe
(E) Poland

35. The use of seed agriculture, the plow, and draft animals started the

(A) First Agricultural Revolution.
(B) Second Agricultural Revolution.
(C) Third Agricultural Revolution.
(D) Fourth Agricultural Revolution.
(E) Green Revolution.

36. Which one of the following does NOT correctly associate a province of Canada with a large immigrant population concentration?

(A) British Columbia—Chinese
(B) Quebec—French
(C) Ontario—British
(D) Nova Scotia—Italian
(E) Saskatchewan—Ukraine

37. Which statement below most accurately describes the relationship depicted in the figure above?

(A) One unit on the Earth's surface equals 24,000 units on the map.
(B) One unit on the map equals 24,000 units on the Earth's surface.
(C) One mile equals 7000 feet on the map.
(D) One mile equals 24,000 units on the map.
(E) One mile equals 24,000 units on the Earth's surface.

38. Using von Thünen's model of rural land use, which of the following agricultural products would be produced farthest from an urban market?

(A) Fruits
(B) Butter and eggs
(C) Corn for cattle feed
(D) Vegetables
(E) Wool

39. National anthems, flags, and holidays are all symbols that promote

(A) irredentism.
(B) nationalism.
(C) supranationalism.
(D) regionalism.
(E) war.

40. The birth rate of any country is greatly influenced by all the factors below EXCEPT

(A) religious beliefs.
(B) the age structure of population.
(C) the government's population policies.
(D) disease.
(E) the sex structure of population.

41. Which one of the following does NOT correctly characterize agribusiness?

(A) A system
(B) A set of relationships to organize food production from seed to loaf of bread
(C) A large corporate entity
(D) A global enterprise
(E) A business enterprise driven by the fast food industry

42. Which of the following statements correctly describes world population distribution?

(A) World population is evenly distributed.
(B) More than one-half the world's population lives between 60 degrees and 80 degrees north of the equator.
(C) Less than half of the world's population lives north of the equator.
(D) A large majority of the world's population lives on a small part of the world's surface.
(E) The world's population increases sharply with an increase in surface elevation.

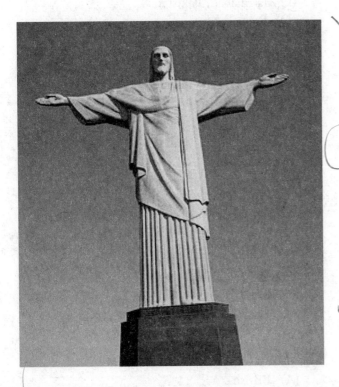

43. On which continent would you most likely find large statues of Christ (Cristo Rey) overlooking cities from hilltops such as the one shown in the photo above?

(A) North America
(B) South America
(C) Europe
(D) Asia
(E) Australia

44. The almost continuous strip of urban centers that extends along the US Atlantic coast from north of Boston to southern Virginia is commonly called

(A) megalopolis.
(B) megacity.
(C) super city.
(D) oligopolies.
(E) triceratops.

45. Which of the following political state shapes would likely be the most efficient for transportation and communication?

(A) Compact
(B) Prorupt
(C) Elongated
(D) Fragmented
(E) Perforated

46. Graveyards and cemeteries are NOT used by

(A) Christians.
(B) Jews.
(C) Hindus.
(D) Muslims.
(E) Animists.

47. A dress store, a shoe store, and a jewelry store located on the same block close to each other is an example of

(A) purchasing power parity.
(B) agglomeration.
(C) deglomeration.
(D) an urban heat island.
(E) concentric zone.

48. Which one of the following is NOT a common reason for state boundary disputes?

(A) Resources
(B) Territories
(C) Linguistic differences
(D) Documents defining boundaries
(E) Exclusive economic zones (EEZs)

49. Which of the following central place functions is most likely to have the highest range of goods and also the highest threshold population?

(A) A dry cleaner
(B) A Chinese restaurant
(C) An elementary school
(D) A cancer treatment clinic
(E) A flower shop

50. The belief that people, not their surroundings, are the forces behind cultural development is called

(A) environmental perception.
(B) possibilism.
(C) environmental determinism.
(D) environmentalism.
(E) a culture system.

51. The conflict in Kashmir is based on which type of boundary disagreement?

(A) Fertile ground
(B) Land use
(C) Irredentism
(D) Document interpretation
(E) Immigration

52. Dishes, axes, knives, and toys are examples of

(A) tools.
(B) artifacts.
(C) mentifacts.
(D) sociofacts.
(E) the built environment.

53. Which one of the following is an example of a vernacular region?

(A) New Hampshire
(B) Bible Belt
(C) Urban zone of working and shopping for Pittsburgh
(D) Little Italy
(E) Texas

54. Which urban model was developed to explain the patterns of American cities in the 1920s?

(A) Concentric zone model
(B) Central place model
(C) Urban realms model
(D) Sector model
(E) Multiple-nuclei model

55. A suburb is

(A) often characterized by sprawl.
(B) the same thing as central city.
(C) a conurbation.
(D) exclusively residential.
(E) separate and not integrated with urban areas nearby.

56. Which one of the following statements does NOT correctly describe truck farming?

(A) It is the main type of farming in Georgia and Florida.
(B) Truck farm produce is shipped long distances.
(C) Truck farming employs low-cost labor.
(D) Mechanization is rarely used.
(E) Highly perishable crops like lettuce and strawberries are common.

57. Which of the following national capitals is NOT a forward-thrust capital?

(A) Brasilia, Brazil
(B) Abuja, Nigeria
(C) Islamabad, Pakistan
(D) Paris, France
(E) Astana, Kazakhstan

58. Which economic sector of the city furnishes goods and services to the larger economy outside the city?

(A) Basic
(B) Non-basic
(C) White collar
(D) Suburban
(E) Blue collar

59. The attachments we have to a specific location and its characteristics is called

(A) placelessness.
(B) sense of place.
(C) location.
(D) cultural landscape.
(E) connectivity.

60. The charter group of Quebec, Canada, was the

(A) British.
(B) Germans.
(C) French.
(D) Irish.
(E) Spanish.

61. Which model below is based on the assumption that growth happens around several major foci, not just the CBD?

(A) Central place model
(B) Concentric zone model
(C) Urban realms model
(D) Sector model
(E) Multiple-nuclei model

62. Which one of the following economic activities is primary?

(A) Pottery production
(B) Electronic assembly
(C) Hydroelectric production
(D) Mining
(E) Selling items on eBay

63. Population growth reflects all of the following factors EXCEPT

(A) birth rates.
(B) death rates.
(C) migration.
(D) age structure.
(E) calculation of the doubling time.

64. Which country below has the highest concentration of Buddhists?

(A) Brazil
(B) Vietnam
(C) France
(D) Russia
(E) Iran

65. What type of land use would you expect to find near the railroad yards?

(A) A Macy's department store
(B) A Walmart
(C) The Wells Fargo Bank headquarters
(D) A steel mill
(E) A penthouse apartment

Use the map below to answer questions 66–67.

66. Which region of China marked on the map above has the highest population density?

(A) A
(B) B
(C) C
(D) D
(E) E

67. In which region of China are the special economic zones (SEZ's) located?

(A) A
(B) B
(C) C
(D) D
(E) E

68. The latitude and longitude coordinates of a place refer to its

(A) absolute location.
(B) relative location.
(C) distance.
(D) situation.
(E) scale.

Map of China with regions labeled A, B, C, D, E. Cities shown: Urumqi, Turan Pendi, Indign claim, Lhasa, Lanzhou, Xian, Chengdu, Wuhan, Beijing, Shenyang, Harbin, Zhengzhou, Nanjing, Guangzhou.

69. Total fertility rates

(A) are increasing in most European countries.
(B) are increasing in Asian countries.
(C) slightly higher than two are at replacement level.
(D) reflect biological constraints.
(E) reflect the level of industrialization in a country.

70. The worldwide trend towards using biofuels has caused all the following to occur EXCEPT

(A) a decrease in use of fossil fuels.
(B) a rise in global food prices.
(C) the conversion of small farms to large mono-culture plantations.
(D) violence.
(E) the eviction of small farmers.

71. Which one of the following factors has NOT contributed to the explosive spread of infectious disease?

(A) World trade expansion
(B) Increased investment in sanitation and healthcare
(C) Migration
(D) Growing global tourism
(E) Rapid population growth

72. A group of people with a common culture and history who occupy an area are called

(A) a state.
(B) a country.
(C) a nation.
(D) a political state.
(E) a nation-state.

73. The outer boundary of a linguistic feature on a map is called

(A) an isogloss.
(B) a dialect.
(C) a toponym.
(D) a vernacular.
(E) a creole.

74. The relationship between the size or length of a map attribute and the same attribute on Earth's surface is called a

(A) mental map.
(B) projection.
(C) scale.
(D) density.
(E) model.

75. Which of the following jobs would NOT be considered a quaternary economic activity?

(A) IRS employee
(B) College professor
(C) Insurance salesman
(D) Computer programmer
(E) Research scientist

END OF SECTION I

Section II: Free-Response Questions

Time: 75 minutes

Section II Comprises 50 Percent of Total AP Score

Directions: Answer each of the three questions below in the allotted time of 75 minutes. You should spend approximately 25 minutes on each question. Answers must be in an essay form, not a list of facts or thoughts, although a formal essay (with an introduction and conclusion) is not required. Use substantive examples where appropriate. Make sure you answer all parts of each question and label each part of your answer to correspond with the part of the question you are answering. Feel free to make a short outline first to capture your thoughts, but only the essay will be scored.

Total Fertility Rates by Region, 1970 and 2004

REGION	1970	2004
East Asia & Pacific	5.4	2.1
Europe & Central Asia	2.5	1.6
Latin America & Caribbean	5.3	2.4
Sub-Saharan Africa	6.8	5.4
High-Income Countries	2.5	1.7
World	4.8	2.6

Source: *World Bank*

1. Use the data in the table above to answer the questions below:
   A. Define total fertility rate.
   B. According to the chart above, identify the two (2) regions experiencing the most rapid decline in fertility rates.
   C. Choose one of the regions you identified in Part B, and discuss why the fertility rate is declining in that region and explain the potential impact of this decline on the region socially and economically.

2. A. Define a universalizing religion.
   B. Give two examples of a universalizing religion and, for each religion, name one country where the religion can be found.
   C. Discuss how the universalizing religion spread to each of the two countries you used as examples in Part B.

3. A. Define a political state.
   B. Describe and discuss two ways a political state can foster cohesiveness and explain how each of these would contribute to a sense of nationalism.
   C. Describe and discuss two factors that can discourage the development of a sense of cohesion and unity in a political state and give an example of each in the real world today.

END OF SECTION II

Answer Key: Section I (Multiple-Choice Questions)

1.	C	39.	B
2.	E	40.	D
3.	D	41.	C
4.	B	42.	D
5.	D	43.	B
6.	B	44.	A
7.	D	45.	A
8.	A	46.	C
9.	C	47.	B
10.	E	48.	C
11.	C	49.	D
12.	A	50.	B
13.	E	51.	C
14.	E	52.	B
15.	D	53.	D
16.	A	54.	A
17.	C	55.	A
18.	C	56.	D
19.	B	57.	D
20.	C	58.	A
21.	D	59.	B
22.	E	60.	C
23.	E	61.	E
24.	E	62.	D
25.	C	63.	E
26.	B	64.	B
27.	D	65.	D
28.	C	66.	C
29.	D	67.	C
30.	D	68.	A
31.	B	69.	C
32.	A	70.	A
33.	B	71.	B
34.	B	72.	C
35.	A	73.	A
36.	D	74.	C
37.	B	75.	C
38.	E		

Explanations for Section I (Multiple-Choice Questions)

1. C—Human geography is concerned with both the physical and cultural environments and how humans function and interact with them. Choices A, D, and E exclude the cultural environment. Choice B excludes the physical environment.

2. E—Scientific study was not a reason for the earliest cities that evolved 4000 to 6000 years ago in culture hearths where sedentary agriculture began to be practiced. They served as centers for religious worship (A), trade and commerce (B), military activities and protection (C), and for the production of commodities requiring additional workers and inputs (D).

3. D—Aspirin production workers labor in manufacturing, which is a part of the value-added secondary economic sector. Computer programmers (A) and government workers (B) are employed in the quaternary sector of the economy. High-level decision makers (C) comprise the quinary sector, and farming (E) and all agricultural activities are primary.

4. B—A general increase in births in the destination country is the most likely result of an influx of young migrants. Increases in the aging cohorts (A) will not occur for some time. The death rate (C) would be expected to decline—rather than rise—as a result of an influx of young migrants. The host country's carrying capacity, or the number of people an area can sustainably support, will not change. An excess of deaths over births (E) would not be expected to be a result of an influx of a large young migrant population.

5. D—The birth rate of a country is greatly and directly influenced by the population policies implemented by its government (A), by the customs and family size expectations of its population (B), and by the age and sex composition of its inhabitants (C and E). The economic policies (D) of its government have only a very indirect and variable influence on the country's birth rate.

6. B—Situation is the relative location of a place in relation to neighboring places. Site (A) is the absolute location of a place and is usually described in physical terms using water bodies, mountains, plains, etc. Absolute location (C) is another term meaning "site." Function (D) in human geography refers to the purpose of a region or place in relation to another region or place. Geological history (E) refers to the scientific study of the Earth's history from its beginning up until now.

7. D—Most people do not move from rural areas into cities to seek a safer environment in which to raise their families or live. Urban crime rates exceed rural crime rates globally; people are aware of this and base their decisions accordingly. Potential employment opportunities (A) are the hope of most rural-to-urban migrants, but while jobs used to be more available in most cities, this is increasingly not always true. Better healthcare (B), generally available in urban areas, and the potential for a better education (C) are reasons why many migrants seek city life for their families. In some cultures, such as the Latin American culture, social and cultural traditions favor life in an urban environment over a rural one.

8. A—A basic assumption of this model says high birth and death rates will drop to lower levels over time as the country develops economically. It traces changes in fertility and mortality that occur as industrialization (not agricultural development) takes place (B). Thus it shows how population growth and economic development (not social development) are linked (E). Thomas Malthus's *Essay on the Principles of Population* states the world's population is growing faster than the food supply (D); his predictions did not take into account the declining birth rates of the *demographic transition model*. The *demographic transition model* has four stages (not six), with some demographers adding a fifth stage to show a continuing drop in the crude birth rate (CBR) seen in the aging populations of wealthier countries (E).

9. C—Environmental determinism is the belief that our environment influences and controls our actions, lifestyle, and culture. Environmental perception

(A) is the theory that people of different cultures look at their environments in different ways. Possibilism (B) is the theory that humans have a choice in how they think, act, and live within a range of available possibilities given to them by their physical environment. Environmentalism (D) is the movement to preserve and protect the physical environment from pollution and misuse by humans. A culture system (E) is a group of culture complexes that form the common identity of a group.

10. **E**—Russia is the largest country in terms of territory (6,591,027 square miles). Canada is the second-largest country in the world in land area. The United States (A) is third largest. China is fourth (C), Brazil fifth (B), and Australia the sixth largest (D).

11. **C**—Physiological density is total population divided by arable land (area in a country that can be farmed). Crude density (A), arithmetic density (B), and population density (E) all refer to the number of people per unit of land. The rate of natural increase (D) is the birth rate minus the death rate for a population in a year's time.

12. **A**—Land in the CBD (central business district) of a city is very expensive (receives the highest bid rent) because it is the hub of the mass transit lines and is the center of the economic and social functions of the city. All public transportation routes lead to it, giving it the highest accessibility and maximum interaction potential.

13. **E**—A nation-state is a state or political territory with only one nation of people within its borders. Iceland and Japan are examples of nation-states because, for the most part, they contain a single nation and are homogenous. A state (A) is a political entity that occupies a definite territory with borders and full sovereignty. The United States and Thailand are examples of states. A country (B) is synonymous with a state. A nation (C) is a group of people with a common culture and history who occupy an area. A political state (D) is another term for a state.

14. **E**—While some believe there was a pre-Columbian transfer of knowledge to the Americas, the majority of scientists and anthropologists believe the Egyptian pyramids and the Mayan temple pyramids were developed independently and not by diffusion of ideas. The other answer choices describe different types of diffusion of ideas.

15. **D**—Forced migration is the involuntary historic movement of people who have no decision-making involvement in the process. Between 1519 and 1867 nearly 11 million African slaves were brought to the Americas from the countries of West Africa. The other answer choices are all forms of voluntary migration in which the immigrant makes the decision to move; most migrations are voluntary.

16. **A**—The country that surrounds another country would view the enclosed country as an enclave. Examples include the Vatican City, an enclave in Italy. An exclave (B) is a part of one country that is separated from the main part. Alaska is an exclave of the United States. A colony (C) is a territory under the control of another political state. An edge city (D) is a new urban complex outside the city center that consists of a large node of office buildings and commercial operations with more workers than residents. A unitary state (E) is a country with a strong central government, such as France.

17. **C**—The carrying capacity of land is the number of inhabitants an area of land can sustainably support given the prevailing technology. It has no direct correlation to living conditions (A) or social development (D), but is related to the level of economic development. Generally, developing countries (B) and traditional societies (E) have low carrying capacities.

18. **C**—Culture hearths such as the Indus River Valley of Pakistan, the Nile River Valley of Egypt, West Africa, and Mesopotamia were birthplaces of major cultures. Culture basins (A) are basins or repositories of culture. Cultural convergence (B) refers to the tendency for cultures to become more alike as they share technologies. A culture complex (D) is a set of traits or practices that revolves around a basic activity in a culture, such as food preparation. Cultural divergence (E) is the trend for two cultures to become more different over time.

19. B—The Hispanic minority group is the fastest growing minority in the United States today. Over 50 percent of US population growth since 2000 has been due to Hispanics, and the majority of that growth is based on higher birth rates, not immigration.

20. C—Using the rank size rule, the fourth-largest city will be one-fourth the size of the largest city; therefore, 200,000 × ¼ = 50,000.

21. D—The cultural landscape is also called the "built environment" and visibly displays human interaction with the environment. Folk culture (A) refers to the collection of culture traits of traditional societies, such as the Old Order Amish or the Hutterites. Carrying capacity (B) is the number of people a piece of land can sustainably support without ecological damage. Environmental determinism (C) is the belief that our environment influences and controls our actions, lifestyle, and culture. The physical environment (E) is the sum of everything around us in the natural world.

22. E—Current research shows a majority of migrants today are young singles with the sex varying by individual case. Migrants rarely represent an accurate or representative slice of either the country they leave (A) or the country to which they are migrating (B). Migrants contribute to both the age (D) and sex (C) of their destination country in an unbalanced and irregular way.

23. E—The threat of severe environmental destruction caused by increasing urban populations has been overestimated by the gloomy UN prediction that megacities would bring catastrophic conditions on the Earth by the year 2015. The other choices correctly describe global urbanization.

24. E—Subsistence economies usually produce only enough for their population to consume with little left over to trade. Free market (A) and commercial (B) economies both refer to an economic system based on supply and demand. Planned (C) and command (D) economies both refer to an economy in which the central government makes most of the production and supply decisions.

25. C—Buddhists do not use pyramids in their religion but instead make use of temple pagodas and shrines to various gods, especially Buddha, "the Enlightened One." They also worship at the bo (bodhi) tree. Those who practice Shinto (A) are basically animists and worship their ancestors at shrines. Muslims (B) worship in mosques, and Jews (D) worship in temples. Christians (E) of all denominations and branches worship in churches.

26. B—The dependency ratio is the measure of the number of economic dependents, old and young, that each 100 people in their productive years must support. The population pyramid represents a population's age and sex composition but not its economic composition (A). It does not show the ethnic composition (C), population density (D), or carrying capacity (E). The carrying capacity of a country refers to the relationship between the number of residents and the area they occupy.

27. D—Culture traits are things that are learned by people of a certain culture. The French learn to speak French, members of certain culture groups learn to weave baskets, and some culture groups share a belief in ancestral spirits. Mentifacts (A) are the main categories of culture's values and beliefs, such as religion, language, folklore, etc. Artifacts (B) are material parts of a culture, such as houses, clothing, tools, etc. A culture hearth (C) is a location where a distinct and advanced culture originated, such as the Indus River Valley or the Nile River Valley. Dialects (E) are variations of a language such as the pronunciation of the word "started." New Englanders pronounce it as "stahted" and Southerners say "stot."

28. C—Ethnocentrism is the practice of judging other cultures by the standards of one's own culture. Ethnicity (A) is identity in a group of people with common ancestry and culture. Assimilation (B) is the process in which people lose cultural traits as they acquire new ones from a host culture. Acculturation (D) refers to the process of adopting new cultural traits while retaining one's own cultural identity and traits. Egocentrism (E) is the view that you are the most important person in your world.

29. **D**—Biofuels like ethanol and methanol are made from biological materials that can be reproduced. Renewable resources (A) are natural resources that can be replenished. Fossil fuels (B) are fuels made from coal and petroleum—both nonrenewable resources since they require thousands of years to be created naturally from decaying organic matter. Agricultural fuels (C) are fuels like gasoline and diesel used to run farm machinery. Farm products (E) are any goods grown or produced on a farm.

30. **D**—There has been no lack of warfare in Europe since 1860—two world wars and several revolutions and and a number of regional armed conflicts have ensued! After 1860, improved sanitation (A) and cleaner drinking water (B) became common in Europe's larger cities. People developed partial immunity to diseases once deadly and widespread in Europe (C). Improvements in the agricultural sector coupled with new food crops, such as the potato, stretched food supplies and increased the overall health of the population (E).

31. **B**—While some cultural traits such as religious beliefs or food preferences determine production decisions, language does not. The physical environment (A) controls economic activity by limiting the type and availability of natural resources at a population's disposal. A government's decisions (C) to encourage (through tariffs and subsidies) or discourage economic activities (by limiting production, for example) greatly influence economic activities. The technology (D) available to a society also guides economic activities of a population. Market conditions of supply and demand (E), whether in a free market or government-controlled economy, strongly influence economic production.

32. **A**—A formal or uniform region is one that is consistent in one physical or cultural characteristic, such as production of corn. Northwest Airlines (B) and the retailing district of Chicago (D) are functional, or nodal, regions of interdependency and have a core and a periphery. Dixie (C) and the Midwest (E) are vernacular, or perceptual, regions based on the way people perceive or feel about them.

33. **B**—High-density apartment complexes, along with retailing centers, malls, and light industries are typically located along high-volume transportation routes. Big box retail stores like Target and Walmart (A) are usually located on the outskirts of the city in suburban areas along major highway transportation corridors. Skyscraper office complexes (C) and major hotels are usually located in the fringes of the CBD. A scrap yard (D) would probably be found beside a railroad or other cargo route. An industrial plant (E) would probably be located near a waterfront, railroad, or other cargo route for easy shipment of both raw materials and finished products.

34. **B**—Thailand is a good example of a prorupt state, or one which is mainly compact but has a long, narrow extension or peninsula. Uruguay (A), Laos (C), Zimbabwe (D), and Poland (E) are all compact states—states with a rounded, or circular, shape.

35. **A**—The use of seed agriculture, the plow, and draft animals allowed humans to greatly expand food production, and these innovations occurred during the First Agricultural Revolution. Each of the succeeding agricultural revolutions (B, C, D, and E) was marked by improved methods and factors that led to increased food supplies.

36. **D**—Nova Scotia is largely populated by immigrants of British descent, and the overwhelming majority of new immigrants to the province are from the United Kingdom. The other answer choices are all correct in associating the province with a large ethnic immigrant population living in the province.

37. **B**—The representative fraction given at the top of the diagram tells us that 24,000 units on the Earth's surface are represented by one unit on the map. In other words, 24,000 feet on the Earth's surface would be one foot on the map. The other answer choices all incorrectly interpret the relationship depicted in the diagram.

38. **E**—Wool would be raised farthest from an urban market since sheep ranching requires lots of grazing land but has lower transportation costs than dairying (B), corn farming (C), or raising more perishable crops such as fruits and vegetables (A and D).

39. B—Nationalism is a strong identification with one's country and what it stands for. National anthems, flags, national holidays, memorials, and even national sports teams all cement one's loyalty to a sovereign state and are strong centripetal forces in a country. Irredentism (A) is the claim by a country's government that an ethnic minority living in another country belongs to the homeland country. Strong irredentist unrest led to a war when Serbia stirred the fires of irredentism in Croatia among the ethnic Serb minority living there in the 1980s and 1990s. Supranationalism (C) is the current global trend for many countries to join organizations for a common goal or good. The United Nations is a well-known supranational organization. Regionalism (D) often develops when a minority group forms a majority in one region of a country and identifies more closely with its group than with the country. War (E) is not promoted by a flag or national symbol. Such iconography may stir nationalism in times of war, but these items do not encourage or promote war in themselves.

40. D—While disease is a factor in the general health of a country's population, it is not an important influence on the birth rate. Religious beliefs (A), the age and sex composition of its population (B and E), and the population policies of the country (C) are the strongest influences on a country's birth rate.

41. C—Agribusiness is not a new or single corporate entity but rather a system (A) that involves a complex set of interrelationships to organize food production (B). It is a global enterprise (D) that is driven in large part by the global fast food industry (E), which requires low-priced farm products to be competitive and profitable.

42. D—More than half of the world's population is concentrated on only 5 percent of the world's land area and two-thirds lives on only 10 percent of the land area. The world's population, in fact, is very unevenly distributed (A) with some parts of the world uninhabited and others very densely populated. The area between 60 degrees and 80 degrees north of the equator is sparsely inhabited because of a very cold climate (B). Over half the world's population lives north of the equator (C). The world's population drastically decreases in numbers with increases in elevation because of increasingly unfavorable living conditions (E).

43. B—There are a number of large Christ the Redeemer (Cristo Rey) statues in South America usually placed on hillsides above cities. There is one in the United States and another in Europe, but the majority are found in South America and are a testament to the widespread Roman Catholic faith on that continent.

44. A—Megalopolis refers to an almost 600-mile-long conurbation stretching from southern Maine to southern Virginia. Several cities and their industrial and market-oriented businesses make up this conurbation. Megacity (B) is a term created in the 1970s to apply to very large cities with a population of 10 million or more that many thought would overwhelm the world's resources. Supercity (C) is the term given to Auckland, New Zealand, by its residents as the city boundaries continue to extend into the neighboring hinterlands, swallowing nearby towns and smaller cities. There is no such term as oligopolis (D), and a triceratops (E) is a species of extinct dinosaur.

45. A—A compact state would have lower transportation and communication costs within the state, leading to more efficient transportation and communication systems. This can lead to greater cohesion among its population. A prorupt state (B) is mainly compact with a narrow extension protruding out of it. An elongated state (C) is long and narrow like Chile or Norway. A fragmented state (D) is composed of more than one disconnected piece of territory. Examples include island states such as Indonesia and the Philippines, as well as states like Italy with regions on both the mainland and on islands. All these shapes of states can be expected to have less efficient transportation and communication systems than a compact state.

46. C—Both Hindu and Buddhist faiths cremate their dead and do not bury the deceased in graveyards or cemeteries. Christians (A), Jews (B), Muslims (D), and most animists (E) make use of graveyards and cemeteries for burial of their dead.

47. B—Agglomeration is process in which businesses cluster together to take advantage of infrastructure or markets. These three stores would likely locate near one another to attract shoppers who might also be interested in their goods. Deglomeration (C) refers to the spreading out of businesses because of crowding and other negatives. Purchasing power parity (A) refers to a formula used to compare the value of a product in various countries. Urban heat islands (D) refer to the increase in temperatures found in urban areas because of increased pavement, population density, and industrial activity. Concentric zones (E) are neighboring zones radiating outward in rings. The *concentric zone model* was developed to explain the urban housing patterns in American cities in the 1920s.

48. C—Linguistic differences are not generally enough to stimulate a heated boundary dispute. Boundary disputes between countries are usually over resources (A), territories they both claim (B), the interpretation of the legal documents that define the boundary between the two (D), or exclusive economic zones (EEZs) offshore (E).

49. D—A central place function with a high range and high threshold would need a specialized group of customers and workers for its services. A cancer treatment clinic provides a special service to certain sick patients who would be willing to travel a great distance to receive their treatment. The other answer choices list services that would have a lower threshold population since they do not require as large a population in order to support their supply of services in their local community.

50. B—Possibilism is the theory that humans have a choice in how they think, act, and live within a range of available possibilities given to them by their physical environment. Environmental perception (A) is the theory that people of different cultures look at their environments in different ways. Environmental determinism (C) is the belief that our environment influences and controls our actions, lifestyle, and culture. Environmentalism (D) is the movement to preserve and protect the physical environment from pollution and misuse by humans. A culture system (E) is a group of culture complexes that form the common identity of a group.

51. C—The conflict in Kashmir is irredentist, therefore territorial in nature, as the Muslim majority in this Indian-controlled territory long to become part of Pakistan. Fertile ground (A) is a resource issue, land use (B), and immigration (E) are functional issues of contention on some borders, and document interpretation (D) is a boundary disagreement based on differing interpretations of how the boundary was defined in writing.

52. B—Artifacts are the material elements of a culture, such as tools, dishes, knives, toys, etc. Tools (A) do not include all the artifacts of a culture, such as toys. Mentifacts (C) are the core elements of a culture and remain relatively constant, evolving only very slowly over time. These include language, religion, and traditions. Sociofacts (D) are the connections between people in a culture and include religious, political, and educational institutions, as well as family and community linkages. The built environment (E) is the material culture of a group, including buildings, roads, and whatever humans have constructed in their environment.

53. D—Little Italy is an urban ethnic community whose residents define themselves as Italian. Answer choices A, B, and E are formal regions defined by a political boundary (New Hampshire and Texas) or a cultural feature (Christianity). The urban working and shopping zone of Pittsburgh (C) is a functional region with a core and a periphery.

54. A—The *concentric zone model* depicts the city as a set of rings radiating out from the CBD and was developed to explain the social patterns of American cities in the 1920s. The central place model (B) was developed by German geographer Walter Christaller in 1933 to explain the patterns and distributions of settlements as they are interconnected with their surrounding hinterlands. The urban realms model (C) is an economic model that states an urban resident's life is mainly lived in one realm within the urban environment. The sector model (D) views urban housing like spokes radiating from a central hub. It states that new housing for the wealthy extends outward on its original axis from the city as it grows, middle-income housing extends in the same way next to higher-income sectors, and lower-income housing fills in the gaps. The *multiple-nuclei model* (E) states that large cities spread out from several nodes of growth, not just one.

55. A—Suburbs are often characterized by "sprawl" or a tendency to spread over time. Central city (B) refers to the central business district (CBD) that is found at the heart of every city. A conurbation (C) is a continuous urban area that has grown to consume what were once separate cities. Many suburbs contain shopping and other facilities as well as homes (D). Suburbs are generally on the outskirts of metropolitan areas and are well integrated with them (E).

56. D—The large-scale agribusinesses that dominate truck farming are highly mechanized. Machinery is used to plant, irrigate, and harvest the crop. Truck farming is big business in California, Florida, and in southeastern states such as Georgia (A). Produce grown on truck farms is often shipped to areas where these crops cannot be grown as easily, if at all (B). Large-scale commercialized farms employ migrant workers who are less costly (C). Perishable fruit and vegetable crops are common crops of truck farming (E).

57. D—Paris, France, is not a forward-thrust capital. All the other answer choices list forward-thrust capitals located on a frontier as a magnet for development or on a contested border as a stance of power.

58. A—Basic jobs in a city's economy generate income for the city by producing goods or services for "export" out of the city. Non-basic jobs (B) provide services to the city's workers and do not usually generate "new" income for the city. White-collar jobs (C) are desk jobs or clerical jobs that require more mental and less physical activity than blue-collar (E), or physical jobs. Suburban (D) refers to the residential communities surrounding American cities and not to an economic sector.

59. B—A sense of place is the feelings of attachment we have to a specific location. Placelessness (A) refers to the absence of distinct characteristics that might make a location special or unique. Location (C) is a description of where a

place is. The cultural landscape (D) defines the Earth's surface as modified by human hands. Connectivity (E) refers to the tangible (highway systems) and intangible (radio waves) ways that places are connected.

60. C—A charter group is the first ethnic group to arrive and start the first effective settlement in a new area. They establish the recognized cultural norms that groups arriving later must follow. The French came to Quebec, Canada, during the seventeenth century to establish a fur trade with the Native Americans and to spread the Catholic faith. Today 75 percent of Quebec's population is of French lineage. Quebec maintains a distinctive Francophone identity distinct from the rest of Canada.

61. E—The *multiple-nuclei model* states that large cities spread out from several nodes of growth, not just one. The central place model (B) was developed by German geographer Walter Christaller in 1933 to explain the patterns and distributions of settlements as they are interconnected with their surrounding hinterlands. The *concentric zone model* (B) depicts the city as a set of rings radiating out from the CBD and was developed to explain the social patterns of American cities in the 1920s. The urban realms model (C) is an economic model that states an urban resident's life is mainly lived in one realm within the urban environment. The sector model (D) views urban housing like spokes radiating from a central hub (the CBD). It states that new housing for the wealthy extends outward on its original axis from the city as it grows, middle-income housing extends in the same way next to the higher-income sector, and lower-income housing fills in the gaps.

62. D—Primary activities such as mining, agriculture, fishing, forestry, and quarrying, involve humans harvesting crops or removing materials from the earth. Pottery production (A), electronic assembly (B), and hydroelectric production (C) are secondary activities that add value to the original material. Internet sales (E) and other retail and wholesale activities involving the business, financial, professional, or clerical sectors are tertiary activities.

63. E—Doubling time is calculated by dividing the country's growth rate (as a percent) into 70. These calculations should never be relied on to accurately predict the future size of a population. Birth rates (A), death rates (B), migration (C), and age structure (D) are all important factors affecting the growth of a population.

64. B—Vietnam practices the Mahayana, the most dominant form of Buddhism. Buddhism diffused to Vietnam during the second century B.C. from India, China, and Central Asia. The other answer choices list countries with only very small minorities of Buddhists. Brazil (A) is a Roman Catholic country. France (C) is nominally Roman Catholic, although in reality it is a very secular country (recent polls show most French seldom attend church). About 80 percent of the Russian population (D) belongs to the Russian Orthodox church, but the Muslim population is rapidly increasing and Islam is Russia's second largest religion. Iran (E) is a Shi'ite Muslim country.

65. D—You would expect to see a steel mill near a railroad yard for cargo reception and product transport. The other choices would not typically be found near a railroad yard.

66. C—The eastern coastal region of China has a population density of over 400 per square kilometer—twice the density of the second-highest which is the central region. The arid basins and deserts of western China (A) and the high, cold mountains of the Tibetan Plateau (E) have very low population densities of less than 10 people per kilometer. Regions B and D represent regions of intermediate population densities.

67. C—The Special Economic Zones (SEZs) of China's east coast enjoy relaxed trade laws that stimulate China's economy.

68. A—Latitude and longitude are the exact location of a place on the Earth's surface in degrees, minutes, and seconds and represent its absolute location. Relative location (B) refers to where a place is in relation to other places. Distance (C) is the space between two points on the Earth's surface, and situation (D) is the relative location of a place in terms of its physical and cultural

features. Scale (E) is the frame of reference for studying something. It is also the size of a unit on a map as a ratio to the same number of units on the Earth's surface.

69. C—Total fertility rates of 2.1 to 2.3 are required to replace a country's population and have been declining steadily in both European (A) and Asian (B) countries over the last decades. The total fertility rate reflects the cultural values of a country and the reproductive behaviors of its women. It does not directly reflect either biological constraints (D) or the level of industrialization (E).

70. A—The development of biofuels has not caused a decrease in the use of fossil fuels as hoped; worldwide consumption of fossil fuels continues to grow, although at a slower pace than it would if biofuels had not been developed. However, the development of biofuels has caused a rise in global food prices as some farmland that used to grow food now produces crops for biofuels (B). In some parts of the world, the transfer of farmland to the production of crops for biofuels has also resulted in the conversion of small farms to large monoculture plantations (C), violence (D), and the eviction of small farmers (E).

71. B—Increased investment in sanitation and government healthcare programs and has worked to decrease the spread of infectious diseases like pneumonia and malaria. The other factors have all contributed to the global spread of infectious disease by increasing contact between people throughout the world.

72. C—A nation is a group of people with a common culture and history who occupy an area. A state (A) is a political entity that occupies a definite territory with borders and full sovereignty. A country (B) is synonymous with a state. A political state is another term for a state (D). A nation-state (E) is a state with only one nation of people within its borders.

73. A—An isogloss is the geographic boundary limit for a linguistic trait. An example is the geographic boundary between the US region where the word "hoagie" is used and the word "grinder" is used. Dialects (B) are different spoken regional versions of the same language. They usually vary in pronunciation, rhythm, and speed. A toponym (C) is a place name such as Cropp's Corners or Oil City. Vernacular (D) refers to the local, nonstandard language spoken in a place. Creole (E) is a language that began as a pidgin language and graduated to a permanent language.

74. **C**—Scale is the relationship between the size of an element on the map and the same element on the Earth's surface. A mental map (A) refers to the images in one's mind about an area.

A projection (B) is the method used to represent the Earth's curved surface on a flat piece of paper (map). Density (D) is defined as the quantity of something per unit on a map. A model (E) is a simplified representation of reality and is used often in human geography to study cause-and-effect relationships.

75. **C**—Sales jobs are a tertiary economic activity. All the other answer choices list "white collar" and professional jobs in the quaternary sector.

Explanations for Section II (Free-Response Questions)

Question 1 (8 points total)

1A. (2 points)
The total fertility rate is the average number of children a woman in her childbearing years would be expected to have if she bore them at the current year's rate.

1B. (2 points)
East Asia and the Pacific's total fertility rate declined 3.3 percentage points and Latin America's declined 2.9 percentage points. They are the only regions on the chart to see a drop of over 50 percent in their total fertility rates between 1970 and 2004.

1C. (4 points)
Note: Your answer should focus on one region only. The discussion below includes both regions to provide an explanation for whichever region you chose.

China decreased drastically from 1970 to 2004, and similar drastic drops in Brazil and other states in both regions reflect a change in cultural values in both regions. In both regions, having fewer children has become acceptable and desirable as economic development continues. Japan's decreasing fertility rate is caused by women deciding not to marry or postponing marriage for career. Japan is offering government incentives to couples to marry, and children receive their high school education free to help with child-rearing expenses. Studies also show that as women are educated, fertility rates fall in some regions. The availability of contraceptives and organized family planning programs has also been shown to influence total fertility rates. Peru showed a decrease in the 1960s in the middle- and upper-income levels because of economic progress and paradoxically again showed a decrease in 1970 among lower-income Andean agrarian people as the economic depression hit Peru.

Economically, this trend of smaller families and fewer children will mean that fewer workers will be entering the workforce in the future, perhaps causing labor shortages. In the long run, retirement ages may rise, taxes increase, and retirement benefits may be reduced since there will be fewer workers to support an aging population. Socially, smaller families may mean a breakdown in the family structure because more mothers will enter the workforce. The increased pressure put on a dwindling labor force may also raise crime rates or require opening borders to immigration to supplement the labor force.

Question 2 (9 points total)

2A. (1 point)
A universalizing religion is a religion in which anyone can become a member.

2B. (4 points—1 point for each religion and 1 point for each country example)
Possible answers include Christianity, Islam, and Buddhism. Country examples for Christianity include Mexico, Cuba, Brazil, the Philippines or any country in North or South America, most countries of Europe, and some countries of Africa. Country examples for Islam include Indonesia, Pakistan, Bangladesh, Egypt, Sudan, Afghanistan, Yemen, Albania, etc. Country examples for Buddhism include Malaysia, Thailand, Sri Lanka, Vietnam, etc.

2C. (2 points—1 point for each explanation of how the religion was spread. To get the point, the country, the religion, and the explanation must all be correct.)
Note: Your explanation will depend on the countries you chose and should specifically describe how the religion spread to those countries. The discussion below is not intended to be a complete answer but only to provide guidance regarding a starting point for your response.

In general terms, Christianity spread by conquest (as in Latin America), immigration (as in the United States and Canada), conversions by missionaries (as in Sub-Saharan Africa). Islam spread by conquest (as in the Middle East) and trade (as in Indonesia). Buddhism spread by missionaries (monks) and by gradual diffusion into other countries that adopted Buddhism and modified it to fit their culture.

Question 3 (9 points total)

3A. (1 point)
A political state is an independent political unit occupying a territory and having sovereign control over its people and territory.

3B. (4 points—1 point for each way a political state can foster cohesiveness and 1 point for each of the explanations)
Note: There are many possible correct answers. The discussion below is not intended to be a complete answer but only to provide guidance regarding a starting point for your response.

Examples of factors that encourage cohesion include a charismatic leader, national icons (flags, anthems, holidays, etc.), royalty, widely revered documents of significance (Magna Carta, a declaration of independence, a constitution), strong national institutions (a school system, the military, the national government), comprehensive transportation and communication networks, etc.

3C. (4 points—1 point for each the two factors that can erode cohesiveness and 1 point for each of the explanations)
Note: There are many possible correct answers. The discussion below is not intended to be a complete answer but only to provide guidance regarding a starting point for your response.

Factors that can discourage national cohesiveness include insufficiently developed transportation and communication networks, conflicts between different religious groups, separatist groups, ethnic division and conflicts, economic instability, political discontent, etc.

STEP 3

Develop Strategies for Success

CHAPTER 4

Tips for Taking the Multiple-Choice Section of the Exam

IN THIS CHAPTER

Summary: Use these strategies to get a higher score on the multiple-choice section of the AP Human Geography exam.

Key Ideas

✪ Always completely fill in the ovals on the answer sheet.

✪ Work quickly but carefully. Remember, you only have 60 minutes to answer 75 questions.

✪ Read the question carefully and read each of the five responses before choosing your answer. Sometimes the correct answer is very close to one or more wrong answers. Only one word or phrase may make a difference.

✪ Four out of five of the answers are wrong—only one answer is correct! Try to eliminate the wrong ones quickly. Draw a line through the wrong answer choices quickly in your booklet.

✪ Sometimes two answers both appear correct. Without taking much time, choose one and move on. Put a quick checkmark beside that question in your test booklet. If you have an extra minute to two after completing this section, you can return to the questions to think further.

✪ **Never leave any blanks!** There is no penalty for guessing. You are only awarded points on correct answers. An educated guess is better than a blank, which will guarantee 0 points for that question.

Introduction

The first section of the AP Human Geography exam contains 75 multiple-choice questions. This is timed and you will be given 60 minutes to complete this section. Your score depends on the number of correct answers you accumulate. There is no penalty for guessing and no chance of ever getting a point if you leave a blank.

How to Attack the Test

Know Your Stuff

With only 60 minutes to read and answer 75 multiple-choice questions, you really need to know AP Human Geography! You have an average of 48 seconds to read the question, read all the answer choices, and think about what to pick. The better your level of understanding, the quicker you can recognize the correct choice and keep moving. Remember, time spent learning and reviewing now means a better score on the exam. And a good score on the exam means time and money saved by not having to take three expensive college credits in college.

Narrow It Down, Then Guess

Each question has five choices—four of these are wrong and are called distracters. Hopefully, the correct answer will "leap out" at you. Don't worry if it doesn't, however. One or two distracters will be "really" wrong and can be eliminated quickly. That leaves three choices— two of which contain errors. Search quickly for the word or phrase that makes two of the remaining choices incorrect. By doing this you will narrow down and find the right answer. If the correct answer is still elusive, make a good guess and move on quickly. Remember, there is no penalty for guessing. Don't skip a "toughie" thinking you will have time later to return and think about it more. You probably won't have time to go back to it. Most students find they cannot complete 75 questions in 60 minutes as it is. Quickly eliminate, then guess, and keep moving!

What Types of Questions Are There?

There are three main types of multiple-choice questions found on the AP Human Geography exam:

- **Conceptual questions.** Most of the questions will ask you to analyze a concept you have covered in AP Human Geography class.
- **Interpretation of maps, graphs, charts.** A few questions will contain a graph, map, or other figure that you will be asked to interpret. You will have to figure out quickly what is being displayed in the figure and see what is being asked in the question. Read each answer choice and see if the answer that came to your mind is listed.
- **Fact-based questions.** Some questions will ask you for a specific bit of knowledge, such as "Which of the political states listed below has recently experienced a resurgence of nationalism?" The distracters will be a list of political states.

Hopefully, one of them will "grab" you and you can mark it and quickly move on. Time is very limited! With less than 60 seconds for each question, you must move quickly through the fact-based questions. The ones requiring interpretation of a map or graph will require extra seconds to read, analyze, and check out the possible answers.

Develop a Strategy

Below is a list of important tips you can use to score your best on the AP Human Geography exam. Follow these recommendations and you will have a strategy for success!

STRATEGY

- Know your stuff! Study and review this book and all vocabulary, models, and concepts.
- Read each test question quickly, but carefully.
- Carefully fill in the answer oval on the answer grid in pencil only. Do not place any other marks on the answer sheet.
- Read each answer choice—some could look correct at first glance but have one word that makes them wrong.
- If you are not 100 percent sure, narrow it down to the *best* two choices and quickly guess.
- Keep moving at a steady pace. Don't get bogged down on one question.
- Check the clock periodically.
- Made a checkmark on the test booklet beside questions you have guessed at. You may have a minute to return and think about them after you have attempted the other questions.
- Never leave a question blank. Remember, blanks will never earn a point but a filled-in answer grid just might get you extra points. If you don't know the correct answer, eliminate the obvious distracters, guess, and move on.

CHAPTER 5

Tips for Taking the Free-Response Section of the Exam

IN THIS CHAPTER

Summary: Use these strategies to get a higher score on the free-response section of the AP Human Geography exam.

Key Ideas

✪ Read the question carefully. Use the strategies in this book to analyze the question.

✪ Write just enough to completely answer the question.

✪ Time yourself. You have 75 minutes to write three essays.

✪ Start with the essay you know most about. Do not spend more than 20 minutes on it, however.

✪ Label each part of your answer to correspond with the part of the question you are answering.

Introduction

In Section II of the AP Human Geography exam, you will have 75 minutes to write three free-response essays. This means you have an average of 25 minutes to write each essay. Each essay is worth a certain number of points from 6 to 12, but you will not be told how many points each essay is worth at the time you are taking the test. Every essay is broken down into two or more parts, which are each worth a certain number of points. When the essays are scored according to the scoring rubric (answer guide), each section of each essay will be awarded points. The total number of points for each essay is based on the sum of the points you earned on each part. When points for each essay are added together, the total is your raw score for Section II of the exam. Your essays are scored according to the rubric. Grammar, spelling, writing style, etc. are not important and do not add or subtract points from your Section II score.

What Types of Questions Are There?

The free-response questions are *not* formal essays! You will not be expected to write a thesis statement, body, and conclusion. In fact, if you do, you probably will not have time to analyze all three questions and write good responses! You will *not* be given points for any pictures, diagrams, or maps you draw, so only do so if you need to lay your facts out in order to write a good response. Make a quick outline if it helps you organize your thoughts for the essay. However, information written in the outline will not earn you points either. Only what is written in your actual essay will earn points.

The questions are usually based on stimulus material that could include a map, chart, graph, photograph, or other spatial display of data. Most questions are three-part and require you to analyze, interrelate, and synthesize concepts and knowledge from multiple areas of human geography in your responses.

Develop a Strategy

The following tips will help you do your best on the free-response essay questions of Section II. Some are *Do*s and some are *Don't*s. Follow them carefully as 10 years of experience writing and scoring AP Human Geography free-response questions have gone into formulating them—and they work! Follow these recommendations and you will have a strategy for success.

1. **Really read the question.** Find the verb (key word asking for action). This will tell you where the points are in the question. Power verbs ask you to perform a very specific action when writing your essay. Below are a list of verbs and an explanation of what they require you to do for the essay. Get to know these verbs and exactly what you are being asked to do when you see them!
   - *Analyze:* Power verb! Find the relationship between two events, concepts, or parts. Tip-off word could be "why?" Write an explanation and a conclusion (or conclusions) based on solid evidence and/or a logical argument. Give details and specifics. You should write *at least* two informative sentences. Use as much AP Human Geography vocabulary as possible.
     Example: Analyze the impact of the Green Revolution on China and India and discuss the need for additional food supplies in these regions.
   - *Assess/Evaluate:* Power verb! Discuss the value or merit of something. List the positive and negative traits of a statement, concept, etc. Talk about advantages and disadvantages. Be clear about the criteria, or standards, which you are using to judge or evaluate. Specific examples should be applied to the criteria to support your answer. Evaluation or assessment means you *must* make clear connections between your argument and the supporting evidence you give.

Example: Assess the impact of urban growth on the housing market in the urban area depicted in the graph and evaluate this growth in terms of population density.

- **Compare:** Put the two statements, countries, concepts, ideas, etc. side-by-side and observe similarities and differences between them. *Always note both similarities and differences!* Be specific and remember, the more relevant information you write down, the better your chances of fitting the rubric and earning points.

  Example: Compare the obstacles to development faced by Bangladesh and Rwanda.

- **Contrast:** Here you are asked to look for the differences between two concepts, ideas, countries, etc. You will need to look for ways in which they are not the same and write these in detail.

  Example: Apply any two urban models to the urban area in the map below and contrast them in relation to the following: population density, housing, socioeconomic factors.

- **Describe:** Power verb! You will need to tell about something or give a picture in words. Write lots of detail in *at least* two sentences. Talk about its most noteworthy characteristics. Tip-off word could be "what?"

  Example: Describe the relationship between land rent and residential density depicted in the graph below. *Another example:* What are the sources of cultural dissonance in many European states today?

- **Discuss:** Power verb! This verb is used a lot on AP Human Geography free-response questions. You are asked to debate or write about something taking both points of view. Write about the topic by presenting both sides. The question will usually give a relationship between two different phenomena or concepts. In your response, identify, describe, and/or explain and be sure and supply ample detail. Discussion requires *at least* three sentences. Remember, if you discuss vacation plans with your parents, you talk for more than a minute and you cover lots of details. That is what you need to do here.

  Example: Discuss how each of the following factors has contributed to the development of the steel industry in China.

- **Explain:** Another power verb! This is another verb you will likely see on the AP Human Geography exam. Here you are asked to make something plain and to use lots of details. Talk about the logical connections between the geographic phenomena in the question. Discuss the cause-and-effect relationships that exist. What is the meaning of this relationship? Use *at least* two sentences and preferably more to give good details as you describe them.

  Example: Explain how boundary disputes between states A and B have led to increasing destabilization of the region in the last three decades.

- **Identify/Define:** You are asked to write down a simple list of characteristics, factors, or give a definition. You do not need to write an explanation. Give a meaning for a word or concept. Always write a good example to ensure points are earned. You will see this verb a lot on the AP Human Geography free-response questions. Usually this part of the question is only worth one or two points, but every point helps! Sometimes it is combined with another verb that requires more thorough analysis as in the first example given below.

  Example: Identify and briefly explain ONE factor that was responsible for population increase in Sub-Saharan Africa during the past two decades. *Another example:* Define the following concepts as they are used in urban geography: (1) ghettoization, (2) gentrification, (3) suburbanization.

2. **Really write.** It is not enough to write a sentence or two; you must *thoroughly* discuss or talk about your response. Don't be chintzy! Don't just answer the question as if this was a routine end-of-chapter review question. The people who will be scoring your

essays (readers) really want to give you points, but they are not miracle-workers. If you write two sentences and the essay is worth 8 points, guess what? There cannot possibly be enough facts and good stuff in those two sentences to wring more than three or four points, if that, out of your essay.

Example, one point out of a possible two-point answer: Revitalization of the residential district of US cities stimulates the increase of a population engaged in economic activities.

Example, two points out of a possible two-point answer: Revitalization of the residential district of US cities stimulates the increase of a population engaged in economic activities. The chance of increased market activity in the business sectors of cities promotes improvement of the landscape to attract more consumers. Tourism is an important incentive to revitalize the central city where tourists will be attracted and improve the economy.

3. **Save the fluff.** Don't write a lot of empty words about nothing. If you have absolutely no clue about the question being asked, find the geographic concept in the question and write a definition. *Always* stick with the topic, even if you cannot really answer the question. Use geographic vocabulary you learned in your class. Find some bit of geographic knowledge from your class and apply it somehow to the question. There is a chance that something in your definition or explanation will accidentally hit on the correct response and earn you a point or two, but please, do not waste your time saying the same thing over and over 10 different ways.

4. **Be a clock-watcher.** You have 75 minutes to write three solid essays for Section II of the exam. Try to limit yourself to 20 minutes for each response and keep an eye on the clock. If you have extra time after writing all three essay responses, go back and review, edit, and make sure each part of every question was completely answered.

5. **Don't skip a question.** Attempt to answer all three free-response essay questions. It will be very difficult for you to do well on the exam if you completely skip just one of these essays! If you try and write something pertaining to the question, even if you do not score points, you will be given a zero and will be better off statistically when your total score is computed. If you leave an essay blank, you will receive a "—" score and it will be impossible for you to get a 4 or 5 score on the AP Human Geography exam.

6. **Answer the question you know the most about first.** However, don't forget to save time for the other two. You can start by writing the third essay response if you choose to do so. It helps to start each new essay on a clean page and not at the bottom of a previous essay, but this is not required. A high-scoring essay will usually take three to four pages to answer completely and comprehensively.

7. **Label each part of your response identifying the part of the question you are answering.** For example, if you are answering Part B of the first essay, write "1B" at the beginning of the first paragraph for that part of your response. This helps the reader who is scoring your essay locate possible points. The reader can go right to the appropriate part of your response and easily check your answer against the rubric. If the reader has to search throughout your response for each bit of correct information, it greatly increases the chances that it will not be located.

8. **Never restate the question in your essay.** Don't write an introductory paragraph or conclusion paragraph either. These actions waste valuable time and get you zero points. You will not be assessed points based on using good grammar, correct punctuation and spelling, and excellent essay structure, but you will not lose points for incorrect spelling and poor grammar either.

9. **Write large and legibly with pen only.** Readers are not handwriting experts, but they do try very hard to read poor handwriting. Make sure you write large enough and as carefully as possible so that points are not missed because of messy, illegible handwriting.

10. **Double-space your essays.** This will give you room to add a few details when you go back and reread your responses. If you have left out an important detail or want to add a supporting fact, you can easily add it in the extra space over or under the sentence.

11. **Review your essays.** Always go back over your essays and make sure that you have:
    - Answered each part of each essay completely. Remember, answer each part of each question with at least two meaningful sentences that *directly* answer the question.
    - Lettered each part of each essay clearly to correspond with the part of the question you are answering.
    - Put the essay number in the small box in the corner of each page of the answer booklet.
    - Referred to the correct region and/or time period referenced in the question.
    - Added specific examples and "for instances" to add more substance and support to your responses.

STEP 4

Review the Knowledge You Need to Score High

Key Human Geography Concepts

IN THIS CHAPTER

Summary: The AP Human Geography course is divided into seven broad content areas:

- ✪ Geography's nature and perspectives
- ✪ Population
- ✪ Cultures
- ✪ Political organization of space
- ✪ Agricultural and rural land use
- ✪ Industrialization and economic development
- ✪ Cities and urban land use

This chapter reviews geography's nature and perspectives by examining the core concepts of human geography (space, place, location, scales, and regions), as well as the necessary skills essential for success in the AP course and on the AP Human Geography exam. In addition, this chapter briefly reviews the new technologies that geographers use to explore the questions of who lives where, how they live, and why they live there. Spatial behavior and interaction are also covered in this chapter.

KEY IDEA

Key Terms

absolute location	formal region
cultural landscape	functional region
density	Geographic Information System (GIS)
distribution	latitude

longitude
meridian
mental map
model
perceptual region
place
projection
region
relative location

remote sensing
representative fraction
scale
site
situation
space
spatial diffusion
uniform region

Introduction

What exactly is human geography? Human geography is the study of why people choose to live where they do. Human geographers seek to discover who lives where, how they live, and why they live there.

Geography as a Field of Inquiry

The study of geography explores where, how, and why different places, people, and environments came to exist and the various effects each has on the other. Geographers examine these places, people, and environments in spatial terms. Their position "in space" can spark as many new questions as it answers, however, so geographers are constantly asking questions such as: Where is it? Why is it located there? How do the people there adapt to their environment? Why do they build dwellings like this? Where do they come from and how do they survive?

We must thank the wisdom of the ancients for starting us off on human geography! The "father of geography," a Greek scholar and mathematician named Eratosthenes, defined the word "geography" calling it *geo* (earth) *graphos* (to write). He is credited with many "firsts." He was the first person to compute the circumference of the Earth, which he accomplished using a measurement called *stades*, or the length of stadiums at that time. He was incredibly accurate. He also used his mathematical genius to invent *pi* and was the first to accurately calculate the tilt of the Earth's axis. He invented the system of latitude and longitude in his spare time, too, and was the first to measure the equator (25,000 miles).

Another ancient Greek scholar, Herodotus, drew the first map of the known world of his time in 450 B.C.E as part of his study of the Greco-Persian Wars. The extent of the known world at that time was the Mediterranean Sea and immediate surroundings.

Core Geographic Concepts

The basic building blocks of human geography are space, place, location, scale, and regions. Since geography is a spatial science, let's begin by talking about what "space" is.

Space is the extent of area that is occupied by something. It can refer to physical and cultural objects on the surface of the Earth. Relative space is concerned with where something is in relation to something else and changes constantly as interrelationships between people, places, and things change. Absolute space is a measurable area with definite boundaries. Absolute space is an essential ingredient in mapmaking (cartography) and spatial analysis of any type. **Site** is the physical location of a place, and **situation** refers to the location of a place based on its relation to other places. For example, the site of Foxburg is on the banks of the

Allegheny River in northwestern Pennsylvania. The situation of Foxburg is that it lies equidistant between Erie and Pittsburgh and is 3 miles upstream from the town of Emlenton.

Place is another word for **location.** We examine place very carefully in human geography to determine the values and attributes that a location possesses. We often refer to a location's sense of place and are talking about all the attributes—physical, cultural, emotional—that a location has to us personally. Conversely, *placelessness* refers to the condition in which a place actually loses its sense of being "special." The unique urban or regional flavor of a location becomes diminished or lost as mass merchandising outlets, fast-food restaurants, and brand-name retail stores erase its sense of place.

Places share similar attributes, and some of them are listed below. All places:

- Have location, direction, and distance from other places
- Change over time
- Interrelate with all other places in some way
- Have size and scale
- Possess a physical aspect and a cultural aspect
- Can be grouped into *regions* based on how they are alike and how they are dissimilar

Location is also important in the study of human geography. **Absolute location** is the actual space a place occupies on the Earth's surface. It is usually referred to in mathematical form using degrees, minutes, and seconds (latitude and longitude coordinates) or even simply a street address for a house or building. The system of describing locations of US places using the township, range, or section is another method of describing absolute location.

Relative location refers to the location of a place in relation to the location of other places. Relative locations vary greatly and depend on your perspective. The phrases, "down South," "up North," "back East," and "out West," are examples of how history and tradition still flavor our speech in the United States. An example of relative location would be "Pittsburgh is located at the confluence of the Monongahela and Allegheny Rivers approximately 90 miles north of Morgantown, West Virginia."

Location is related to the global grid system of latitude and longitude. Latitude is the distance north and south of the equator and is measured in equidistant lines called parallels, which decrease in length as they get closer to the north and south poles. Longitude is the distance east and west of the Prime Meridian in meridians, or lines of equal length that meet at the north and south poles.

Scale, or the degree of generalization on a map, is used in two very important ways in geography. First, scale can mean the frame of reference for studying something—the agricultural practices of the world (global scale), a region (regional scale), or a community (local scale). Scale also can mean the size of a unit on a map as a ratio of its size on the map to the same units on the Earth's surface. It is important to know which meaning you are talking about when using the term. For example, reference to your study of large-scale desertification using a small-scale map can be confusing! (A small-scale map shows a smaller amount of detail for a larger area. A large-scale map shows a larger amount of detail for a smaller area.) In the example above, your study of large-scale desertification refers to desertification on a global or multiregional scale.

Two Examples of How Scale Is Shown on a Map

Representative fraction (RF):   1:250,000

Verbal scale: 0   1   2

                                   miles

Regions are an important concept because they allow us to study space, place, and locations in better detail by allowing us to generalize about a common characteristic and thus group them. A region is an area that displays a common trait such as culture, government, language, landform, etc. Regions can be mapped and analyzed. Just as historians group events in a specific era as "periods," geographers group area spatially into "regions." Examples of this type of grouping result in the Sunbelt, Silicon Valley, the Bible Belt, the Heartland, etc. The table below defines and gives examples of some important regions you should know.

TYPE OF REGION	DEFINITION	EXAMPLES
Formal (uniform)	A region with a high level of consistency in a certain cultural or physical attribute	French-speaking region of Canada Dairying region of North America Political boundaries demarcating states (such as Poland, Thailand, etc.) or their subdivisions (Iowa, Manitoba, etc.) Tropical region Desert region
Functional (nodal)	A region with a node, or center hub, surrounded by interconnecting linkages. Usually connections relate to trade, communications, transportation, etc.	Metropolitan Area of Chicago Bank of America Port of New Orleans and its hinterlands Mall of America's surrounding area
Perceptual (vernacular)	A region defined by feelings and prejudices that may or may not be true. A construct of one's mental map.	Dixie Bible Belt Rust Belt Hillbilly region Society Hill Urban street gang's turf Chinatown

Key Geographic Skills

In AP Human Geography, we use several key geographic skills. The five main skills involve analyzing human actions as they relate to their environment. Since geography is a spatial discipline, these key skills revolve around learning to interpret, analyze, and apply data spatially in the form of maps, graphs, and charts. Information can be displayed and problems solved by applying the concepts learned in AP Human Geography!

The five key geographic skills presented in AP Human Geography class are:

1. **The ability to interpret maps, graphs, tables, charts, and other spatial data.** Since it is impossible to represent a globe accurately on a flat piece of paper, a map always distorts, or misrepresents, some item of information. The type of information you want to find on a map will tell you which projection, or type of map you need to use.

2. **How to understand and interpret the implications of relationships among observable facts (phenomena) in places.** Geographers study the interaction of the major elements that give character to a place. When you are engaged in geography, you are trying to understand the value of places!

3. **How to recognize and interpret relationships among patterns and processes at different scales.** Patterns of vegetation, fauna, precipitation, house types, or agricultural activities are all the result of various processes. Geographers figure out how these different processes relate to each other at various scales.

4. **How to define regions and evaluate the regionalization process.** It has been said that making regions is the highest form of a geographer's art.

5. **How to characterize and analyze changing interconnections among places.** One of the most important aspects of geography is the effort to understand how places are interconnected and how these interconnections change with technology and over time.

Maps and Models

Maps and models are essential to the study of human geography (see Fig. 6.1). Maps usually display data spatially in a flat, two-dimensional manner, which means all maps are flawed in some way. **Projections** are versions of maps that try to minimize one attribute of the map but do so at the expense of the other attributes. Distortions in conformality (location), distance, direction, scale, and area always result from this process. The type of projection you should choose is the one that shows what you most need to know about an area (see Fig. 6.2).

When relationships between points based on angles are needed, as in navigational or meteorological charts, a conformal projection such as the Mercator projection or the Lambert Conformal Conic projection is used. Equidistant projections, such as the Equidistant Conic projection or the Equirectangular projection, are used when accurate distances from the center of a map are required. When directional relationships from a given central point, or azimuth, are important, the Lambert Azimuthal Equal-Area projection is often chosen. All projections require a compromise in one or more of the following map attributes—shape, area, distance, or direction. World maps, such as the Winkel Tripel projection and the Robinson projection, display a compromise in one or more of these characteristics.

Some maps, however, are in our minds—**mental maps**. They are mental images in our heads that enable us to get to our friend's house without getting lost or help us get from one class to another at school. These maps are as real as a highway map of Ohio and just as useful! Besides helping us navigate our daily lives and get from one place to another, mental maps also contain perceptions about safety, pleasure, or neighborhood, as well as other emotional variables. The mental map shown is a sketch map drawn by an AP Human Geography student of his neighborhood (see Fig. 6.3).

Different types of maps show different types of information. All maps are biased in some way, so be sure to recognize the map author's purpose and intention and take that into account when studying the spatial display of data on the map.

Figure 6.1   Ottoman map of Africa.

Figure 6.2   Azimuthal map projection of the United States. Source: *United States Geological Survey.*

Figure 6.3   Mental map of a neighborhood.

Check out the table to see some kinds of maps geographers use and the best purpose for each type.

TYPE OF MAP	WHAT IT DOES	EXAMPLE
General-Purpose or Reference Map	Displays general features of an area	Topographic, highway, atlas
Thematic Map (types of thematic maps are listed below)	Displays a single type of information	Population, median income, annual beef production
• **Graduated Circle**	Size of circle conveys number of occurrences of event in an area	
• **Dot**	Displays pattern, distribution, dispersion of data in an area	(see example below)
• **Choropleth**	Displays an average value of data in an area	(see example below)

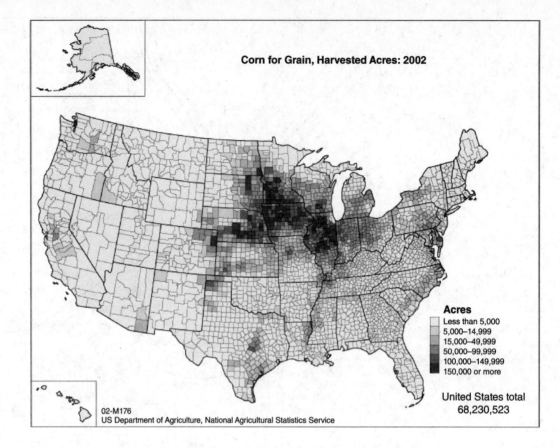

Figure 6.4   Example of a choropleth map.

The two maps in Figs. 6.4 and 6.5 are both examples of thematic maps displaying the same data but in two different ways. The first is a choropleth map and the second is a dot map. Compare them and see which one makes better sense to you.

A **model** is a simplified generalization of something in real life. Maps are a special form of model that depict information in two dimensions and usually on paper. Most models eliminate unnecessary details and isolate one or two important ideas in order to study them. AP Human Geography applies several important models that we will review in later chapters of this manual.

New Geographic Technologies

The use of satellite imagery provides us with images of Earth's features that aid us in mapping and studying various processes as they occur. This process of detecting the nature of an area from a distance is called **remote sensing** and has actually been around for over 150 years. People have attached cameras to airplanes, kites, and hot-air balloons in an attempt to photograph places from a distance for many years. Various processes such as water pollution, desertification, and even military surveillance can be accomplished with remote sensing through the use of infrared film and thermal scanning. Today, American Landsat satellites relay images from outer space to receiving stations, which digitally convert them into images for scientific study and mapping use.

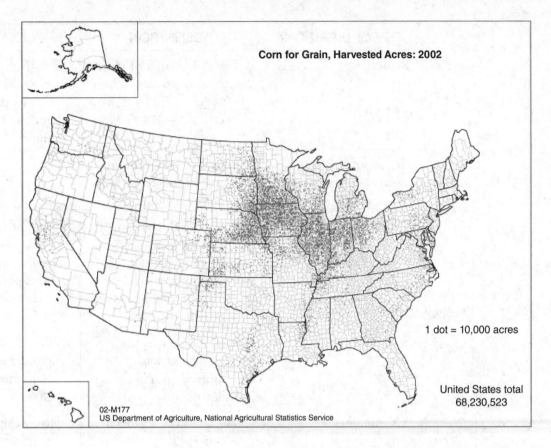

Figure 6.5 Example of a dot map.

Geographic Information Systems (GIS) marry mapping software with a database for the purpose of overlaying various data layers on a basic locational map grid. An abundance of data sets today have made GIS a valuable tool for human geographers studying questions about regional, social, and economic problems or analyzing physical processes as they impact human behaviors.

Spatial Behavior and Interaction

The two main questions geography answers are "Where?" and "Why?" Maps have long been the primary tool of geographers when answering the question of "where" places and activities are located on the surface of the Earth. To answer the "why" question, geographers must turn to the processes of **spatial interaction** and **diffusion.** The relationships between the members of your community depend on the type and kind of human interaction that occurs among the community members. In the same way, the interconnectedness between places depends on the amount of spatial interaction between them.

Diffusion is the movement of people, ideas, customs, and information between places. **Spatial diffusion** is the spread of something over time or space. The two basic types of diffusion are relocation and expansion. The table here defines and gives examples of these two forms of diffusion. **Spatial distribution** refers to the array of items on the Earth's surface. All spatial distributions have density, dispersion, and some type of pattern.

TYPE OF DIFFUSION	DEFINITION	EXAMPLES
Relocation	Physical transfer of idea, trait, or artifact to new region	Christianity to the New World by Spaniards; Islam to Indonesia by Muslim traders
Expansion (Types of expansion are shown below.)	Spread of idea, trait, or artifact usage to neighboring region	
• Hierarchical	Spread of ideas, etc. first to ruler, king, or highest authority and then downward to subjects or less prominent people	Spread of English in India under British rule so those in prominent positions needed to learn it first
• Contagious	Idea, trait, etc. spreads evenly outward from diffusion origin or hearth	Christianity's spread throughout Europe from monasteries and Roman settlements
• Stimulus	The spread of a general concept throughout a population	The development of a written language by Native American groups

Density is the number of an item within a unit of area. It is more than just a count of an item—it refers to how many of that item are in a limited space or area. One million people in a country the size of Switzerland will look a lot different than one million people in the People's Republic of China, for example! Density is an important concept when studying spatial issues. We will discuss the different types of density in the chapter reviewing population.

❯ Rapid Review

Human geography is the study of why people choose to live where they do. The study of human geography involves the use of maps, models, and spatial analysis technologies as a means of abstracting and simplifying space and all it contains for study. Maps depict a three-dimensional Earth in two dimensions, are inherently flawed due to this, and are designed with special purposes that should match the needs of the map-user.

› Review Questions

1. Chinatown is an example of a

   (A) functional region.
   (B) nodal region.
   (C) perceptual region.
   (D) formal region.
   (E) uniform region.

2. The map created by Lewis and Clark could be called a

   (A) thematic map.
   (B) choropleth map.
   (C) graduated circle map.
   (D) general purpose map.
   (E) topographic map.

3. If you wanted to see the location of the city building in Seattle, Washington, you would need a

   (A) large-scale map.
   (B) small-scale map.
   (C) topographic map.
   (D) graduated circle map.
   (E) choropleth map.

4. Human geography is the study of

   (A) the physical processes of the Earth.
   (B) who lives where, how they live, and why they live there.
   (C) the psychology of the human race using maps.
   (D) the culture of the human race minus environmental influences.
   (E) how humans evolved through time.

5. The Christian religion in South America first spread by

   (A) stimulus diffusion.
   (B) relocation diffusion.
   (C) contagious diffusion.
   (D) hierarchical diffusion.
   (E) force.

› Answers and Explanations

1. **C**—Chinatown is an example of a perceptual region—a region defined by feelings and prejudices that may or may not be true. There may not be a Chinese majority living in Chinatown anymore, but people's mental maps still reflect the old images of a Chinese-majority population there. Functional (A) and nodal regions (B) mean the same thing and refer to regions with a center hub surrounded by interconnecting linkages of transportation, communication, markets, etc. Formal (D) and uniform regions (E) are the same thing and refer to regions with a high level of consistency in a certain cultural or physical attribute, such as a part of the United States in which Hispanic culture is dominant.

2. **D**—A general purpose map shows general features of an area. Choices A, B, and C are all thematic maps. A thematic map (A) displays a single type of information, such as population or corn production. A choropleth map (B) is a thematic map that displays an average value of data in an area by using colors and shading or cross-hatching. A graduated circle map (C) is a type of thematic map in which the size of circle conveys the number of occurrences of the event in an area. A topographic map (E) is a general-purpose map that displays the natural landscape features (elevation, rivers, streams, etc.) of an area but also some cultural features such as railroads and buildings, too.

3. **A**—Large-scale maps, such as a city map of Seattle, show a small area and display a large amount of detail. Small-scale maps (B) show a large area but in less detail. Topographic maps (C) show landscape features of a fairly small area. Graduated circle maps (D) show the frequency of occurrence of an event using circles of different sizes. Choropleth maps (E) display the average value of the data in an areal unit.

4. **B**—Human geography studies why people live where they do. Physical geography (A) is the

study of the physical processes of the Earth, such as atmospheric conditions, landforms, climatic processes, etc. Choices C, D, and E are all *part* of the study of human geography in some small way but are only a very tiny piece of the total puzzle.

5. **B**—The Spanish conquerors and priests brought Christianity across the Atlantic Ocean thus physically introducing it into a new region—the Western Hemisphere. Stimulus diffusion (A) refers to the spread of a general concept throughout a population. Contagious diffusion (C) happens when an idea, trait, etc. spreads evenly outward from a diffusion origin or hearth. Hierarchical diffusion (D) is the spread of ideas, etc., first to a ruler or the highest authority and then downward to subjects or less prominent people. Force (E) may have spread various religions and certainly played a role in Christianity's spread to the indigenous people of the New World, but it *first* had to relocate across the Atlantic Ocean by means of coming across the water on ships.

CHAPTER 7

Population

IN THIS CHAPTER

Summary: In AP Human Geography, we look at population through the double lenses of space and place. Human populations have moved and settled in various locations for many years. What factors cause them to move to a new location? What makes up a population? What determines whether a population will grow or decline? This chapter reviews the basic concepts of population composition, dynamics, movements, settlement patterns, and how people relate to places.

KEY IDEA

Key Terms

agricultural density
carrying capacity
chain migration
channelized migration
crude birth rate (CBR)
crude death rate (CDR)
crude density
demography
demographic transition model
dependency ratio
distance decay
doubling time
ecumene
human capital theory of migration
internally displaced person

intervening opportunity
life course theory of migration
migration
place utility
physiologic density
population density
population momentum
population pyramid
pull factor of migration
push factor of migration
rate of natural increase (NIR)
replacement level
step migration
total fertility rate (TFR)
zero population growth (ZPG)

Introduction

The study of population and migration is an important subject area that is heavily tested on the AP Human Geography exam. It is important to know and be able to apply the concepts discussed in this chapter at every scale from local to international. What comprises a human population and the dynamics, movements, and composition of that population are both interesting and complex topics for geographers.

Population Density, Distribution, Composition, and Scale

Demography is the study of the characteristics of a human population. It is useful to examine some facts about a population before studying the human-environmental interactions that follow. **Population density** is the number of persons per unit of land area. In Fig. 7.1, you will see which regions of the world have many inhabitants per unit of land area and which regions have very few, if any. Which regions have the most inhabitants? The largest cluster lives in East Asia (20 percent) with South Asia, Southeast Asia, and Europe following in order of population. The remainder of the world's population is dispersed unevenly over the remaining ecumene. The northeastern coast of the United States and upward into the southeastern coastline of Canada comprises the fifth-largest cluster of population and the largest concentration of humans in the Western Hemisphere. The part of the Earth that is fit for humans to live is called the **ecumene.** Nearly 75 percent of the Earth's inhabitants live on 5 percent of the Earth's surface, and 50 percent of these people live in urban centers.

There are different ways of expressing the density of humans on the surface of the Earth. Perhaps the most helpful is **physiologic density**, which is the number of persons per unit of agricultural land. This number is helpful because it gives us a rough estimate of how many people a parcel of farmland can reasonably support. It could be useful in studying population pressure and overcrowding. Is the land very fertile and productive, or is the soil poor and overworked? Since the productivity of the land makes a difference, physiologic density is not a

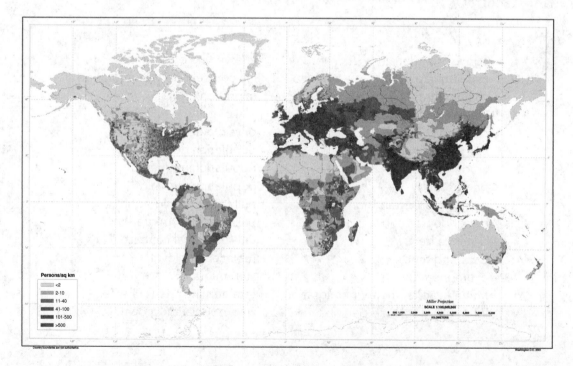

Figure 7.1 World population density, 1994. Source: *US Department of Agriculture (USDA).*

foolproof statistic. **Agricultural density** refers to the number of farmers living in rural areas per unit of agricultural land. This figure omits people who live in cities and provides an estimate of the number of people actually living off the farmlands. Possibly the most general and least useful statistic is that of **crude density**, or arithmetic density. This is the number of people per unit of land. All you have to do is divide the total land area of a region, country, or other land area by the total population to compute the arithmetic density. As the unit of land area increases in size, the crude density figure becomes less meaningful since it "blends in" the urban populations and masks the sparsely inhabited areas into one fairly useless average. Although it could be useful for quick estimates because it is easy to calculate, crude density is not very meaningful. It is most useful for homogeneous areas, such as single towns, that have evenly distributed populations.

Carrying capacity, defined as how many people an area can support on a sustained basis, relates to density because together, they define whether or not an area is overcrowded. An area may be very densely populated and yet not overcrowded, if it also has a very high carrying capacity, perhaps because of fertile soil and modern agricultural techniques. On the other hand, a place like Greenland, with a very low carrying capacity, could be over-populated at a density that would make other places underpopulated.

Population distribution is the pattern of where humans live. Humans are not spread evenly throughout the world. Most people live in the Northern Hemisphere, on continental margins, and in lowlands. The table summarizes the place characteristics that produce high and low population densities in the world.

CHARACTERISTIC	DESCRIPTION	EXAMPLE
Place Characteristics That Produce Low Population Densities		
Extreme climate	Too hot, cold, arid, or wet	Antarctica (too cold and too arid)
Extreme relief	Too high or too steep	Himalaya Mountain peaks
Extreme remoteness	Too hard to access	The island of Tristan da Cunha (the world's remotest inhabited island)
Infertile land	Unproductive land supports fewer farmers	Amazon River Basin (tropical rainforest or *selva*)
Place Characteristics That Produce High Population Densities		
Moderate climate	Not too hot or too cold	England
Adequate water supply	Ample rainfall year-round	Thailand
Fertile farmland	Many small farms feed many people	France
Mineral resources	Provision of jobs, raw materials, and energy for industries	Germany
Lowlands and river valleys	Flat or gently rolling land provides easier transportation and communication	China, Western Europe
Coastlines	60 percent of world's population live within 60 miles of the ocean	US Eastern Seaboard, South America

Migration is the movement of humans from one place to another. Migration flows occur at every possible scale from the family that moves from one neighborhood to another to the huge intercontinental flows of migrants from one continent to another. The reasons for these often large movements of humans have varied over the centuries, but these migrations are usually flights from dangerous or difficult circumstances in migrants' home regions. For example, after the collapse of the USSR, large number of refugees fled their homelands for Western Europe where jobs and new lives as guest workers opened doors of opportunity for both them and their host countries. Migrations also occur between countries on a continent (intercontinental), within a country (interregional), and from the rural countryside to urban centers (rural to urban).

Population Growth and Decline

While both the **crude birth rate (CBR)** and the **total fertility rate (TFR)** reflect on the number of births in a population, they differ in important ways. The crude birth rate measures the number of babies born per 1000 people, and the total fertility rate measures the number of babies born per reproductive-age woman. The total fertility rate is a more accurate measure of the amount of reproduction occurring in a population. A population with large amounts of reproduction occurring would have a high fertility rate (many children per woman), but could still have a low crude birth rate if most of the population were male or very old or young, that is, not reproductive-age women.

The **crude death rate (CDR)** refers to the annual number of deaths per 1000 people. Improved antibiotics, vaccinations, pesticides, and access to medical care and safe water supplies have reduced death rates (also called mortality rates) since 1945, but the concentrations of very youthful populations in less developed countries (LDCs) is equally important when considering populations. The greatest drop in death rates has occurred in the "infants one-year-and-under" age cohort. This is the age group with the highest mortality rate, so the changes in healthcare availability have had the greatest impact on this group. The drop in the infant mortality rate has been the most important factor impacting death rates all over the world.

HIV/AIDS is the fourth most common cause of death worldwide. It is a sexually transmitted phenomenon that is ravaging many Sub-Saharan African countries at an alarming rate. Since AIDS kills more women (who perform the majority of farm work as well as family care) than men in this region, food shortages threaten the survival of many families in Sub-Saharan Africa.

The **rate of natural increase (NIR)** is found by subtracting the crude death rate from the crude birth rate. (Immigration is not included in computing the NIR). The NIR is very large in the Southern Hemisphere (especially Africa), actually negative in Europe, and low in the United States. As a general rule, less developed countries (LDCs) tend to have higher rates of natural increase than more developed countries, although the pattern is not universal. Hence, population growth is usually faster in LDCs.

The **doubling time** is the length of time it takes for a country's population to double in size if the growth rate stays the same. Simply use the Rule of 70 and divide 72 by the NIR to compute the doubling time of a population. A 2 percent rate of natural increase (medium-high) would double population in 35 years. The exponential growth of a growing population can be seen in the J-curve, which looks like a big letter J on a graph with the curve heading into the universe as population growth explodes. Population projections suggest reason for concern in some world regions as population appears to be approaching a point that exceeds available resources.

Because of **population momentum**, it can be very difficult to project what a population will be like in the future. Population momentum means that even though the fertility rates may be decreasing, the population can still be increasing. Developing countries (such as those in Asia and Latin America) have a much greater population momentum than the industrially developed countries because of a high proportion of the population in their reproductive years.

The **demographic transition model** attempts to show the link between population growth and economic development. The stages in demographic transition are as follows:

- Stage 1: Slow population growth, when the birth and death rates are both high
- Stage 2: The population increases greatly as the death rate drops and birth rate stays high
- Stage 3: The population growth slows because of a falling birth rate
- Stage 4: The rate of natural increase is low or decreasing because of low death rates and low birth rates

Most of the world before the Industrial Revolution was in Stage 1. Because both birth rates and death rates were high, the population remained stable. Pandemics, wars, and weather catastrophes had big effects on population. In Stage 2, death rates, especially among children, drop due to improvements in medical care. Birth rates remain high so population growth occurs at a fast pace. Today many of the least developed countries (LDCs) are in Stage 2. In Stage 3, birth rates slowly decrease due to improvements in the economic conditions, status of women, and access to contraception. Population continues to grow but at a slower rate. More Developed Countries (MDCs) are in Stage 3 today. Stage 4 finds both birth and death rates low and a stable population. Countries in Stage 4 have higher levels of education, stronger economies, improved healthcare, more women in the workforce, and a fertility rate of approximately two children per woman. Most developed countries (DCs) are in Stage 4 today.

There appears to be a fifth stage, which is represented by many European countries and Japan that have achieved the final stage of demographic transition and have subreplacement fertility rates (below 2.1 children per woman). These countries have higher death rates than birth rates, and the population of elderly is greater than the youthful population. Most of the other developed countries, like the United States, have achieved the fourth stage of demographic transition, as can be seen by their low rates of natural increase. Some analysts doubt the applicability of demographic transition to all parts of the world because of the effects of population momentum and the fact that some countries have lowered their death rates without accompanying economic development.

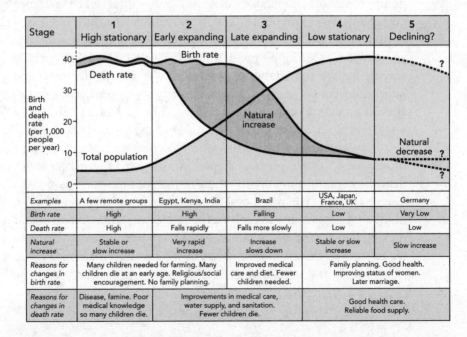

The Demographic Transition Model. Source: *Financial Sense (http://www.financialsense.com/contributors/michael-shedlock/2012/01/10/what-level-of-human-population-is-sustainable).*

With over 7.4 billion inhabitants, the Earth is becoming a well-populated rock! Over the years, various theories have attempted to predict what will happen if our numbers continue to grow. Overpopulation is a value judgment (subjective determination) based on a person's viewpoint about the Earth's limited resources. Thomas Malthus, a British scholar, made the assumption regarding the relationship between population growth and food supply that population always grows geometrically, while food supply only grows arithmetically. This assumption is not always valid as we now realize today. Neo-Malthusians, on the other hand, believe that population growth has a tendency to exceed food supply growth (as did Malthus) but suggest that governmental policies can keep population growth in check. Governmental policies of birth control and family planning to reduce birth rates are implicit in the neo-Malthusian population growth model.

Now, some geographers are concerned about population implosion, or too few people on the Earth. Since the 1970s, several countries—many in Europe—have TFRs below the **replacement level** of 2.1 necessary to assure the population continues to replace itself. Many European countries developed pro-natalist policies and economic incentives designed to encourage families to produce more children, but reproduction rates still kept falling. Currently, many more developed countries (MDCs) and newly developed countries (also called newly industrialized countries or NICs) have fertility levels below replacement levels. These countries are concerned with the implications of a growing cohort of aging adults and a decreasing group of children and working-age adults to bear the socioeconomic costs. Achievement of **zero population growth (ZPG)**, a condition in which births plus immigration equal deaths plus emigration for individual countries, would present unique socioeconomic problems. These socioeconomic problems would be made worse by shrinking national and international economies.

Patterns of Population

The composition of a population is represented in a **population diagram,** or age-sex diagram. This graph shows the number of males and females in any given population by age group, or cohort. Population diagrams can help predict the future needs of a country's population. For example, a triangular population diagram (see Fig. 7.2) with a very broad bottom structure and tapering apex suggests a population with a large number of babies and children. This might predict immediate needs for social services, immunizations, and schools for the too-young-to-work crowd. A rectangular or cylindrical pyramid with a larger aging cohort (see Fig. 7.3) can predict the future needs of a large population of aging adults for medical care and services. Japan has the highest percentage of aging adults in the world with over 21 percent of its citizens in the age 65 and older cohort.

The **dependency ratio** (the ratio of people under age 15 and those 65 and older to those aged 15 to 65) gives us a good idea how many workers are required to support the dependent population. Many countries in Europe such as Sweden, Austria, Italy, and Greece as well as Japan will experience a decrease in their workforce at the same time as the number of dependents to each worker increases. Government spending for adult daycare, nursing homes, and home care social services will increase while government expenditures for education, child welfare and health services, and maternity services will decrease.

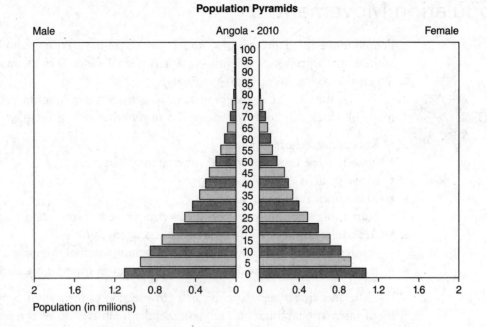

Figure 7.2　Age-sex diagram for Angola, 2010. Population diagrams.
Source: *US Census Bureau.*

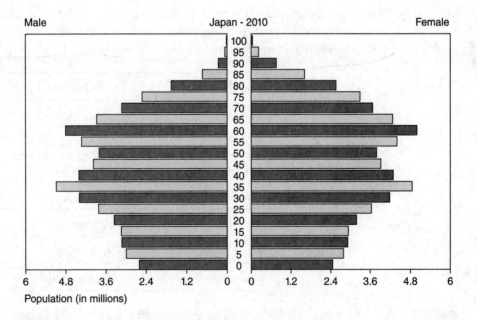

Figure 7.3　Age-sex pyramid for Japan, 2010. Source: *US Census Bureau.*

Population Movement

People move for many reasons, and geographers have created models and theories that address the processes of migration. When people move *into* a country, they **immigrate**. When they *exit* a country, they **emigrate**.

E. G. Ravenstein, a geographer, proposed several migration principles in the 1880s, many of which still hold true today. To summarize these principles, most migrants:

- Move only a short distance.
- Usually settle in urban areas if moving long distances.
- Move in steps.
- Move from rural to urban.
- Start a migration flow that produces a movement in the opposite direction.
- Are adults (families with children are less likely to move).
- If international, are young males whereas more internal migrants are female, but this has changed recently. Now, from 40 to 60 percent of international migrants are female.

Migrants are *not* representative of a cross section of their sending population. The majority of international migrants are young adults in all regions of the world. Female migrants usually move for better economic opportunities and send remittances (money) home to their families. Many migrants send remittances back home to their families. For example, since the early 1990s, Indians working abroad in oil-exporting countries of the Persian Gulf send remittances back home to India that contribute more to the Indian balance of payments than all other forms of capital inflow added together. Migrants also are typically well educated, and this often creates a "brain drain" back home in the sending country.

Push and Pull Migration Factors

There are many reasons why migrants move. The table here shows some of the major reasons people leave their homes and move. It is divided into push factors (factors that encourage leaving) and pull factors (factors that "pull" the migrant to the new location.

PUSH FACTORS	PULL FACTORS
Famine	Better jobs
War	Lower taxes
Lack of jobs	Nicer climate
Disease	Better schools
Violence	More room
High crime	Low crime
Overcrowding	Better medical care

All moves are influenced by **place utility**, which is the person's satisfaction or dissatisfaction with a place. People will choose whether to remain or move based on place utility. **Distance decay** is the principle that says migrants try to minimize the friction of distance. This means that migrants will be more inclined to move to locations closer to them; they will be less interested in moving to distant locations. **Intervening opportunity** is the idea that migrants will choose a location closer rather than farther if all other factors are roughly the same. The closer opportunities will appear more attractive to the migrant than those farther away. We usually know more about locations we are already closer to, and we are less aware of facts about distant locations. Also, the costs in time and money increase the farther away the new location is from the present location.

Voluntary and Involuntary Migrations

Not everyone who migrates really wants to make the move. Sometimes forced, or involuntary, migrations occur as people are forced out of their homes by the government or some other group. Here is a list of the types of migrants:

- **Immigrant:** A person who is entering another country with the intention of living there
- **Emigrant:** A person who is leaving one country with the intention of living in a different country
- **Refugee:** A person who is residing outside the country of his or her origin because of fear of persecution because of religion, ethnicity, race, or political ideology
- **Internally Displaced Person (IDP):** A person who is forced out of the home region because of war, political or social unrest, environmental problems, etc. but does not cross any international boundaries

Refugees have become a huge problem in the world today with the regions of Africa, Europe, Southeast Asia, and Southwest Asia facing the worst problems. Fighting in the Darfur region of the Sudan, for example, has generated thousands of refugees; 250,000 refugees have fled from the Darfur province to Eastern Chad since the conflict began. Refugees typically flee their home in fear without official documents, taking only the clothes on their backs, and traveling on foot or using some other basic mode of transportation.

Refugees place demands on the host country's resources, which are usually already strained to capacity. Several African countries have asked the international aid community to share the refugee burden by contributing financial resources to infrastructure projects that would benefit both nationals and refugees. They contend that they absorbed the extra migrants instead of closing their borders and thus prevented a humanitarian crisis requiring the assistance of the developed countries (DCs).

Spatial Patterns and Theories of Migration

How long do migrants usually stay when they move? Short-term migration occurs when a person moves to another country for a period of at least three months but less than a year. Local movements or internal migration occur as people leave an area in a country or region and go to another part of that same country or region. Sometimes a drought or other agrarian hardship in one part of the region makes life intolerable, and people living there go to another part of the region as occurs in India, for example. The ability to move within the country or region helps people survive hardships without going too far from home. Cyclic movement, or movement away from home for a short period, includes commuting, seasonal movement, and nomadism.

Once considered short-term migrants, guest workers are migrants permitted into a country to fill a labor need on the assumption that the workers will go "home" once the labor need subsides. They generally have short-term work visas and send remittances back to their home country. Increasingly however, guest workers from Southwest Asia and North Africa are bringing their families to live with them in Europe.

One type of local movement that is prevalent in Western nations is residential relocation because of the desire for a better school district, a more convenient location, changes in life cycle, income level, job location, perceived safety of neighborhood, etc.

Migration takes many spatial forms. Some migrants make a large move from one continent or culture to another, but often migrants make small, incremental moves. What are the typical spatial patterns of migration? The table here summarizes the forms of migration.

FORM OF MIGRATION	DEFINITION/ DESCRIPTION	EXAMPLE
Step migration	Series of small moves to reach destination	Rural to big city by moving to village, small town, larger town, and then big city
Chain migration	Part of a migrant flow that follows former migrants to an area	Turkey to ethnic enclave in Berlin, Germany
Counter or return migration	Generally, about 25 percent will return to home area eventually	Ohio to West Virginia
Channelized migration	Repetitive pattern of migration not linked to family or ethnicity	Retired persons to Arizona and Florida

Barriers to Migration

Moving is not always easy! There are barriers to migration that affect the flow of persons from one region or country to another. Limiting factors on migration include financial and emotional costs, knowledge of opportunities in the new place, and personal characteristics such as gender, economic status, and age. The elderly and the poor are *least* likely to migrate whereas educated males between the ages of 18 to 34 are *most* likely to migrate. In addition, migration is usually controlled by government policies. Immigration laws restrict or allow migration of certain groups into a country. Government immigration quotas may limit the number of persons from each region entering a country. Restrictive immigration prevents certain individuals from entering a country.

Human Capital Theory of Migration

KEY IDEA

National and international economies require a fluid movement of both labor and capital to function smoothly. When migrants move from one location to another, they shift human capital. The **human capital theory of migration** states that educated workers often migrate from poor countries to wealthy countries seeking better-paying jobs. This movement of human capital benefits both countries. The capital-rich country gains talented labor and the labor-rich country receives much-needed capital as the migrants send remittances home to their families. The loss of labor in the poor country also increases the wage rate for those who do not emigrate. When workers migrate, their education benefits the country where they move to work. Any healthcare needs or retirement benefits will be paid in the new country. Most countries now practice selective migration by requiring certain immigrants to possess specific qualifications such as skills, youth, and health.

Life Course Theory of Migration

The **life course theory of migration** states that the interaction of life course events (becoming married, having a child, becoming divorced) with migration has important repercussions on a society. Recent life course studies of internal and international migration show that changes in education and occupation are regarded as major reasons why individuals decide to change their region or country. Also, migration influences life course decisions in both individuals and families. Studies show that married individuals are less likely to move than are singles and that their relocation is generally more successful.

Childbearing is an important cause for housing- and environment-related moves. These are mostly moves within a labor-market area or they are migrations from urban regions to surrounding suburban or rural areas. The need for additional space or the desire to live in a more pleasant environment in which to raise children are major reasons why families decide to change their residence. Second, as the family grows, the likelihood for families to make job-related long-distance moves, especially to urban sites, declines strikingly. The economic and psychological costs of moving from one region to another increase as the family with school-age children grows in size.

› Rapid Review

Population and human migrations are themes that are integral to the study of AP Human Geography. Geographers study the spatial distributions of humans and their movements by looking at demographic statistics such as CBR, CDR, TFR, and age-sex pyramids, and by analyzing the impact and rationale for migrations.

› Review Questions

1. The three largest population clusters in the world are in

   (A) East Asia, South Asia, Southeast Asia.
   (B) East Asia, South Asia, South America.
   (C) Africa, South Asia, East Asia.
   (D) Australia, South Asia, East Asia.
   (E) Australia, East Asia, Europe.

2. In what stage of the demographic transition model are most LDCs?

   (A) First
   (B) Second
   (C) Third
   (D) Fourth
   (E) Fifth

3. Which one of the following demographic statistics best measures the level of reproduction occurring in a population?

   (A) Composite birth statistics
   (B) Natal rate
   (C) CDR
   (D) CBR
   (E) TFR

4. Which one of the following statements is a law of migration according to E. G. Ravenstein?

   (A) Most migration is urban to rural.
   (B) Most migrants move a great distance.
   (C) Every migration flow creates a return or counter migration.
   (D) Most migrants consist of families.
   (E) Most international migrants are senior citizens.

› Review Questions

5. Which one of the following statements is most characteristic of a refugee?

(A) They usually move with official documentation.

(B) Their first steps are often made on foot, by boat, wagon, or bicycle.

(C) They take all of their physical possessions with them.

(D) Their chief motivation is to get new jobs.

(E) They move at a leisurely pace.

› Answers and Explanations

1. A—The three largest population clusters in the world are in East Asia, South Asia, and Southeast Asia, in that order.

2. B—Most LDCs are in Stage 2 of the *demographic transition model*. This is the stage in which death rates are falling (because of improved health conditions for infants and children and improved food supplies) and population is increasing. No country is in Stage 1 (A) today. In Stage 3 (C), a decrease in the fertility rate and the birth rate causes countries to stabilize in terms of economic growth. Malaysia, Mexico, and Vietnam are in this stage. In Stage 4 (D), both birth and death rates are low, and the population is high and stable. Most MDCs are in this group. Japan and some European countries may be in Stage 5 (E) in which the population is rapidly aging and declining because fertility rates are below replacement level.

3. E—TFR, or total fertility rate, best measures the level of reproduction that is occurring in a population. There are no statistics called composite birth statistics (A) or natal rate (B). The CDR, or crude death rate (C), is the total number of deaths per 1000 annually. The CBR, or crude birth rate (D), is the total of live births per 1000 annually in a population. The CBR does not reflect age and sex differences in a population and thus is not as good a measure of the level or production as the TFR, which measures the number of babies born per reproductive-age woman.

4. C—Every migration flow creates a counter flow or return flow. Most migration is rural to urban, not urban to rural (A). Most migrants move a short distance (B). Most migrants are young and single males (D), and most international migrants are young (E).

5. B—Refugees usually have very little time or money to arrange for anything more than the most basic form of transportation to escape their situation. Refugees rarely have any official documentation to take with them (A). Usually refugees are only able to take a few small possessions with them as they are often fleeing on foot (C). Refugees leave under duress and are usually fleeing for their lives; a search for new jobs is not part of the motivation for their flight (D). Refugees leave as quickly as they can and do not take their time (E).

CHAPTER 8

Culture

IN THIS CHAPTER

Summary: This chapter focuses on the cultural traits, behaviors, and patterns that make a group of people different and unique from other groups. It also reviews the spatial patterns and diffusion of culture traits and look at how cultural landscapes evolve over time.

Culture, or what makes a group of people special and unique, is an important part of AP Human Geography. All the parts of a culture—both material and nonmaterial—create unique landscapes called **cultural landscapes** that help human geographers differentiate between groups and societies. The study of the diffusion and spread of innovations, cultural traits, and culture systems is integral to AP Human Geography.

KEY IDEA

Key Terms

acculturation
animism
artifact
assimilation
built environment
charter group
creole
cultural barriers
cultural diffusion
cultural landscape
culture
culture hearth
culture region
culture trait
dialect

environmental determinism
ethnic enclave
ethnic island
ethnic religion
ethnocentrism
first effective settlement
folk culture
ghetto
globalization
hierarchical diffusion
host society
innovation
language family
land survey
language family

lingua franca	race
long-lot system	rectangular-survey system
material culture	secularism
mentifact	sense of place
mete-and-bounds system	sequent occupance
monotheism	shamanism
nonmaterial culture	sociofacts
pidgen	syncretism
placelessness	taboo
polytheism	tipping point
popular culture	transculturation
possibilism	universalizing religion
protolanguage	vernacular region

Introduction

What is **culture**? It includes everything about the lifestyle, beliefs, and values of a group of people. Even the definition of "family" is a part of a group's culture. Culture is transferred within a society by imitation, instruction, and example and is learned, not inherited, from one's parents. Geographers investigate how and why a culture is found in a particular location.

Cultural Concepts

Culture Traits: Material and Nonmaterial

A **culture trait** is a single feature of a culture. For example, the type of clothing and the system of religious beliefs of a group of people are culture traits. A **culture complex** is a group of individual cultural traits that are interconnected. For example, keeping cattle is a cultural trait of the Maasai society of Kenya and Tanzania. The culture complex is comprised of related traits of cattle as a measure of wealth, the imbibing of milk and cattle blood, and the elevated status of herders in Maasai society.

Material culture is composed of **artifacts** (tangible things) such as tools, weapons, and furniture. **Nonmaterial culture** is made up of **mentifacts** (language, religion, artistic pursuits, folk stories, myths, etc.) and **sociofacts** (educational and political institutions, religious organizations, family structure, etc.). The distinctions are not always clear-cut. For example, a house is an artifact because it provides shelter for its owners. This house can also be a sociofact because it expresses the nature of the family it houses, and it is also a mentifact because it reflects a culture group's beliefs about architecture, building design, and housing materials.

Diffusion: How Culture Begins and Spreads

Culture spreads from one region to another in a process called **cultural diffusion.** Diffusion involves the movement of people, ideas, and goods from one location to another. A culture trait such as language, religion, or housing style is spread from one area to another through a form of cultural diffusion. A **culture hearth** is a place where innovations and new ideas originate and spread outward (diffuse) to other regions. Examples of culture hearths are Egypt, Mesopotamia, the Indus River Valley, and West Africa. Agriculture and trade were essential attributes of each culture hearth and led to the stratification of each society

Photo by author, 2005

Figure 8.1   Two-headed jaguar throne, Uxmal, Mexico.

into farmers, administrators, rulers, artisans, soldiers, and priests. All culture hearths were urban-centered, and cultural traits such as religion, forms of architecture, and writing spread and diffused outward from each one as **innovations**, or new inventions. The two-headed jaguar throne in Fig. 8.1 is found at Uxmal, Yucatan (Mexico), and is one of many still-standing structures from the Maya, a Mesoamerican culture hearth.

Sometimes **cultural barriers**, or hindrances to diffusion, occur in a society and keep cultural traits from spreading. A **taboo** is a potent form of cultural barrier that prevents certain habits or new ideas from establishing themselves in a society because of already-established prohibitions, customs, and rules. Many societies have food taboos (dietary restrictions) that prohibit the consumption of a certain kind of meat. For example, Hinduism prohibits consumption of beef, Muslim and Judaism prohibit consumption of pork, and most Somali clans restrict the consumption of fish.

Acculturation, Assimilation, and Globalization

Acculturation is the change that occurs within a culture when it adopts a practice from another culture. An example of acculturation occurred when the Mongols under Genghis Khan swept down for the Central Asian steppes to conquer China in the thirteenth century. The Mongolian occupiers largely adopted Chinese culture within a generation and were acculturated by the society they had conquered. **Transculturation** occurs when an equal exchange of traits or influence between two culture groups occurs. **Syncretism** is the birth of a new culture trait from blending two or more cultural traits. An example of this is folk Catholicism in which the indigenous religions of the Maya and Aztec were blended with Roman Catholicism brought across the Atlantic by the Spanish. The Spanish conquerors forced the natives to convert, but the natives incorporated the old gods and goddesses of their indigenous religion into statues of Catholic saints and altarpieces so the natives could worship their old gods while feigning compliance. The resulting folk Catholicism is a rich synthesis of two religions.

Acculturation is the process of adopting *some* of the values, customs, and behaviors of the host culture (the larger group into which the minority culture migrated). Immigrants may adopt the language and a few other customs of the host group but will still retain many of the distinctive customs and traditions of their cultural group.

Assimilation is the process in which immigrants become *totally integrated* into the host culture. The immigrants are still often aware of the differences between the two cultures, thus retaining their ethnic identity. The United States and Canada actively incorporate their immigrant minorities into their host societies (in different ways and to different degrees), but many other countries marginalize minority cultures and either demand total assimilation or ban the use of minority languages and religion.

Globalization is the increasing interconnection of all regions in the world through politics, communication, transportation, marketing, manufacturing, and social and cultural processes. The increasing amount of connectivity in the world today presents a multitude of spatial advantages and also some problems. Rapid and intensive sharing of knowledge has the ability to improve quality of life and transmit news faster than the speed of light due to globalization. The downside of globalization includes the loss of cultural uniqueness, loss of languages, and a general "sameness" that follows the spread of pop culture.

Culture Regions

A **culture region** is a portion of the Earth's surface occupied by populations sharing recognizable and distinctive cultural characteristics. An example of a culture region would be the spatial extent of the Muslim religion or the area in which English is widely spoken.

Cultural Differences

Cultures vary greatly in many ways, and they are constantly changing and never remain the same. For example, the culture today in the United States is much different from the culture when your parents were children. Differences *between* cultural groups are usually much greater than differences *within* a single cultural group, however. The greatest areas of difference lie in the following culture traits: language, religion, and ethnicity.

The physical environment helps form culture. Cultural ecology is the study of how the natural environment shapes and influences a culture group. While geographers today agree that the environment is important in shaping cultures, geographer Ellsworth Huntington and others endorsed the theory of **environmental determinism**. This theory states that human behavior is controlled by the physical environment. Therefore, people who live in the cold, brisk climates of Europe will be energetic, hard workers, and generally achieve more than people living in hot, humid tropical environments, which were thought to contribute to a slow, sluggish tendency. Of course, this theory is no longer accepted. How did the Maya flourish and establish a highly advanced civilization in tropical Mesoamerica? How could the majority of culture hearths be located in the lower latitudes if this theory held true? **Possibilism**—the theory that the physical environment merely establishes limits of what is possible on the human population—has been more widely accepted in recent years, although it, too, raises questions. The human race has pushed beyond the limits imposed on it by the physical environment thanks to advanced technology and communications.

Language

Language is the most important channel for the transmission of culture. The linguistic diversity of the world is rapidly decreasing. Of the thousands of languages still spoken today, over half of the Earth's inhabitants speak one of only eight languages. Many languages are no longer spoken (dead), and many more are on the verge of extinction.

A **language family** is a group of languages that are related and derived from a single, earlier language—the **protolanguage**, a reconstructed ancestral language. It can be further divided into subfamilies, branches, or groups of languages that are related. Linguists often show this historical relationship between languages in tree form. The Indo-European language family is the largest language family, and the languages in this family are spoken by roughly half the world's population. It includes most European languages and many of those spoken in Asia, as well as the introduced languages of the Americas. The Indo-European people probably came from Eastern Europe and spread throughout Europe and Asia taking their language with them to the people they subjugated. The map in Fig. 8.2 shows the main language families.

The map in Fig. 8.2 also shows the processes of cultural diffusion at work. You can see where the Indo-European languages have spread by expansion diffusion and then jumped every ocean in the world by relocation diffusion. In many areas, **hierarchical diffusion**, or the adoption of an official language by the ruler or administration, diffused a language downwards into the society. Where obtaining a government post or well-paying job depended on the ability to speak the official language of the land, a person had to learn the new language of governmental administration.

This image shows the six world languages that have the most speakers (first language). Roughly one-third of the world's inhabitants speak one of the six languages as their first language.

Language tree. Source: *http://static5.businessinsider.com/image/54c856a86bb3f7e1721 6e935-1250-938/language%20family%20tree_cropped.jpg*

Language is one of most important factors in maintaining local and national cultures. **Globalization** (the increasing interconnections between countries and cultures of the world) threatens indigenous cultures and their languages. Schools as well as all forms of media, from the Internet to magazines and newspapers, contribute to the loss of a language. When a family migrates from one country to another, their children attend school and are educated in the language of the country and not in their native tongue. In Indonesia, there are languages that are endangered—even though tens of thousands of people speak

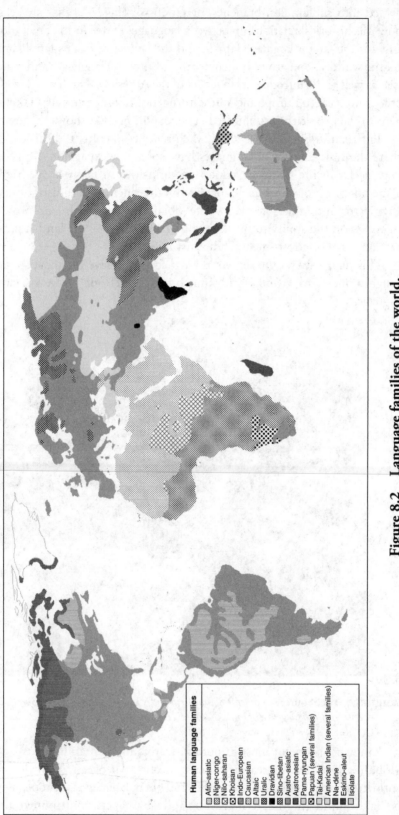

Human language families

- Afro-asiatic
- Niger-congo
- Nilo-saharan
- Khoisan
- Indo-European
- Caucasian
- Altaic
- Uralic
- Dravidian
- Sino-tibetan
- Austro-asiatic
- Austronesian
- Pama-nyungan
- Papuan (several families)
- Tai-Kadai
- American Indian (several families)
- Na-déne
- Eskimo-aleut
- Isolate

Figure 8.2 Language families of the world.

them—because children are being educated in the national Indonesian language instead of the language native to their region. Sometimes a country with many different regional languages adopts a **lingua franca**, a language that is informally agreed upon as the language of business and trade. For example, Hindi, Mandarin Chinese, and Swahili are used in India, China, and many countries of Sub-Saharan Africa, respectively, as lingua francas because of the great diversity of native languages spoken in each of these regions.

Language can also be a tool of separatism in a country. Many Basques in the Pyrenees Mountains of Spain speak Euskara, a language dating back to the pre-Indo-European era. The Basques' steadfast insistence on retaining their language as an important part of their culture has kept it alive. Catalan, Gaelic, and Breton are just a few other localized languages that ethnic groups are striving to retain. Language can also serve as a potent unifier in a country of diverse ethnicities. In India, for example, the return to old Hindu place names signifies a resurgence of Hindu nationalism and a rejection of any lingering vestiges of colonialism.

A language may have several **dialects** or speech variants, which reflect the local region in which they are spoken. In the United States, English can sound very different depending on what part of the country you are visiting! These regional variations can be understood by other English-speakers and are based on differences in vocabulary and accent. Many Scandinavian languages are mutually intelligible, meaning that a Norwegian can understand a Swede speaking in Swedish although they are two separate languages. **Pidgin** or **creole** languages are simplified mixtures of two or more languages that are adopted in areas of cultural diversity. A pidgin is no one's native language and contains a fairly even mixture of vocabulary from the languages of the people who created it. A pidgin language is usually a result of trading between groups of people who do not share the same language. Swahili is a pidgin language composed of various Bantu dialects and Arabic. A creole language is a mixture of two languages that is a native language of a group of people. The majority of the vocabulary comes from the original language. The grammar changes that occur in the first language make the creole language different enough that the first language speakers cannot understand the creole speakers. The second language has a great impact on the first language over time because of slave conditions, plantation culture, or military campaigns. Afrikaans, Haitian and Louisiana Creole, and Bazaar Malay are other creole languages widely used in other regions of the world today.

Religion

Religion is a dynamic cultural trait—a mentifact—that can identify, unite, or divide a group of people. The changing spatial patterns of religion over the centuries reveal wars, conquests, conversions, and revivals. See Fig. 8.3 to review the distribution of major religions in the world today. Universalizing religions diffused throughout the world because of missionaries, while smaller ethnic and tribal religions tended to remain spatially localized in isolated areas unless the members themselves migrated.

The six major world religions are Christianity, Judaism, Buddhism, Hinduism, Islam, and Sikhism. Of course, there are many more religions practiced in the world today (Sikhism, Voodoo, Rastafarianism, Baha'i, etc.), but the first six mentioned are the ones you need to know for the AP exam.

Religions are classified in one of three groups: universalizing, ethnic, or traditional (tribal). A **universalizing religion** is one in which anyone can become a member. Christianity, Buddhism, and Islam are the three main universalizing religions. Their members actively proselytize, or seek new converts, by sending missionaries throughout the world to spread their beliefs. An **ethnic religion** is one that is a part of a particular ethnic or political group. Outsiders cannot join because they must be born into this ethnic group to practice the religion, although one can marry into an ethnic religion. Judaism and Hinduism (as practiced

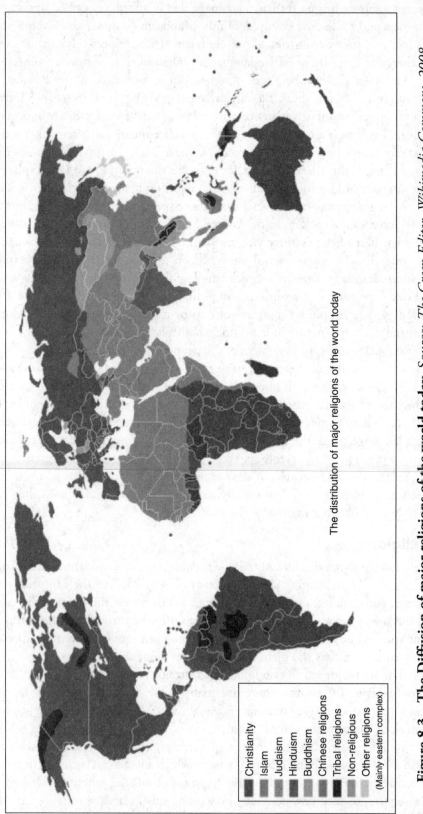

The distribution of major religions of the world today

Christianity
Islam
Judaism
Hinduism
Buddhism
Chinese religions
Tribal religions
Non-religious
Other religions
(Mainly eastern complex)

Figure 8.3   The Diffusion of major religions of the world today. Source: *The Green Editor, Wikimedia Commons, 2008.*

in India) are examples of ethnic religions. The third major grouping of world religions is **traditional**, or **tribal religion**. Traditional religions are ethnic religions that are practiced by small, local cultural groups. They are typically blended religions that combine the belief system of the ethnic group, tribe, or village, with animism and, perhaps, imposed religions. In Indonesia, for example, with its multilayered cultural landscape showing a rich **sequent occupance** (the process by which a landscape is gradually modified by a succession of occupying groups), there are numerous tribal religions being practiced, but they are each classified under one of the many major religious groups and most show syncretism.

There are some other religious belief systems that you should also know for the AP exam. **Animism**, the belief that spirits (including ancestral) live within objects such as animals, rivers, rocks, trees, and mountains, is practiced in Malaysia, Africa, Australia, and by most indigenous groups throughout the world. **Shamanism** is a form of tribal, or traditional, religion that reveres a particular person, the shaman, as one with special healing or magic powers. **Secularism** is the rejection of all religious beliefs and is spreading rapidly in certain areas of the world such as Europe. For example, France and Italy possess large Roman Catholic majorities yet are secular countries where very few people attend church regularly. Secularism is on the rise in Europe. The European Union's European Court of Human Rights forbids any religious symbols such as crucifixes, crosses, etc. on public school walls and calls them a violation of religious and educational freedom.

In the table below, you can see the approximate percentage of the world's population who ascribe to each of the world's major religions. Make sure you know which religions have the most adherents and where they live for the exam.

MAJOR RELIGION	PERCENTAGE OF WORLD POPULATION
Christianity	33.32%
Roman Catholic	16.99%
Protestant	5.78%
Orthodox	3.53%
Anglican	1.25%
Islam	21.01%
Hindu	13.26%
Buddhism	5.84%
Sikh	0.35%
Jews	0.23%
Other religion	11.90%
Non-religious	11.77%
Atheist	2.32% (2007 est.)

Source: *CIA World Factbook, 2010*

Hinduism is the oldest major world religion; it arose in the Indus River Valley in Pakistan. This ethnic religion spread by contagious diffusion into the Indian subcontinent displacing native religions. Later, Indian traders spread Hinduism into Southeast Asia and the Indonesian island of Bali. Hinduism spread elsewhere in the world by relocation diffusion as devout Hindus moved for jobs and education. Today over 80 percent of the world's Hindu population lives in India. One must be born into this belief system of hundreds

Figure 8.4   A *Gujarat* (ornamental tower) at the Hindu temple entrance in Madurai, India.

of gods and multitudes of rituals to participate. Its caste system (social structure) strongly influences Indian society and traditionally dictates a person's job, social standing, and even the foods some eats and clothing a person wears. The cultural landscapes of South and Southeast Asia are rich with displays of the ornate, colorful Hindu temples and shrines. Figure 8.4 is a good example of the elaborate carvings of gods that adorn Hindu shrines and temples. This is one of several towers that comprise a typical Hindu temple.

Judaism emerged slightly later than Hinduism, around 3000 to 4000 years ago, in the Mesopotamian culture hearth in Southwest Asia (the Middle East). Judaism is the oldest of the three main monotheistic (one God) world religions. Christianity and, later, Islam, were direct offshoots of Judaism; they also are monotheistic and share a Mesopotamian birthplace. All three regard Jerusalem as a sacred city. Judaism is an ethnic religion in which members are bound by a strict set of rules and dictates that include dietary restrictions. Religious persecution led to a diaspora (dispersion) of Jews throughout the world, but their homeland is Israel. The Jewish cultural landscape is understated compared to most other religious forms of architecture. Jewish temples are simple buildings, and their cemeteries are equally unremarkable.

Christianity began with the birth of Jesus, a Jewish carpenter, whom Christians believe is the Messiah promised by God. Christianity is a universalizing religion because Jesus proclaimed God's love and salvation to everyone, not just the Jewish people. The expansion of the Roman Empire throughout Europe spread Christianity throughout most of Europe by expansion and hierarchical diffusion. Later, relocation diffusion brought the faith to the New World at the hands of Spanish priests and conquistadores. The Protestant

Reformation in Europe during the fifteenth and sixteenth centuries occurred as a rebellion against the excesses of the Catholic Church. The spread of the British Empire carried Protestantism into South and East Asia and the Pacific Islands, but India, China, and Japan proved resistant because of strong ethnic and cultural beliefs. Today, South Korea has a majority population of Protestants, but it is an exception in East Asia. Protestant missionaries spread their religious beliefs to Sub-Saharan Africa and Latin America, but traditional religions maintain dominance in much of Sub-Saharan Africa, and Catholicism has deep roots in Latin American culture. The cultural landscape throughout the world is greatly influenced by the diversity of Christian religious architecture. Cathedrals, Spanish missions, Protestant churches, and monasteries are some of the types to be found today.

Islam, the last of the three main monotheistic religions to be birthed, is based on the teachings of Mohammed, a prophet who followed in the footsteps of Abraham, Moses, and David. The Koran is the sacred book of Islam, and Muslims adhere closely to the strict tenets of the religion as stated in this book. The Five Pillars of Islam are (1) repetition of the Muslim creed, (2) prayer five times daily, (3) observance of Ramadan (a month of fasting), (4) almsgiving, and (5) a pilgrimage to Mecca before one's death. Islam spread rapidly by expansion diffusion throughout Southwest Asia and into India after Mohammed's death in A.D. 632. The Ottoman Empire helped disseminate Islam in Eastern Europe (Bosnia, Kosovo, Albania) as well. The Muslims conquered and ruled Spain for nearly 700 years until the Spanish, during the Christian Reconquista, regained control of Spain and expelled all Muslims in 1492. Islam spread by relocation diffusion into Southeast Asia, Sub-Saharan Africa, and the Western Hemisphere through trade and human migration. The two main branches of Islam are Sunni and Shi'ite with Sunni having 80 to 85 percent of the adherents to Islam. The cultural landscape of Islam revolves around the mosque—a center of worship that varies from a very simple, plain structure to one that is quite ornate and elaborate in design and decoration. Figure 8.5 depicts the Dome of the Rock in Jerusalem.

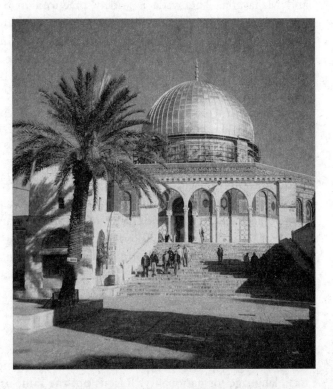

Figure 8.5 The Dome of the Rock is the oldest Islamic structure in existence in the world today. The site is sacred to both Jews and Muslims.

Figure 8.6   Buddha in Louyang, China (Longman Grotto).

This structure is the oldest Islamic structure still in existence today and is considered part of the sacred heritage of both Judaism and Islam.

Buddhism is a universalizing religion (some say it is a philosophy) that does not believe in worshipping gods but rather in seeking and discovering the truth for oneself. Buddhism began in the sixth century B.C.E in present-day Nepal (then part of India). It is based on the meditations and teachings of Buddha (Siddhartha Gautama), the Enlightened One, an Indian prince who spent his life pondering the mysteries of life, death, and suffering. There are two main branches of Buddhism—Theravada (the oldest surviving branch) and Mahayana. Theravada is widely practiced in Sri Lanka and Southeast Asia, while Mahayana (which includes Tibetan and Zen Buddhism) is found throughout East Asia. Contagious diffusion spread Buddhism throughout India. Monks and missionaries carried Buddhism to other parts of Asia. Buddhism slowly became reabsorbed into Hinduism, and it competed unsuccessfully with Islam in northern India. Buddhist temples, or pagodas, and stupas (shrines), as well as monasteries where Buddhist monks pray, meditate, and seek enlightenment, color the cultural landscape in most parts of Asia. Statues of Buddha such as the one shown in Fig. 8.6 are located throughout the cultural landscape of Asia today.

East Asian Ethnic Religions

Buddhism merged with ethnic religions when it arrived in Asia. In Japan, the syncretism of Shintoism (traditional religion based on nature and ancestor worship) and Buddhism formed a special type of Buddhism. In China, Confucianism (system of ethics and family behavior) and Taoism (a philosophy based on living a peaceful life in tune with nature) blended with Buddhism to form a syncretic religion that combined elements of all three belief systems.

Ethnicity

An **ethnic group** is a population that shares common roots based on culture, religion, race, language, or nationality. Race is not the same as ethnicity. **Race** refers to a group of people with a common biological ancestor. The members of a race have distinguishing physical characteristics that make them look different from members of other races. Since we all share a common ancestor, these racial differences have clearly evolved as humans spread out over the Earth and adapted to the different environments they encountered. **Ethnocentrism** is the belief that one's own ethnic group is superior to all others.

Ethnicity is a very spatial concept. Ethnic groups have long migrated to other locations in search of a better future for themselves and their families. Geographer Wilbur Zelinsky used the term **first effective settlement** to refer to the first group—or **charter group**—of settlers to establish a new and lasting culture and society in an area. For example, the chief charter group to colonize the United States came from England, Ireland, Scotland, and Wales.

Ethnic homeland areas are areas that contain an ethnic group that seeks autonomy or self-rule. The Croatians, Slovenes, and Bosnians of Eastern Europe, and the Basques, Welsh, and Bretons of Western Europe are examples of ethnic minorities with their own homelands and very specific ethnic territories. An **ethnic island** is a small ethnic settlement centered in the middle of a larger group of the population. Ethnic islands of Germans exist in the Hill Country of South Central Texas and throughout much of western Ohio and eastern Illinois. Scotch-Irish ethnic islands are found throughout the Appalachian and Ozark Mountain regions of the United States. The cultural landscapes are imprinted with the architecture and symbolism of their rich cultural backgrounds. **Ethnic enclaves** are small areas of cities that are inhabited by a minority cultural group. Most large cities have ethnic enclaves, and the **toponyms** (place names) may hint at the ethnicity of the original settlers even though the neighborhoods may not be strictly ethnic anymore. Chinatown, Polish Hill, and Little Saigon are just a few easily guessed ethnic enclaves, but there are many more with toponyms that do not hint at the strongholds of immigrant solidarity that once occupied them. In Western Europe, ethnic enclaves of Muslims from North Africa live in highly segregated neighborhoods where they deliberately restrict contact with the **host society** (dominant culture group receiving a minority group) as much as possible. When a charter group neighborhood reaches a critical number of minority inhabitants, the **tipping point** is reached and the charter group quickly leaves the neighborhood. A **ghetto** is an ethnic enclave where the residents are either forced or voluntarily live segregated (separated) by race, religion, or ethnicity.

Gender Roles

Men and women have different roles based on their culture. Throughout the world, cultures assign roles to people based on their gender (male or female). In Sub-Saharan Africa, a woman's traditional role is to care for the old, the young, and the sick, while working in the fields to grow food, gathering firewood for cooking use, and fetching water. The man's role is to converse with other men at length and work in fields growing cash crops or perhaps work at a job in the city for family income. Young women in many developing countries are expected to work to add to the family income, and many leave their homes and travel to other countries. As recently as the 1940s, big sisters in the United States worked in factories or offices to provide college funds for a younger brother. Gender roles change very slowly and usually with great difficulty. Societies construct identities for men and women based on the society's cultural norms. "The woman's place is in the home" is still a prevailing attitude in most regions of the world today. She may also have a place in the full-time workplace, however, and the multitude of roles she fills often is a source of family and societal stress.

Figure 8.7   Old Order Amish going fishing in Pennsylvania.

Popular and Folk Culture

Popular culture (pop culture) refers to the ever-changing cultural norms associated with a large, diverse group of people who are very influenced by mass media, mass production, and mass merchandising. Examples of pop culture include Harry Potter, Shrek, and Netflix. Pop culture is widely distributed throughout the Earth because of the means of dissemination—the mass media.

Folk culture refers to a homogenous group of people with a strong family structure who follow a simple, traditional lifestyle of self-sufficiency and independence from the society's cultural mainstream. The Old Order Amish are a folk culture in the United States (see Fig. 8.7). Folk culture tends to be highly localized and clustered with little interaction with the main cultural group. Their **material culture**—physical items of culture such as furniture and clothing—differs greatly from that of mainstream American culture. Their **nonmaterial culture**—the intangible mentifacts and sociofacts such as customs and social behaviors—also differs greatly from those of most Americans.

Cultural Landscapes and Identity

The **cultural landscape** is made up of the structures placed on the physical landscape by human activities, or how people arrange the physical space around them. It includes any change to the natural landscape such as roads, fields, cities, houses, bridges, etc. **Sequent occupance** is the concept that successive societies leave their cultural imprints on a place, each contributing to the cumulative cultural landscape. For example, the cultural landscape of Bolivia includes imprints from the early Incan civilization, and from the Spanish colonists who conquered them, and finally from the period after independence. Remnants of each of these successive cultures make up the cultural landscape of Bolivia today.

Land survey methods for parceling out land to its occupants differ according to the charter group's ethnicity in the United States and Canada. The English settlers to the original 13 colonies used the nucleated-village-and-outlying-farmlands method used in their native England. A central village (town) with a commons and meetinghouse was surrounded by farmlands worked by the villagers. From Pennsylvania south, the land was allocated by royal land grant. Natural boundaries such as rivers, trees, and large rocks marked land boundaries. This **metes-and-bounds system** led to numerous disputes whenever a boundary tree was uprooted by a storm! After independence from England, the United States adopted a **rectangular-survey system** with rectangular grid divisions to divide new land settlements. The French charter group in the Mississippi and St. Lawrence River valleys used the French **long-lot system** to give each settler access to river frontage and fertile alluvial soil while extending the long lots outward several acres to give them additional grazing and farm lands. Spanish colonists adopted the long-lot survey system wherever they settled, too.

In the United States, the chief settlement pattern of isolated farms scattered throughout the countryside has been based on the rectangular land survey system. The French and Spanish long lots encouraged settlers to live close together along the rivers or main roads. The towns and villages of the English charter group found in New England were adopted by utopian religious communities including the Mormons. Because of the extensive blending of cultures and assimilation of immigrants in the United States, the ethnic regions are less pronounced than in other world regions. For example, Basque houses are easy to pick out because of their dark green shutters, and blue, thatched-roofed Croatian homes are easy to identify in the Croatian countryside.

The types of housing built reflect the cultural identities of those who live there and also depend on environmental constraints. House construction materials (wood, brick, stone, mud, palm thatch, etc.) reflect the natural resources in the area and the climate and precipitation patterns. For example, houses in northern Europe typically have steeply slanted roofs to allow snow to slide off easily during long, cold winter months. In the regions of North America where cold, snowy winters prevail, northern European immigrants built similar houses. In the Yucatan Peninsula, Maya villagers use palm thatch roofing because it is easy to obtain and will withstand the frequent tropical storms by allowing violent winds to pass through unhindered. Although mass construction and pop culture are slowly destroying the regional diversity in US housing, you can still see the New England salt box, the Charleston single house (see Fig. 8.8), and the shotgun house of the Deep South.

Photo by author, 2010

Figure 8.8 Charleston single house.

Symbolic Landscapes and Sense of Place

Vernacular regions are popular regions named for the way people perceive them. For example, most people in the United States think of the Midwest as the region occupying the center of the country—a broad, rolling heartland of plains, grains, and livestock where people have solid, family values and a hard work ethic. When you say the South, they think of the states in the southeastern portion of the country and think about sunshine, tobacco and cotton, grits, and a slower way of life. Vernacular regions are based on a sense of place that people develop based on popular media images, books, and historical and cultural differences between regions.

Geographer D. W. Meinig believed that there were three symbolic landscapes in the United States, and he arranged them chronologically and historically. First in chronological order, Meinig described the New England village with its central village green, Protestant church, and meeting house. This landscape of religion and community laid the very foundations of American democracy from the seventeenth through the nineteenth century. Throughout the nineteenth century, Main Street represented the second symbolic landscape with its courthouse, banks, and retail establishments serving as the heartbeat of the Northeast and Midwest towns as they grew economically. The third symbolic landscape, Meinig believed, was the suburb of Southern California. He felt this defined the twentieth century with the family car, single-family dwelling, and the white picket fence with racial and class tensions left behind in the city.

Sense of place is the special perception we have of a certain place based on our feelings, emotions, and associations with that place. **Placelessness** is the loss of a place's unique flavor and identity because of the standardizing influence of popular culture and globalization. As Walmarts and other "big-box" stores move into communities, the mom-and-pop small businesses are slowly phased out. On a global scale, the uniform nature of pop culture is smoothing out the cultural individuality between groups and results in a different material and nonmaterial culture from the folk and ethnic ones that were first in place.

Impact of Culture on the Environment

Both popular and folk cultures have an impact on the physical environment. Popular culture is usually imposed on the environment in a uniform fashion, while folk culture seems to evolve naturally out of the physical surroundings of the culture group. For example, fast-food restaurants impose a "like image" on the **built environment** (the material culture of an environment) that is easily recognizable no matter what country you are visiting. McDonald's "golden arches" are present in every country in the world, and even though the menu is culturally modified to suit the host society, the architecture is fairly uniform. The negative impact of culture on the environment is increasingly evident as whales are overfished because of cultural food preferences, and fur-bearing animals are overharvested for their valuable furs. Both popular and folk culture can pollute the natural environment. Pop culture creates a lot of waste that is not always biodegradable (able to decompose) such as Styrofoam containers and plastics. Folk cultures can also harm the natural environment by soil overuse, erosion, and overhunting some species of animals.

❯ Rapid Review

Culture is a combination of material artifacts, values, and political traditions. Language, religion, and ethnicity are cultural values. Human geography is interested in how these values are distributed and diffused spatially throughout the various regions of the world.

❯ Review Questions

1. The process by which the English language diffused throughout India under British colonial rule was

    (A) assimilation.
    (B) hierarchical diffusion.
    (C) expansion diffusion.
    (D) contagious diffusion.
    (E) stimulus diffusion.

2. When an ethnic group completely blends with the larger society, it is called

    (A) assimilation.
    (B) expansion diffusion.
    (C) hierarchical diffusion.
    (D) contagious diffusion.
    (E) acculturation.

3. Which one of the following is the best example of a cultural landscape of pop culture?

    (A) Central business district (CBD)
    (B) Commercial strip
    (C) Shopping mall
    (D) Hotel and convention complex
    (E) Bed-and-breakfast

4. The standardization of location that erases cultural variety can result in

    (A) place image.
    (B) popular culture.
    (C) folk culture.
    (D) placelessness.
    (E) a sense of place.

5. Which of the following world religions is one that proselytizes, or actively seeks converts?

    (A) Judaism
    (B) Hinduism
    (C) Animism
    (D) Shamanism
    (E) Buddhism

❯ Answers and Explanations

1. **B**—The British raj brought a new administrative system to India. Anyone desiring to hold office needed to learn English, which was the language of the new ruling authority. This diffusion of a cultural trait downward from a ruler or top government authority into the population is called hierarchical diffusion. Assimilation (A) is the process in which immigrants become totally integrated into the host culture. Expansion diffusion (C) is the spread of a cultural trait to a neighboring region. Contagious diffusion (D) is the evenly outward spreading of a cultural trait from a source.

Stimulus diffusion (E) is the spread of a cultural trait throughout the general population.

2. **A**—Assimilation is the process in which immigrants become totally integrated into the host culture. Expansion diffusion (B) is the spread of a cultural trait to a neighboring region. Hierarchical diffusion (C) is the diffusion of a cultural trait downward from a ruler or top government authority into the population. Contagious diffusion (D) is the evenly outward spreading of a cultural trait from a source. Acculturation (E) is the process of

adopting some of the values, customs, and behaviors of the host culture.

3. **C**—A shopping mall is a large complex of retail stores with mass-produced and mass-marketed items that have wide appeal to a high-consumption population. Because of a shopping mall's widely advertised and highly promoted merchandise and easy-access availability to the general population, it is a good example of a pop culture landscape. The central business district (CBD) (choice A) is the downtown business district of an urban area. A commercial strip (B) is usually composed of small businesses and retail shops. Hotel and convention complexes (D) are service islands that provide a service to a segment of the population. Bed-and-breakfast establishments (E) offer quaint and comfortable short-term lodgings to guests.

4. **D**—Placelessness is the loss of a place's unique flavor and identity because of the standardizing influence of popular culture and globalization. Place image (A) is simply one's image of a place. Popular culture (B) is the ever-changing cultural norms associated with a large, diverse group of people who are very influenced by mass media, mass production, and mass merchandising. Folk culture (C) is a homogenous group of people with a strong family structure who follow a simple, traditional lifestyle of self-sufficiency and independence from the society's cultural mainstream. A sense of place (E) is the special perception we have of a certain place based on our feelings, emotions, and associations with that place.

5. **E**—Buddhism is one of the main religions (along with Christianity and Islam) that seek to convert others. Judaism (A) and Hinduism (B) are ethnic religions into which you must be born to participate. Animism (C) is the belief that spirits (including ancestral) live within objects such as animals, rivers, rocks, trees, and mountains. Shamanism (D) is a form of tribal, or traditional, religion that reveres a particular person, the shaman, as one with special healing or magic powers and is not a proselytizing world religion.

CHAPTER 9

The Political Organization of Space

IN THIS CHAPTER

Summary: This chapter reviews how humans have organized the surface of the Earth into countries (also called states) and the conflicts that sometimes arise. The political geography of the Earth changes constantly as boundaries and borders change. The boundaries of countries change suddenly sometimes (for example, in war and armed conflict) or change gradually as states devolve (for example, in the case of the USSR). Alliances and the forces of globalization greatly impact the political geography of the Earth today.

KEY IDEA

Key Terms

alliances
antecedent boundary
centrifugal force
centripetal force
colonialism
confederation
consequent boundary
conservation agriculture
decolonization
devolution
domino theory
enclave
exclave
exclusive economic zone (EEZ)
federal state

forward capital
fragmented state
gerrymandering
growth pole
heartland-rimland theory
imperialism
irredentism
Mediterranean agriculture
nation
nationalism
nation-state
organic farming
relic boundary
separatism
sovereignty

state
subsequent boundary
superimposed boundary
supranationalism

terrorism
unitary state
Von Thünen's agricultural land use model

Introduction

The concepts of political geography involving states, territories, borders, and alliances are important in the study of AP Human Geography. These concepts help us understand the news headlines about territories and conflicts that we read on a daily basis. Spatial concepts of territory, state, and nationalism revolve around the political arrangement of space.

The Concept of Territoriality

The Earth is divided into political units called **states**, or countries. (The term "state" refers to a country and **not** a political subdivision within the United States, such as Nevada or Maine.) Each country has a defined population and borders, in other words, boundaries that are defined. There are many examples of states in the world today. A **nation** is a unified group of people with a common culture. Examples of nations without a state or political territory of their own are the Kurds, the Navajo, and the Roma or "Gypsies" (see Fig. 9.1 below). **Nation-state** refers to a state in which over 90 percent

Legend
• The size of the wheel symbol represents the total size of the Roma population in each country. Romania = 1.85 million.
• The shade of each country's background represents the percentage of the Roma population with respect to the country's total population. Romania = 8.5%.

Figure 9.1 Distribution of the Roma nation.

of the population is comprised of a specific culture or group of people. Japan, Iceland, Armenia, Bangladesh, and Lesotho are examples of nation-states. Antarctica is the southernmost continent in the world and is neither a nation nor a state. Although several countries conduct scientific research on Antarctica, it has no permanent residents and does not belong to any country.

Countries have heartlands, or core areas, where economic development is usually the greatest. Many times the capital of the country is located within its core, but sometimes it is found in a former core area. Capital cities are often relocated for various reasons. Brazil moved its capital from Rio de Janeiro inland to Brasilia to draw economic development into the country's interior. Brasilia then became a **growth pole,** drawing people and jobs into the undeveloped interior. Pakistan moved its capital city from coastal Karachi to Islamabad near the contested territory of Kashmir to make a bold and aggressive statement to its rival (India) for control of the territory. Islamabad is a **forward capital** that makes a bold statement to the rest of the world.

Boundaries and Their Influence

The shape of a country influences how easy it is to develop economically. A country's shape either helps or hinders transportation and communication between different parts of the country and between the capital and the outlying areas of the country. The table here summarizes the categories used to describe the shapes of countries and gives some examples of each type.

SHAPE OF COUNTRY	DEFINITION	EXAMPLES
Compact	Round. Easy for defense and communications among all areas.	Belgium, Poland, Bhutan, Hungary
Prorupt or protruded	Round with a large extension (panhandle). Increases access to resources such as water.	Thailand, Myanmar (Burma), Mozambique
Elongated	Long, narrow. Difficult communications between areas.	Chile, Italy, Vietnam, Argentina
Fragmented	Two or more areas separated by another country or body of water. Difficult communications between areas.	Philippines, Denmark, Indonesia, Malaysia
Perforated	Totally surrounds another country.	South Africa surrounds Lesotho; Italy surrounds Vatican City and San Marino
Landlocked	No access to water. Trade difficulties because of lack of ports.	Bolivia, Laos, Rwanda, Paraguay, Serbia, Switzerland

Approximately 30 percent of the countries in Africa are landlocked as a result of the colonial era. Uganda, Central African Republic, Rwanda, Burundi, and Malawi are just a few of these countries without access to the ocean.

Frontiers and boundaries are important ways of delineating space. Frontiers are almost totally uninhabited areas, such as those found on the Arabian Peninsula and Antarctica. Unlike frontiers, which are areas not controlled by any state, boundaries are thin, invisible markers that are physical or cultural or a combination of both. Because they represent barriers to travel, physical boundaries such as mountains, deserts, and water often serve to separate states.

Cultural boundaries sometimes closely follow ethnicity and separate two or more cultural groups from each other. Most of the time, however, boundaries are geometric with lines drawn during colonial times with no respect for ethnic divisions. When the British partitioned India, religion dictated the boundary lines. Language was a major influence when the Versailles Peace Conference met to redraw the boundaries of Europe.

Antecedent boundaries are boundaries placed before the cultural landscape developed (in other words, very early in the area's settlement history). **Subsequent boundaries** are drawn after the cultural landscape is in place, and **consequent boundaries** are a type of boundary that is drawn to accommodate existing language, religious, or other cultural boundaries. **Superimposed boundaries** are sometimes forced on existing boundaries as in the case of the division of Africa by European colonial powers during the nineteenth century. **Relict boundaries** are old boundaries that are no longer used between countries such as the now nonexistent boundary between North and South Vietnam. Another example of a relict boundary is the Great Wall of China (see Fig. 9.2), which was built during the third century B.C.E. (Ch'in dynasty) as a defensive border to repel invading Mongols from the north.

Disputes often arise over boundaries. Positional disputes occur when countries disagree about the interpretation of boundary documents. Sometimes boundaries are disputed because of superimposed boundaries that split an ethnic group into two different countries. **Irredentism** is the situation that arises when an ethnic group supports

Figure 9.2   Relict boundary: the Great Wall of China.

and seeks to reunite with its ethnic population in a neighboring country. Somalia has many border conflicts with Ethiopia over the rights of Somalis living in Ethiopia. Resource disputes often occur as two countries dispute ownership of a natural resource that lies on the border. Dispute over a rich oilfield on Iraq's border with Kuwait was a major reason for Iraq's invasion of Kuwait in 1990 to 1991 and the resulting Persian Gulf War.

Evolution of the Contemporary Political Pattern

All culture hearths developed some form of political organization of space so they could control and rule their people and lands. The idea of the modern political state developed in the early eighteenth century in Europe. Friedrich Ratzel, a German geographer, compared the political state to a living organism that had to expand and absorb nearby territories in order to survive. Germany used this theory to justify its invasion of neighboring states during World War II. **Imperialism** is the use of military threat, cultural domination, and economic sanctions to gain control of a country and its resources. **Colonialism** imposed a set of formal controls by the mother country over its colonies or outside territories. Today many countries with multiethnic populations still suffer conflict because of the superimposed boundaries placed by European colonial powers. **Decolonization** is the process by which former colonies gain their independence. The United States gained independence in the eighteenth century, Latin American colonies gained their independence during the nineteenth century, and most African colonies became independent during the twentieth century.

Halford Mackinder, an English geographer, developed the **heartland-rimland theory** to justify European colonization during the nineteenth century (see Fig. 9.3). He claimed the core of Eurasia was the heartland, and the surrounding territories comprised the rimland. The heartland was well positioned to dominate the world because of the immense size of its land mass. Since Russia formed a major part of the heartland, Mackinder influenced politicians of the day to try to limit Russia's expansion by colonizing the territories near Russia.

The policy of containment was a direct offshoot of Mackinder's heartland-rimland theory after World War II. The United States joined several European countries in various

Figure 9.3   Mackinder's heartland-rimland theory.

regional alliances such as the North Atlantic Treaty Organization (NATO) to prevent Soviet domination of Europe. In addition, the **domino theory** was a popular anti-communist theory between 1945 and 1990 that greatly influenced the foreign policy decisions of the United States during this time period. This theory stated that once a country became communist, the neighboring countries around it were likely to also become communist, like a column of dominoes falling over, one by one. The Vietnam War was a direct result of this theory as the United States tried to stop the spread of communism. During the Cold War era between the end of World War II and the dissolution of the Soviet Union in 1991, the balance of power between the world's two superpowers, the United States and the Soviet Union, was a struggle between the noncommunist "free world" and the forces of communism.

In recent years, the use of **terrorism** as a tool of intimidation and coercion has increased. Terrorism is the use of violence in a controlled and intentional way to force attention onto issues. Terrorist attacks are aimed at a population and not a particular person (which is called assassination). The question of whether an act of violence is committed by a rebel or a terrorist is not easily answered at times. State-sponsored terrorism is different from terrorism and contains three escalating levels of participation: (1) the state provides sanctuary for those who have committed acts of terrorism; (2) the state provides weapons, military intelligence, and money to terrorists; and (3) the state plans acts of terrorism. A state guilty of any one or all of the above is to be viewed as a state that sponsors terrorism.

Challenges to the Contemporary Political-Territorial World Order

A number of factors today present interesting challenges to the world's contemporary political system dominated by national governments. These challenges raise questions about the role of national governments in a global political system in which other types of organizations are increasingly acting on the international stage. These groups range from stateless terrorist groups to multinational organizations to transnational corporations and nongovernmental organizations. Some challenges to the traditional world order are explored here.

- Globalization of the economy and the new transnational corporations present an interesting challenge to the modern political order today. Transnational corporations make decisions for a level that transcends that of the state. Resource, staffing, production, and marketing decisions may involve several countries and economies and have direct implications for those economies.

- **Supranational** (an association of three or more states for mutual benefit) and multinational organizations require a surrender of at least partial authority of the individual state. Membership requires giving up individual rights for the common good and goals of the supranational group. The European Union (EU) and North American Free Trade Association (NAFTA) are two supranational trade blocs that supersede individual countries' decisions regarding trade.

- Nongovernmental organizations (NGOs) reflect special interest groups such as women's and children's rights, AIDS prevention, etc. They often use the media to pressure the central governments of countries to take action or limit action. Thus national governments often must respond to international groups and pressures in making domestic policies.

- Immigrants find it much easier to retain close ties with their homelands through modern communications technology. This often leads to a lessened response to assimilation into the new country and continued loyalties to the old one. The result is a challenge to traditional ideas of national citizenship and unity.

Sovereignty, Fragmentation, Unification, and Alliance

Sovereignty refers to the internationally recognized exercise of a country's power over its people and territory. A **federal state** is a type of government that gives local political units (such as states or provinces) within a country a measure of power. The United States, Canada, Germany, Australia, Switzerland, and India are examples of federal states. Recently, there has been a trend toward federal government in the world. **Unitary states** allocate most of the power to a strong central government. France and Sweden are examples of unitary states. Sometimes the devolution, or breakup, of a multinational state can create a host of problems. Over 200 different ethnic groups resided in the Soviet Union. After the breakup of its strong centralized authoritarian government, most of the former Soviet republics joined a **confederation** of states to retain some cohesion.

Some countries are geographically fragmented with a portion of their territory completely surrounded by another country's territory. An outlier (piece of a country that is separate from the main territory) that is enclosed within the borders of another country is called an **exclave.** Nagorno-Karabakh is an Armenian exclave located totally within, and under the jurisdiction of, Azerbaijan. Armenia (and Nagorno-Karabakh) are Christian, but Azerbaijan is a Muslim country so tensions are always present. An **enclave** is a piece of territory that is completely surrounded by another territory of which it is not a part. Nagorno-Karabakh would be the enclave to those living within the territory.

Countries are constantly subjected to **centripetal forces** that unite and **centrifugal forces** that divide. When unifying forces (centripetal) dominate, the country will stand strong in the face of international challenges and conflicts, as well as conflicts within its borders. When forces within threaten to divide the country (centrifugal), a breakdown of central authority may occur. Forces such as a strong, charismatic leader, national anthems, national holidays, and national institutions such as schools are all strong centripetal forces in a country. **Nationalism**, or the strong love of and loyalty to one's country, is also a potent unifying force. Nationalism also involves the concept that a nation has the right to govern itself without the interference of others.

Centrifugal forces such as religious differences and poor transportation and communication systems can be strong divisive forces within a country. Nationalism can also serve to divide a country when an ethnic or a cultural minority seeks political autonomy or the right to self-governance. This **separatism** sometimes leads to **devolution** (a breakdown or weakening of central authority) as the central government ends up giving the minority separatist group some of its demands to keep the peace. Separatist groups include the Moros of the Philippines, the Basques of Spain, the Bretons of France, and the Sikhs in India. The collapse of the former Soviet Union has led to several challenges to ethnic individuality and rights. Most separatist groups operate on the periphery and suffer from unequal treatment both politically and economically. This neglect coupled with poor linkages to the central government leads to a feeling of marginalization and resentment that spawns further unrest and strife.

Alliances are associations among countries for the purpose of mutual defense or trade. Some alliances are on a regional scale, such as the Association of Southeast Asian Nations (ASEAN), and some are on an international scale (the United Nations). Some are for political, military, or defense purposes, and other alliances are economic in purpose, such as the European Union (EU), North American Free Trade Agreement (NAFTA), Caribbean Community and Common Market (CARICOM), etc. Countries realize they need to cooperate with other countries to keep their borders secure and to guarantee economic and trade advantages, so they join with other countries to provide these benefits. International alliances water down an individual country's authority while, at the same time, giving that country the assurance that members of the alliance will back it up. The United Nations (UN) attempts to include all countries of the world, but it does exclude some countries such as Taiwan (with the opinion that Taiwan is a province of the People's Republic of China). The UN's increasing use of the policy of intervention to protect human rights without regard to matters of state sovereignty or jurisdiction has created a supranational organization with the right to override a country's absolute sovereign jurisdiction over its inhabitants. While the UN cannot force countries to agree on a disputed issue, it can exert the force of a majority consensus in the eyes of the world, which can be a powerful influence to wield!

The Law of the Sea

Starting in 1982, the oceans of the Earth have been regulated by a treaty known as the United Nations Convention on the Law of the Sea (although the United States has never officially ratified it). This convention sets up rules regarding water boundaries and rights of usage for the Earth's oceans.

Under this treaty, a coastal state has:

1. Exclusive fishing rights and sovereignty over a territorial sea of up to 12 nautical miles from its coast.
2. Limited jurisdiction over a territorial sea up to 24 nautical miles from its coast (the right to enforce laws of immigration, sanitation, hot pursuit).
3. An **exclusive economic zone (EEZ)** of up to 200 nautical miles off its coast for natural resource exploration and exploitation (see Fig. 9.4 below).

Figure 9.4 Exclusive economic zones of the United States.

The high seas beyond the EEZs of coastal states are open for free use by all political states. Any country can fish, fly over, perform scientific research in, and pass through these high seas at will. Of course, competing claims to EEZs overlap in many areas of the Pacific Ocean, the South China Sea, etc., so countries must negotiate terms of use or face future conflicts and tensions.

Geography of Representation

Territorial organization refers to government representation determined by spatial area. In a representative form of government like that of the United States, residents of a spatial area (congressional district, for example) elect representatives to stand for their views and interests in the larger governing body. Periodically, the boundaries of voting districts are redrawn to better represent the voting interests of the residents and to ensure fair and equal representation. The state legislatures take care of this in the United States, but in Europe, independent commissions are charged with redrawing boundaries. **Gerrymandering** is the process of redrawing territorial district boundaries to benefit a certain political party. Political opposition can be spread over several districts and thus diluted (wasted vote) or it can be concentrated into a few districts (excess vote). The drawing of odd-shaped boundaries is an attempt to corner like-minded voters who are spread out spatially into one district.

❯ Rapid Review

The countries of the world (states) are political units with constantly changing boundaries, associations, alliances, and concerns. They are subject to forces that unify and divide and are greatly influenced by conflicts both within and outside their borders.

› Review Questions

1. Which one of the following is the best example of a nation-state?

   (A) Germany
   (B) Italy
   (C) Vietnam
   (D) Japan
   (E) England

2. A part of a country that is separated from the main country by the territory of another country is

   (A) an island.
   (B) ghetto.
   (C) an enclave.
   (D) a peninsula.
   (E) a colony.

3. The celebration of a national holiday is an example of

   (A) centrifugal force.
   (B) centripetal force.
   (C) terrorism.
   (D) insurgency.
   (E) revolution.

4. Mackinder's heartland-rimland theory predicted

   (A) the Muslim takeover of the world.
   (B) the rise of British colonialism.
   (C) that the Japanese would conquer the Pacific Rim.
   (D) that a nation from Eurasia would conquer the world.
   (E) the rise of nationalism in Europe.

5. What would probably be the easiest shape of a state for national defense?

   (A) Compact
   (B) Elongated
   (C) Prorupt
   (D) Fragmented
   (E) Perforated

› Answers and Explanations

1. **D**—Japan is a nation-state or a country with a large, homogenous population living within its borders. The other answer choices are all states with more diverse populations comprised of several nationalities.

2. **C**—An enclave is a piece of territory that is completely surrounded by another territory of which it is not a part. An island (A) is a piece of land surrounded by water. A ghetto (B) is an ethnic enclave where the residents live segregated by race, religion, or ethnicity in a voluntary—or sometimes forced—manner. A peninsula (D) is a piece of land surrounded on three sides by water. A colony (E) is a territory under the political control of a state.

3. **B**—National holidays, songs, symbols, flags, and other similar icons are unifying (centripetal)

forces in a country. A centrifugal force (A) is one that divides a country. Terrorism (C) is the use of violence in a controlled and intentional way to force attention onto issues. An insurgency (D) is an organized and armed uprising against authority within a country. A revolution (E) is a fundamental change in power or organizational structures that takes place in a very short period of time.

4. **D**—Mackinder's theory focused on the effects of Eurasia's potential domination of the world from its base of being the largest and most-populated landmass in the world. Mackinder did not address religious domination of the world (A). Britain (B) was already a huge naval empire that ruled the seas, so his theory was in direct conflict with the existing world order. Mackinder's theory had

nothing to do with predicting the dominance of Japan (C). The theory was concerned with the future power relationship in the world, not with the rise of nationalism in Europe (E).

5. **A**—The generally round shape of a compact state makes communication and transportation among all areas easier, thus also making it easier to defend. The other answer choices list shapes of states that would be more difficult to defend because communications between distant parts of the countries would be more difficult, and the borders would be much longer relative to the size of the country.

CHAPTER 10

Agricultural and Rural Land Use

IN THIS CHAPTER

Summary: Agriculture is a primary economic activity that is found in almost every country of the world. Everyone depends on agriculture to survive. Over the centuries, agriculture has changed from a small and isolated practice into a worldwide mega-industry. Agriculture is constantly changing as new technologies and products make it increasingly efficient. It takes many forms and has gone through distinct changes and phases as it globalizes. The effects of agriculture—both large and small—on the human population are an important part of the study of AP Human Geography.

KEY IDEA

Key Terms

agribusiness
biotechnology
conservation agriculture
desertification
First Agricultural Revolution
genetically modified organism (GMO)
Green Revolution
intensive subsistence agriculture
modern commercial agriculture
monoculture
organic farming
pastoralism
plantation agriculture

polyculture
primary economic activity
Second Agricultural Revolution
sedentary
shifting agriculture
specialty farming
subsistence agriculture
sustainability
swidden agriculture
transhumance
truck farming
urban subsistence farming
vertical integration

Introduction

Agriculture is the raising of crops and livestock to provide food and other products, such as fertilizer, feed crops for animals, hides and plant fiber for clothing, etc. It is called a **primary economic activity** because it involves taking something from the Earth. The history of agriculture is long and marked with infrequent, but major, changes that greatly impact human life on this planet.

Development and Diffusion of Agriculture

The earliest humans on Earth hunted animals, gathered plants and other items, and fished for their sustenance, living on whatever was available to eat in their region of the world. Almost simultaneously, in approximately nine different culture hearths around the world, humans began to domesticate plants and animals. This enabled people to settle down in one location, or become **sedentary**. It marked the transition of humans from hunting and gathering groups to sedentary groups who lived in villages and towns. This transition involved the use of seed agriculture and farm and draft animals and marked the **First Agricultural Revolution**, often referred to as the Neolithic Agricultural Revolution. These sedentary societies modified their natural environment so they could grow surplus crops by using irrigation and storage techniques. Because of these settlements of high-density population, the societies could utilize division of labor, establish trade relationships, and develop a culture enriched with art and architecture. The sedentary nature of societies led to the need for centralized administrations and political structures, too, and populations grew.

The **Second Agricultural Revolution**, which started in the seventeenth century in Europe and North America, increased efficiency of crop production and distribution. Initially, as crop yields increased because of the horse-drawn hoe and seed drill in England, people ate healthier because more food was available at lower prices. This led to a surplus of crops in England and spread throughout Europe, permitting more people to move to the cities as the Industrial Revolution got under way. The eighteenth century's European colonies became sources of raw agricultural and mineral products for the industrializing nations. As death rates decreased, populations increased rapidly.

Agriculture blossomed into an industry through the use of mechanization and industrial methods in the early twentieth century. Mechanization led to greatly increased farm production on a much larger scale than ever before thought possible. The internal combustion engine led to the first tractors, which were used to pull combines and reapers until the 1930s when self-powered harvesting equipment was invented. Farming changed from a family farm enterprise into commercial enterprises (**agribusinesses**) that emphasized single crops and profits. Mechanization replaced humans in the fields with machinery and chemical fertilizers replacing the use of animal fertilizers to increase soil fertility and crop production.

Today agricultural industrialization completes the industry's transformation. Machines have replaced human labor, and new seeds, chemical pesticides, and fertilizers have placed the farm as only one of many links in the chain of agricultural processing. Industrial substitutes are replacing natural crop products during this current phase.

The **Green Revolution** began in the mid-1970s when scientists developed hybrid higher-yield seeds and new fertilizers to use with them. Scientists were trying to use intensive agricultural technology to help poor countries produce larger harvests without farming larger acreage. These new seeds and fertilizers were diffused from core to periphery countries during this time to aid in producing a larger harvest and to help eradicate hunger. New high-yield rice, wheat, and maize seeds were used to increase harvests worldwide.

Figure 10.1 Rice-growing in India.

China and Southeast Asian countries saw rapid increases in rice harvests, and India doubled its rice production (Fig. 10.1). Rice is the chief food for over half the world's population, with China and India alone contributing over half the total rice production. However, poor farmers cannot afford pricey seeds and fertilizers and irrigation to improve their harvests; as a result, they have not benefited much from the Green Revolution. Also, Africa's chief food crops are millet, sorghum, yams, and cassava, which haven't been much affected by the Green Revolution; only maize hybrid seeds have helped increase harvests there.

While it has increased yields, the Green Revolution's increased use of irrigation has caused environmental damage. Soil salinities have caused many soils to become less productive. Irrigation has also decreased groundwater levels while causing conflicts over water usage. Another negative side effect of the Green Revolution is the loss of biodiversity and native food crops (plants, etc., that are adapted to the climate and agricultural practices of the native populations). Many indigenous societies try new technologies to increase harvests while at the same time maintaining highly diverse cropping. This is not easy to do in the face of increasing market pressures to produce and export a single crop. Encouraged by government agencies to adopt new agricultural practices, traditional societies are usually hesitant and slow to adopt them.

Modern commercial agriculture is large-scale agricultural production for profit using specialized methods, technologies, and genetically engineered seeds. More developed countries (MDCs), like the United States and Canada, use specialized agricultural methods to raise crops for profit. The table below shows countries of the world ranked by agricultural output. Make sure you know the main crops that the top five countries produce for the exam. The law of supply and demand influences farmers to raise the crops for which there is market demand. Prices for these crops typically bring the highest profits (selling price minus costs to raise the crop). Governments often distort the market influence by subsidizing certain key crops (rice in Japan or milk in the United States) in order to protect local production (Japan) or guarantee prices in the market (United States). Farms that produce a single crop that minimizes risks (climate, costs of inputs like labor and fertilizer, market demand, etc.) and maximizes profits (choice of crop best suited for growing conditions and soil, potential pricing, etc.) have been the norm in the United States since the 1950s.

Countries Ranked by Agricultural Output, 2009

RANK	COUNTRY	OUTPUT (IN MILLIONS, US DOLLARS)
1	China	520,352
—	*European Union*	*312,498*
2	India	210,116
3	United States	171,075
4	Brazil	96,016
5	Japan	81,089
6	Russia	57,774
7	Spain	48,313
8	France	48,167
9	Australia	40,885
10	Italy	38,129

Vertical integration (contracts between farmer and purchasing/processing company) caused farm outputs to increase by the 1990s. This evolution from the single farm to the integrated production and marketing partnership model is called **agribusiness**. The fast-food industry has driven this evolution with its demand for uniformly grown livestock and produce that meets certain specifications. Because this form of agriculture is so efficient, a food surplus now exists, which keeps prices down in the face of stagnant demand.

The map in Fig. 10.2 shows the net trade in agricultural products for countries and regions of the world. The darkest areas are regions that produce and export more food crops than they import. The lightest areas import more food crops than they export. If you compare this map to a climate map of the world, you can readily see the regions with climate extremes are unable to produce sufficient crops for their inhabitants whereas middle latitude regions generally possess more favorable conditions for agriculture.

Major Agricultural Production Regions

In less-developed countries (LDCs), at least two-thirds of the population is involved in growing crops for food or in herding livestock. In most of Africa, Latin America, South Asia, and East Asia, farming is the chief occupation. In Bhutan, 90 percent of the people are employed in farming and herding. While agriculture is a large part of the economies of LDCs worldwide, employment in agriculture is declining steadily and matches global trends in MDCs. Farming for local domestic markets and for export globally is a crucial part of an LDC's national income.

Subsistence agriculture, the consumption of everything that is grown, gradually took over hunting and gathering. The various forms of subsistence agriculture have important differences. **Shifting agriculture** is based on growing crops in different fields on a rotating basis. For example, the Maya in the Yucatan grow maize by rotating fields (milpas) on a seven-year cycle. The fields are cut and burned off each year to enrich the soil with nutrients. Seeds are planted just in time for the rainy season. The cleared area

% (exports-imports)/consumption

<   −50   −25   0   25   50   >   No data

Figure 10.2   Net trade in agricultural products, 2000–2002.

is only cultivated for two or three years until all nutrients are used up and the farmers move on to clear another area for their crops. This is also called **swidden agriculture** or **slash-and-burn** and is prevalent in locations such as the Amazon Basin.

Intensive subsistence agriculture depends on heavy inputs of fertilizer and human labor on a small piece of land for substantial crop yield. China, India, and Southeast Asian countries rely on this type of agriculture to double-crop (two harvests of a crop per year), or even triple-crop (three harvests of a crop per year) rice to support their large and rapidly growing populations.

Usually several crops are produced (**polyculture**), and animals are also raised for labor, food, or clothing. **Urban subsistence farming** in the form of small city gardens is a rapidly growing activity and accounts for one-seventh of the world's food production according to recent UN figures. These gardens form an important source of sustenance for poor urban families unable to buy adequate food for their families. Waste and garbage is recycled as fertilizer, and both contribute to reducing the need for waste disposal while at the same time contributing to the spread of infectious disease and water pollution. Some cities like Bulawayo, Zimbabwe, strictly regulate urban farmers by destroying crops grown on land not owned by the farmers.

Pastoralism is a form of subsistence agriculture in which animals are herded in a seasonal migratory pattern. Today there are nearly 200 million pastoralists in the world who breed and herd cattle, goats, sheep, camels, and reindeer. Pastoralism is found in arid, marginal lands, such as deserts and steppes where rainfall is scarce and unreliable—sufficient for grazing grasses but not enough for other forms of subsistence farming. Pastoralism is widely practiced in North Africa, the steppes of Central Asia, and the Middle East. When pastoralists move their herds constantly in a set seasonal pattern of grazing (from mountain to valley pastures, for example), the movement is called **transhumance**.

In MDCs, agricultural activities range from large livestock and grain-producing farms to smaller farms that service local markets. In the United States, mixed crop and livestock farming is the most prevalent form of commercial agriculture west of the Appalachian

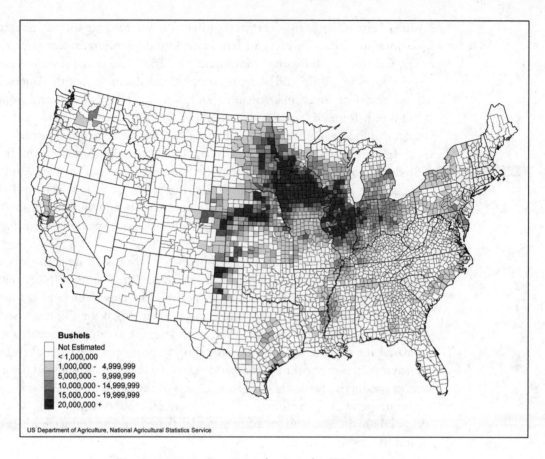

Figure 10.3   Corn production by US county, 2009.

Mountains. Northern and western Europe also engage in this type of farming most often. In this type of farming, most of the grain crops are fed to the livestock, which are then sold in the markets. Because they are able to grow both the livestock and the crops to feed them, this is an efficient, risk-reducing farming lifestyle.

Grain farming is a specialized agricultural activity where farmers grow one crop (**monoculture**) corn, wheat, or rice for commercial markets. The map in Fig. 10.3 shows the corn production by US county in 2009. The United States produces over 70 percent of the corn and a large percentage of the wheat for world markets. The use of machinery, fertilizers, pesticides, and genetically modified seeds (a type of genetically modified organism, or GMO, discussed later in the chapter) has made this a highly efficient and very productive means of growing cereal crops for market. These agribusinesses have largely taken the place of the traditional small family-owned farms of the past.

Dairy feedlots near large cities operate like factories in their efficiency. The high levels of mechanization and automation allow these dairies to not only serve the nearby urban markets but also compete effectively in the globalized market for dairy products.

Plantation agriculture (also called monocropping) on a large estate is a specialized form of agriculture that is usually located in former colonial areas in Latin America, sub-Saharan Africa, and Asia. Plantations are most often found in tropical regions of the world where ample rainfall and fertile soils allow the crop to be produced in abundance. Climate is the most important requirement for producing a plantation crop (rice, cane sugar, rubber, cacao, tea, coffee), and most plantations are located near the coasts for easy shipping access. Plantations generally use an alien labor force of immigrants from various other LDCs but require foreign investment and management to function efficiently. **Mediterranean agriculture** is another form of specialized agriculture that is known for producing grapes, olives, citrus, and figs—crops requiring a warm year-round climate with plenty of summer sunshine. This type of farming is found in countries bordering the Mediterranean Sea, California, Chile, southwestern South Africa, and southwestern Australia.

Ranching (cattle and sheep grazing) is prevalent in South America on the pampas (grasslands) of Argentina, Australia and New Zealand (sheep), and South Africa (sheep) but is only found in Spain and Portugal in Europe. Since it is more profitable to raise crops than livestock, ranching is declining in areas that have adequate rainfall.

In the United States, **truck farming**, or commercial gardening and fruit farming, is the predominant agricultural activity in the Southeast. Most of the fruits and vegetables grown are sold to large processing companies, but some are also sold to individual consumers. Migrant farm workers and large-scale automation and mechanization maximize profits while keeping costs at a minimum. In New England, **specialty farming** provides upscale customers with fresh produce.

Access to markets is a huge problem for farmers all over the world. *Von Thünen's model*, as shown in Fig. 10.4 below, helps explain the relationship between the cost of land and the cost to transport the crop to market. The closer the land is to the city, the more expensive it is, and the farther away, the cheaper it is. Von Thünen was a German farmer who wrote *The Isolated State* in 1826 in an attempt to resolve a farmer's dilemma—how to balance the cost of land with the best crop to produce. The costs of transporting different farm products to the central market determined the agricultural land use around a city. The most productive activities will locate closest to the market on more expensive land, and less productive activities will locate further away on cheaper land.

The main assumptions of this model (based on early nineteenth-century urban-rural land use conditions) are:

- **Isolated state:** no trade with the outside world
- **Land characteristics uniform:** flat land with uniform fertility around the city
- **Transportation:** no roads or rivers, just farmers with carts and horses for transportation of products

Farmers who supplied fresh milk and dairy products to the city market needed to locate close to the marketplace or risk delivering soured milk and cream. Perishable fruits and vegetables also needed to be grown closer to the marketplace because of perishability concerns. These crops were grown in the intensive farming area, whereas forest resources (needed then for fuel) could be grown and harvested further out from the market. Grain farming was in the next ring outside the city because grains could be grown, harvested, and stored easily and cheaply until needed. Livestock could be raised in the outer ring where cheap pastureland was plentiful. In von Thünen's day, livestock destined for market were driven into the city market "on the hoof," and large refrigerated tractor-trailer rigs were not needed to transport the packaged meat.

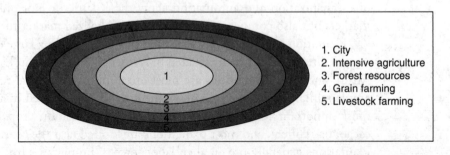

1. City
2. Intensive agriculture
3. Forest resources
4. Grain farming
5. Livestock farming

Figure 10.4   Von Thünen's agricultural land-use model.

Rural Land Use and Settlement Patterns

Settlements in the United States were originally based on resources such as agriculture, fishing, and forestry and proximity to water (coastlines, rivers, etc). The impact of increasing globalization in agriculture combined with the possible reduction of price supports to farmers contribute to the changeover of rural farmlands to alternative land uses. Land use functions such as housing, employment, recreation, and water storage are also putting increasing pressures on rural land use. For example, when people move to the rural countryside for amenities such as a rustic, simpler lifestyle in picturesque surroundings, they become agents of change and build housing developments that modify the environment, making it less rural.

Today, 75 percent of the US inhabitants live in urban areas with the remaining 25 percent of US inhabitants living in rural areas. Rural areas consist of open country and settlements with fewer than 2500 residents and have population densities as high as 999 per square mile or as low as 1 person per square mile. Three factors affect the pattern of rural settlement:

1. The kind of resource that attracts people to the area (forests, farmland)
2. The transportation methods available at time of settlement (rivers, roads)
3. Role of government policy, especially the land survey system (metes-and-bounds, long lot, rectangular, etc.)

Modern Commercial Agriculture

On the journey from subsistence agriculture to commercial agriculture, agriculture has greatly changed. Modern commercial agriculture is large-scale agricultural production for profit using specialized methods, technologies, and sometimes, genetically engineered seeds. Commercial agriculture has diffused from the core countries (MDCs) where many of the techniques were developed into the peripheral countries (LDCs) that use them to increase crop yields and feed their growing populations. We have already discussed the three revolutions, so let's take a quick look at some elements of modern commercial agriculture today.

Biotechnology is the application of scientific techniques to modify and improve plants, animals, and microorganisms to enhance their value. A **genetically modified organism (GMO)** is created when scientists take one or more specific genes from an organism (including plants, animals, bacteria, or viruses) and introduce those genes into another organism. An organism that has been transformed using genetic engineering techniques is called a transgenic organism, or a genetically modified organism. Approximately 65 to 70 percent of food products on store shelves may contain at least a small quantity of crops produced with these new techniques.

The first genetically modified food product was a tomato which was transformed to delay its ripening. Certain food plants (tomatoes, potatoes, and tobacco) have been genetically modified to produce insulin and certain vaccines. If these vaccines are proven successful in trials, they give the LDCs hope that they can cheaply grow and provide vaccines locally for their populations. See Figure 10.5 for a glimpse at how quickly the use of GMO's has grown in the United States over the past several years.

Organic Farming and Local Food Production

Organic farming is the process of producing food naturally. Organic farming avoids the use of synthetic chemical fertilizers and genetically modified organisms to influence the growth of crops. The organic farmer strives to protect the Earth's resources and produce

The HT varieties of soybeans, cotton, and corn genetically engineered to be herbicide tolerant (HT). This allows a particular herbicide to be used to kill weeds without harming the crop. Bt varieties are engineered to be resistant to particular pests (insects, worms, etc.). Many varieties of genetically engineered plants are both Bt and HT.

Figure 10.5 The adoption of genetically engineered crops in the United States.
Source: *US Department of Agriculture (USDA)*

safe, healthy food for consumption with "zero impact" on the environment. Farmers grow their crops without the help of artificial fertilizers and harmful chemical pesticides, and organic ranchers and dairy farmers raise their livestock free of drugs and animal hormones. Organic food products are increasing in demand as consumers try to avoid harmful toxins and residues of pesticides in the food supply.

Locally produced foods are fresher, more nutritious, and tastier than those found in supermarkets because they travel a much shorter distance from field to shelf. Buying from local farmers also helps the local economy by enabling farmers to stay in business. Farmers' markets, roadside produce stands, and local specialty stores emphasizing local produce are just a few of the ways local food production is manifested today.

Environmental Impacts of Agriculture

Agricultural practices worldwide have caused many adverse impacts on the environment. Intensive farming techniques are often too hard on the soils, and they become too depleted or polluted for further use. Clearing land for farmland or cattle ranching has caused massive deforestation in many countries. Dry or semiarid regions such as the African Sahel are at risk of **desertification**, which is the turning of agricultural land into deserts through use of overgrazing and the subsequent erosion of unprotected topsoils by winds. The use of pesticides and fertilizers pollutes soil and drinking water supplies and also kills off useful insects that provide natural pest control. Widespread use of water for irrigation depletes water tables and changes the ecology of rivers and streams. People working in agricultural industry often suffer health problems caused by working with agricultural chemicals. As farmers strive to produce enough food for the growing global population, can we produce it in a sustainable way? **Sustainability** is the principle that we must meet our present needs without compromising the ability of future generations to meet their needs. Sustainability emphasizes the stewardship of both natural and human resources.

Conservation agriculture is a new way of farming based on optimizing crop yields and profits without depleting soil, encouraging erosion, and harming the environment. Conservation agriculture methods include reduced use of fossil fuels, pesticides, and other pollutants thus keeping the environment safer for the inhabitants, too. Some common conservation practices include:

- **Conservation crop rotation:** planting low-residue (low-fiber) crops such as soybeans in one year, followed by a high-residue crop such as corn in the following year on the same field
- **Conservation tillage:** allowing the crop residue to stay on top of the field, rather than being plowed under when planting begins
- **Terraces:** creating an embankment (a terrace) at a right angle to sloping land in order to allow water to soak into the soil rather than to move down the slope, taking the soil with it
- **Grassed waterways:** creating a broad and shallow depression, usually below a terraced area, that is planted with grasses to prevent erosion by slowing the flow of runoff, holding a bank, and filtering out soil particles

› Rapid Review

Agriculture is a global industry that has changed and evolved through the years from being an isolated family farm to a multimillion-dollar commercial agribusiness. The foods we eat every day come from global communities far away. Can we raise crops in a sustainable way without harming our planet?

❯ Review Questions

1. The practice of shifting cultivation is

   (A) slash and burn agriculture.
   (B) agribusiness.
   (C) found primarily in the tundra regions.
   (D) commercial agriculture.
   (E) pastoralism.

2. The Green Revolution introduced the use of

   (A) maize.
   (B) chemical fertilizers.
   (C) mechanization.
   (D) slash-and-burn agriculture.
   (E) organic farming methods.

3. Which one of the following statements does NOT correctly describe plantations?

   (A) They are usually found in tropical regions.
   (B) They often employ alien laborers.
   (C) They usually specialize in producing one crop.
   (D) The soil type is the main element determining what a plantation produces.
   (E) They satisfy a demand in temperate regions for tropical crops like sugar, bananas, or coffee.

4. All of the following factors are serious negative consequences of the Green Revolution EXCEPT

   (A) excessive salinity of soils.
   (B) serious groundwater depletion.
   (C) increased crop production.
   (D) loss of traditional agricultural practices.
   (E) loss of traditional crop varieties (land races).

5. The goal of commercial agriculture is

   (A) minimal food security.
   (B) genetic diversity of seeds.
   (C) establishment of seed banks throughout the world.
   (D) profit maximization.
   (E) sustainable farming practices.

❯ Answers and Explanations

1. **A**—Slash-and-burn agriculture is based on growing crops in different fields on a rotating basis and usually starts with the cutting and burning of stubble left from previous harvests. Agribusiness (B) refers to an integrated production and marketing partnership in agriculture that has evolved over the years as farming becomes "big business." No agricultural activities except reindeer herding take place in the tundra regions of the world (C). Commercial agriculture (D) involves the production of agricultural goods for sale. Pastoralism (E) is a form of subsistence agriculture in which animals are herded in a seasonal migratory pattern.

2. **B**—Chemical fertilizers and the higher-yield seeds that required their use were introduced by scientists in the 1970s when the Green Revolution attempted to help periphery countries grow larger

harvests. Maize (A) has been in existence as a food crop for centuries. Mechanization (the use of mechanized equipment in agriculture) (C) really accelerated in the early twentieth century when the internal combustion engine introduced the first modern tractors. Slash-and-burn agriculture (D), which is based on growing crops in different fields on a rotating basis and usually starts with the cutting and burning of stubble left from previous harvests, existed long before the Green Revolution and was largely unaffected by it. Organic farming methods (E) avoid the use of synthetic fertilizers and produce food naturally.

3. **D**—Climate, not soil type, is the main factor to consider when producing a crop. All the other statements correctly describe plantations. Plantations are usually located in the tropical

regions (A) and often employ workers from other countries (B). Plantations specialize in large-scale production of one agricultural product (C) such as tea, coffee, bananas, coffee, etc. When colonial powers created the plantation system in their colonies, they did so to supply themselves with tropical crops they could not grow at home (E).

4. **C**—Increased crop production is a major benefit of the Green Revolution. Increased soil salinity—and infertility—is one negative consequence of the Green Revolution (A). Serious groundwater depletion (B) often occurs from the increased irrigation required for Green Revolution techniques.

Loss of traditional agricultural practices (D) and traditional crop varieties (land races) (E) occur in traditional societies asked to implement the Green Revolution technologies and higher-yield hybrid seeds.

5. **D**—Profit maximization is the chief goal of commercial agriculture. Minimal food security (A) is *never* a goal in any society. Genetic diversity of seeds (B), the establishment of worldwide seed banks (C), and sustainable farming practices (E) are never as important as making a profit in commercial agriculture.

CHAPTER 11

Industrialization and Economic Development

IN THIS CHAPTER

Summary: This chapter reviews the spatial nature of industrial economies and contemporary global patterns of industrialization and resource extraction. The world's industrial regions and major industrial location theories are largely based on human behavior, as well as the workings of a market economy. What is happening now in the world's industrial regions is not always the same as what occurred in the early days of the Industrial Revolution. Today, as industrialization occurs in one region, deindustrialization happens in another.

KEY IDEA

Key Terms

agglomeration effects
backwash effects
commodity chains
creative destruction
deindustrialization
dependency theory
developed countries (DCs)
developmentalism
export-processing zones (EPZs)
fixed cost
footloose firm
Fordism
globalization
gross domestic product (GDP)
gross national product (GNP)

import substitution
Industrial Revolution
least-cost theory
less-developed countries (LDCs)
localization economies
locational interdependence theory
maquiladora
Millennium Development Goals
neocolonialism
Neo-Fordism
offshoring
outsourcing
quaternary economic activities
quinary economic activities
Rostow's model of economic development

secondary economic activities

spread effects

sustainable development

tertiary economic activities

transnational corporations (TNCs)

world-systems theory

Introduction

Although industries existed long before the Industrial Revolution, after this amazing event the economies of Europe and, later, all countries, would never be the same. As the more advanced countries deindustrialize, newly industrialized countries (NICs) compete for global markets. What are the factors guiding economic behaviors in an economy, and how do they influence location, profits, resource allocation, and other important aspects of industry?

Industrialization and Development

Economic development is spatially very uneven. **Developed countries** (**DCs** or "the core") and more developed countries (MDCs) have the highest levels of economic development. Countries such as the United States, Great Britain, Australia, Germany, France, Japan, etc., comprise the core countries. **Less-developed countries** (**LDCs**) are located on the semi-periphery or periphery of the global economy and include the former communist countries (such as Romania and Bulgaria, for example) and formerly referenced Third World countries (such as Nigeria and Kenya, for example) (see Fig. 11.1 below). These countries are seeking an improved standard of living that is often achieved by industrialization of the economy and the transition from an agrarian-based system to one centered on manufacturing or trade.

The United Nations developed the Human Development Index (HDI) to measure the development of every country. The HDI is computed based on three factors: access to knowledge, a decent standard of living, and the ability to lead a long and healthy life.

The level of development in a country is dependent on economic development and activity as measured by using the **gross domestic product (GDP)** and the **gross national product (GNP)**. The GDP is an approximation of the total value of all final goods and services produced by a country per year. "Final" refers to the finished end product to avoid

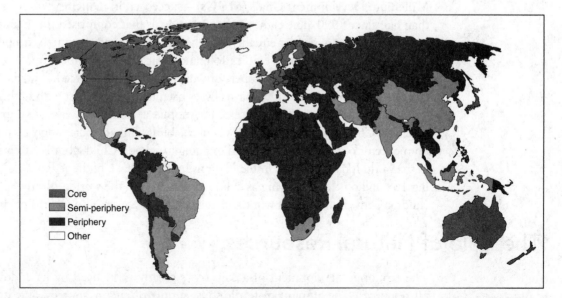

Core
Semi-periphery
Periphery
Other

Figure 11.1   World map of countries by trading status in the late twentieth century.

double counting. For example, raw steel sold to General Motors is not counted since the finished automobile is counted in GDP when sold to the consumer. The GNP is the GDP plus the value of income from abroad such as earnings from a US company like Intel, which produces silicon chips in Leixlip, County Kildare, Ireland.

Generally, technology transfer from core countries to periphery and semi-periphery countries leads to advanced participation in the world's economic system. If the country fails to achieve technology transfers, the quality of life for its inhabitants does not usually improve. The standard of living is influenced by economic progress with analysis of multiple criteria (GNP, per capita energy consumption, percent of workforce engaged in agriculture, and calorie intake per capita) required to correctly evaluate a country's economic progress.

Regions *within* countries also differ in terms of levels of economic development. Some regions are substantially above the national income average whereas others fall short. Scarcity of resources, lower levels of skills, and a shortage of investment all combine to produce a region with lower economic performance. Sometimes the physical geography of a region combines with lack of infrastructure (such as decent roads) to cause regional economic inequality. Even portions of DCs are often underdeveloped and lack adequate economic resources. The Appalachian region of the United States is an example of a region that has continually lagged behind the rest of the country in terms of economic growth and standard of living. The export-oriented coast of China is far more economically advanced than the less-developed interior provinces.

Women in Development

Changes in the global economy have resulted in a rapid increase in the number of women engaged in industrial employment in LDCs. Women are paid lower wages than men for the same work (even in DCs such as the United States) and are required to work *in addition to* their family responsibilities. Women also work longer hours than men in every country (both in paid and unpaid labor), except the United States, Canada, and Australia. The increased job opportunities for women have led to better healthcare, education, and child-care for women worldwide. Women in many LDCs now have access to microcredit (Grameen Bank microcredit loans in Bangladesh, for example) that gives them the opportunity to start small businesses. Similar practices cropping up around the world are helping families and individuals rise out of poverty. The United Nation's mandate to erase poverty – **Millenium Development Goals (MDGs)** – succeeded in reducing extreme poverty by more than half since 1990. The eight development goals that comprised this mandate are targeted at the promotion of gender equality and the empowerment of women through the provision of better healthcare, hunger eradication, and basic universal education.

The impact of growing numbers of women in the labor force has taken its toll on world families, too. Children in LDCs have always been required to assist with both paid and unpaid family labor needs, but the absence of the mother at home has seriously impacted the family structure. Children not only babysit younger siblings but are increasingly employed in the economic sector of the economy instead of going to school. Child labor is a tremendous problem in the world today with the United Nations International Children's Fund (UNICEF) estimating 168 million children living as child laborers around the world. Nearly 85 million of these children perform hazardous work and a wide percentage are also victims of child trafficking.

The Role of Natural Resources

The economic development of a country is greatly influenced by its endowment of natural resources. The amount of fertile soils, supply of energy sources, and stores of valuable minerals all contribute to a country's level of economic development. However, natural resources are unevenly distributed throughout the world with some countries possessing more than others. Core regions where the highest demands often occur do not possess adequate supplies for their needs and depend on periphery countries to fulfill their needs. Trade is very helpful in supplementing a country's resource base. Core countries such as Japan, with its lack of minerals and cultivatable farmland, make up for their deficit through trade. Energy sources and other natural resources can also be exchanged sometimes, should a shortage in one resource occur. Countries that depend on a single raw material's export are in trouble should the global market for that resource drop (see Fig. 11.2 below).

Natural resources are unequally distributed throughout the world. While high levels of natural resources and energy are necessary to fuel continued development on a world scale, concerns are growing about the impact this is having on the environment. Rainforests and fragile ecosystems are destroyed, natural environments are polluted, and biodiversity is lost on an alarming basis in the world today. The preservation of biodiversity is vital to ensure that species extinction slows down. Future implications on the world's demographics, including mass migrations, famines, and civil unrest will rest largely on the stabilizing influences of sustainable development practiced on a global scale. Core countries increasingly acknowledge the need to address resource issues in periphery and semi-periphery countries to maintain global stability and survival.

KEY IDEA

Sustainable development is the concept that it is possible to balance economic growth without jeopardizing the environment and equitable human access. It is important to determine what level of development a country can maintain without jeopardizing the future of its inhabitants to continue at that level. Unfortunately, many governments support development strategies that fuel resource usage at the expense of the global environment. Until very recently, global organizations such as the World Bank have provided loans for this type of economic development. Geographers believe that the global environment can be protected while economic development continues in the periphery. They also believe that humans must continue to develop renewable resources as supplies of nonrenewable resources dwindle.

Economic Activities

The economic activities of a country can be classified according to the table shown here.

ECONOMIC ACTIVITY	DEFINITION	EXAMPLES
Primary	Extraction of natural resource	Farming, mining, forestry
Secondary	Processing of raw materials into finished goods by manufacturing	Steel manufacturing, furniture production, food processing
Tertiary	Provision of services	Retail, restaurants, tourism, police and fire provision, sanitation, advertising
Quaternary	Information and knowledge processing	Education, data processing, research and development, banking and finance, medical, entertainment
Quinary	Highest-level decision making	Top-level government officials and business executives, research scientists, financial consultants

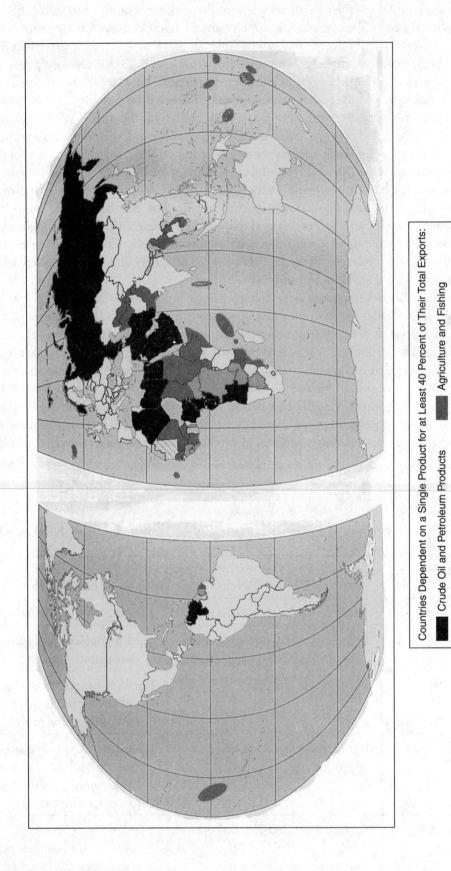

Countries Dependent on a Single Product for at Least 40 Percent of Their Total Exports:

Crude Oil and Petroleum Products

Metals and Minerals

Agriculture and Fishing

Countries Not Dependent on a
Single Product

Figure 11.2   Countries dependent on the export of a single commodity.

Countries on the periphery employ the majority of their workers in primary economic activities such as mining, fishing, or agriculture. **Secondary economic activities** that add value by changing a material into a more useful product (form utility) are generally performed in the core and semi-periphery countries. **Tertiary economic activities** are those that provide services such as wholesale and retail jobs, tourism, and restaurant work. **Quaternary economic activities** are really high-order tertiary activities that the most developed countries abound in such as white-collar workers in education, information processing, and government. The highest level of quaternary economic activities is sometimes classified as quinary. **Quinary economic activities** are reserved for those who are the highest-level decision makers in both the government and private sectors of the economy. Sometimes there is disagreement about how to classify an economic activity, but in general, primary refers to basic extraction of a resource from the earth, secondary is the processing of that resource into a finished product, tertiary refers to the service sector, and quaternary deals with information handling and processing. Core countries have the highest levels of economic development and employ workers in the quaternary and quinary groups whereas primary economic activities dominate in the peripheral countries.

Theories of Economic Development

W.W. **Rostow's model of economic development** (also called modernization theory) is based on stages of economic growth and modernization (see Fig. 11.3). The first stage of development is a traditional subsistence economy based mainly on farming with very limited technology. When the levels of technology within a country develop and the development of a transportation system encourages trade, the second stage—preconditions for take-off—is reached. During the third stage—take-off—more transportation systems and infrastructure are built and manufacturing industries grow rapidly. Growth poles emerge as investment increases. By stage four—the drive to maturity—growth is self-sustaining, and leads to an increase in the number and types of industry. During this stage, more complex transport systems and manufacturing expand as transportation develops, rapid urbanization occurs, and traditional industries may decline. In Rostow's fifth and final stage—the age of mass consumption—a rapid expansion of tertiary industries occurs while manufacturing declines. Rostow's model assumes periphery countries only need to modernize to achieve

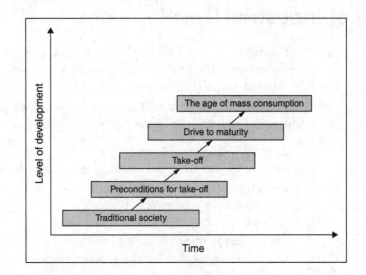

Figure 11.3 Rostow's stages of economic development.

greater economic development and that the role of core countries is to provide foreign aid and industrial technology to help them. The Green Revolution with its transfer of agricultural technology from core to periphery is an example of this theory in action.

Rostow's theory is criticized for the following reasons:

- It attempts to fit all countries into the Western/European historical mold.
- It is geared toward large countries, thus leaving out small ones, such as Gambia and Burundi.
- It is linear when many times economic development occurs nonlinearly in "fits-and-starts."
- It is based on high-consumption Western ideals.

Countries and regions are interdependent in the world's current global economy. The fortunes of a country are increasingly linked with those of many others. Rostow's model keeps alive the myth of **developmentalism**—the notion that every country and region will eventually make economic progress toward a high level of mass consumption if they only compete to the best of their ability within the world economy. The chief weakness of developmentalism is that it is not fair to compare the prospects of periphery countries to the experience of countries that were among the first to reach take-off. The early starters arrived in a world free of effective competition, obstacles, and precedents. Today's less-developed countries must compete in a crowded global economy while facing numerous barriers.

During the 1970s, a new approach to examining the world's economies began. Andre Gunder Frank's **dependency theory** is a theory of economic development based on the periphery's dependence on the core. He believed that the core exploits resources in the periphery resulting in the periphery's dependence on the core as it imports the core's finished products. The periphery is then forced to take on a dependent role in the global economy, starting in colonial times and continuing today in the form of **neocolonialism**. Frank proposed that the periphery is underdeveloped today because of the development of the core and the uneven trade, profits, and resource and labor exploitation that resulted. Following in this line of thinking, Immanuel Wallerstein developed the **world-systems theory** at a time (1970s) when the Third World and the Cold War were commonly accepted terms. He claimed there is only one world—a complex world-system—in which nation-states compete for capital and labor. He saw the global economy as a market system with a fluid and dynamic flow of countries and economies from periphery to semi-periphery to core.

Location of Industrial Development

We have already reviewed how von Thünen's theory explained the location of agricultural activities based on market location in Chapter 10. In similar fashion, location of an industry is also based, in part, on market access. However, other locational factors must also be considered. For example, the best location is also based on relative costs of input needed to produce the product. The following principles help determine the location of industrial activity:

1. Accessibility to material inputs such as raw materials and energy
2. Relative importance of the following inputs:
   a. Labor needed to produce the product
   b. Cost of land, plant, machinery (fixed costs)
   c. Wages, salaries, utility bills, local taxes, etc.
   d. Demand of the market for the good or service
   e. Transfer costs (transporting inputs from sources and outputs to markets; costs of storing, insuring, unloading, etc., of raw materials and finished goods)

3. Influence of government policies and cultural factors
4. Influence of behavioral considerations

Least-cost theory, developed by Alfred Weber, states that three main expenses must be minimized in locating an industry—labor costs, transportation costs, and agglomeration costs, with transportation costs being the most important. He used a locational triangle diagram to determine the optimal location using the approximate weights of raw materials and finished products along with distances.

An industry location is based on many variables, called inputs, which can change over time. Three of the most important variables are shown above: raw materials, labor, and markets. The Substitution Principle states that the benefits of one input could offset the negatives of another.

Agglomeration effects are also important in determining where to locate an industry. They are the cost advantages (external economies) for an individual company gained by locating near similar functional industries or companies. For example, a tanning salon might choose to locate in a strip mall containing a hair salon, dress shop, and shoe store since these stores attract a certain type of customer. **Localization economies** are cost savings for individual industries as a result of grouping together in a certain location. For example, Silicon Valley (see Fig. 11.4 below) and its software and electronics industries

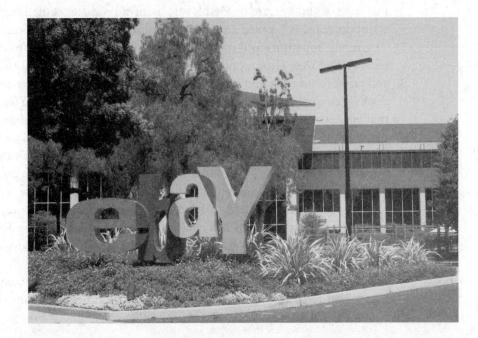

Figure 11.4   Silicon Valley benefited from agglomeration effects.

clustered together to take advantage of a highly skilled and specialized labor force and intense competition among competing firms.

Gunnar Myrdal, a Swedish economist, called this buildup process of advantages by agglomeration and localization cumulative causation. He proposed that flows of people and investment dollars from other regions (often the closest) into the location accumulate and cause economic growth of that region. Sometimes this also causes a negative spiral of economic disadvantage as nearby regions lose talented workers and suffer reduced capital flows. The **backwash effects** (negative impacts) to the peripheral regions often include a reduced local tax base, which means fewer dollars for schools, highways, and other activities. **Spread effects** also occur in which the peripheral region benefits from the economic growth of the core region by growing too. The need to provide more goods and services often outstrips the core's ability to provide them, leading to a trickle-down effect that provides the periphery regions with the opportunity to step in and do so.

Growth poles are locations for economic activity that are specifically grouped around a high-growth industry. The location of dynamic, high-growth industries in a region gives that region a valuable economic "boost." French *technopoles* (high-tech industrial sites) are an example of this type of growth pole.

"Paris is a **regional growth pole**. Unfortunately, the "pull" of Paris is so strong that very few industries have chosen to locate in the surrounding region. This negative polarization effect in France is called "Paris and the French desert." Sometimes profits influence locational decisions even more than costs. **Locational interdependence theory** is a theory developed by economist Harold Hotelling. This theory suggests competitors, in trying to maximize sales, will seek to limit each other's territory as much as possible by locating close to each another in the middle of their combined customer base. If both sellers are equidistant from their potential customers, neither has a greater advantage.

Profit maximization theory is the third important theory in locating a new industry. It is based on finding the location where net profit would be greatest. Sometimes the substitution principle is used to determine if a less expensive input can be substituted for a more expensive one. The spatial margin of profitability is computed based on transport costs of raw materials and finished product, and the firm could be located anywhere within this margin and operate profitably. If the firm produces something that requires minimal transport costs, it is called a **footloose** industry (for example, computers).

Import **substitution** is the production of goods and services internally by the periphery country that were once supplied by the core. By subsidizing local industries and using taxes and tariffs to protect them from outside competition, countries like Brazil and Peru have successfully enabled their economic development. When a core region witnesses decreased industrial employment as industries respond to decreased profits, **deindustrialization** occurs. The decline in industrial employment that occurred during the 1960s and 1970s in the Rustbelt of the northeastern United States is an example of this concept. This also occurred in the older industrial regions of Europe and the United Kingdom during this time period.

Creative destruction is the reinvestment of funds in new, profitable ventures and regions that once were used to fund older, less profitable ventures and regions. The US Sunbelt now benefits from receiving funds once invested in the Rustbelt region. Capital flows from one region to the other sometimes occur when a declining region reinvents itself. Pittsburgh experienced a postindustrial renaissance during the 1980s and 1990s after its demise as a steel-producing giant. New investment capital powered the city to transform into a high-tech, cutting-edge software and medical research giant (Fig. 11.5).

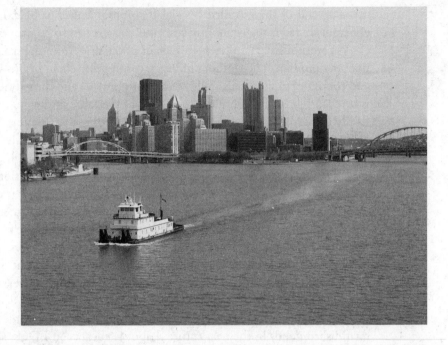

Figure 11.5 Pittsburgh—product of deindustrialization and renaissance.

Growth and Diffusion of Industrialization

Industrialization involves the process of manufacturing products in a factory. The **Industrial Revolution** began in the late 1700s in England and led to the astronomical growth of population for the next two centuries as industrialization diffused outward first across the Atlantic Ocean into British colonies in North America and then east into Europe. Before the invention of the machines that enabled the Industrial Revolution to occur, there was industry, but it operated at a very small scale in the homes of individuals (called a cottage industry). James Watts's steam engine expedited the processing of iron, and the textile industry soon adapted various machines into its manufacturing processes. Industries began to cluster around coal deposits—the new fuel-of-choice for the growing number of steam engines that powered this new industrial growth.

Engineering developed new products and manufacturing techniques on an accelerating basis, fueling the fires of industrialization and contributing to transportation innovations such as railroads. Industry diffused into the countries of northern and western Europe first and into countries of southern and eastern Europe during the twentieth century. The chief areas of industrialization in western Europe are found in the United Kingdom, the Po River Basin of northern Italy, and the Rhine and Ruhr River valleys in Germany and France.

Changes streamlined the manufacturing process. **Fordism** is the process of using assembly-line techniques and scientific management in manufacturing and is attributed to Henry Ford. **Neo-Fordism** is the evolution of mass production with a more responsive system geared to the nuances of mass consumption. It uses flexible production systems that allow production processes to be shifted quickly from production of one product to another with very little "downtime" in the assembly line. Components are often delivered to factories "just in time" to be used so that parts inventories are minimal. **Export-processing zones (EPZs)** are small areas with exceptional investment and trading conditions that governments create to stimulate and attract foreign investment. China's coastline is made up of several of these (called Special Economic Zones or SEZs), and China has benefited enormously from the economic stimulus this creates to its economy.

A **commodity chain** refers to a chain of activities from the manufacturing to the distribution of a product. The clothing industry commodity chain begins with the growing of cotton and continues to the textile mills where cloth is made and the garment factories where clothing is stitched. The chain continues to firms that specialize in design, marketing, distribution, and finally the last link of the chain—retailing, or selling the clothing to the consumer. Peripheral countries such as Mexico and Turkey are low-profit, labor-intensive links in the clothing commodity chain, while core countries (almost always) reap the high profits and function as the specialized links at the end of the chain. **Transnational corporations (TNCs)** (also referred to as multinational corporations or MNCs) are found at the high-profit end of the commodity chain and specialize in brand names, high technology, and design and marketing functions.

Transnational corporations (TNCs) are companies that have facilities and processes spread among several countries (global assembly line). A few examples of transnational, or global, corporations are Apple, Bayer, GlaxoSmithKline, and Xerox, but there are many, many more. Investment dollars flow unevenly in the global economy, however, and few investment dollars typically flow to LDCs. MDCs such as China, Brazil, and Mexico receive the lion's share of investment money because they are viewed as emerging economies that will become markets for finished goods in the near future. Labor is cheaper in LDCs, so the more labor-intensive operations are usually performed there. Final details and assembly are done in the DCs near the end markets for the products. Banking and finance are also global industries; they provide investment funds, thus controlling the economic direction of many LDCs. **World cities** (New York City, London, Paris, Tokyo) are those in which a very large proportion of global finance and banking transactions take place.

Contemporary Patterns and Impacts of Industrialization and Development

Globalization is more than just the homogenization of cultures and ideologies created by better technology and communications networks. It also involves the increasingly fluid movement of economic goods and services between and among countries and regions of the world. What does our future hold as globalization increases and our future is increasingly intertwined with that of others?

Comparative advantage is the production of a commodity by a country that has the most favorable ratio of advantage or the least unfavorable ratio of disadvantage compared to other countries. Countries can use specialization to gain an advantage in supplying or producing a commodity that they can exchange for another commodity more cheaply than they could produce that commodity within their own country. **Outsourcing**, the practice of shifting production of a product to a third party either in the country in which you are based or in another country, is an offshoot of comparative advantage. Taking advantage of less expensive labor and producing goods in another country angers some who view this as stealing jobs and production potential from one's own country. Outsourcing is often used to refer to sending service sector and production work to other countries where lack of labor unions keeps the labor costs low. **Maquiladoras** are foreign-owned assembly companies located in the United States–Mexico border region. These companies are able to take advantage of cheaper labor, favorable tax breaks, lax environmental regulations, and otherwise keep costs minimal while operating close to the core markets for the products. **Offshoring** is the practice of contracting with a third-party service provider in another country to take over or supervise part of the business operations. The offshore staff functions just like the employees in the home office, and customers may not even be aware they are dealing with staff overseas.

Half of the world's energy resource consumption now occurs in semi-periphery and periphery countries, because of their rapid industrialization. This increased demand for scarce natural resources has already driven up market prices with the result that shortages are already occurring. In many periphery and semi-periphery countries, natural resources are being extracted and exploited in an unsustainable fashion. Unfortunately, developing countries are industrializing so rapidly that they are unable, or unwilling, to limit the corresponding high levels of environmental pollution. China's skyrocketing industrialization has led to its possessing 16 of the 20 most polluted cities in the world, according to the World Bank.

Technological advances are creating time-space convergence through transportation and communication on a scale once thought unattainable. Advances in materials technologies, biotechnology, and information technology are occurring at such a rapid rate that many researchers and social scientists no longer even attempt to predict what our future holds!

› Rapid Review

Industries are spatially distributed throughout the world in an uneven pattern. Four major areas—Eastern North America, East Asia, Western Europe, and Eastern Europe dominate, but China is rapidly becoming more important than these regions. Factors influencing the location of industries are based on costs, labor markets, and proximity to markets. Industrial location theories discuss how the location of each industry is determined, and overall concerns with resource distribution, usage, and sustainability are increasingly of importance.

› Review Questions

1. Advertising, legal services, and retailing are examples of

   (A) primary economic activities.
   (B) secondary economic activities.
   (C) tertiary economic activities.
   (D) quaternary economic activities.
   (E) quinary economic activities.

2. The Industrial Revolution first diffused from Great Britain to

   (A) Germany.
   (B) Russia.
   (C) Italy.
   (D) British colonies in North America.
   (E) France.

3. Which one of the following statements does NOT correctly describe commodity chains?

   (A) They usually begin in periphery countries.
   (B) They reap the highest profits for core countries.
   (C) They involve several locations around the world.
   (D) They are located near cheap sources of labor.
   (E) They are centered around periphery markets for finished goods.

4. Which theory below explains why two competing pizza parlors both position themselves in the middle of their customer base?

   (A) Dependency theory
   (B) The stages of economic development theory
   (C) World-systems theory
   (D) Locational interdependence theory
   (E) The domino theory

❯ Review Questions

5. All of the following factors are important in locating an industrial activity EXCEPT

   (A) the cost of labor.
   (B) the cost of land.
   (C) the market demand for the good.
   (D) government policies.
   (E) climate.

❯ Answers and Explanations

1. **C**—Tertiary economic activities are those that provide services. Primary economic activities (A) deal with the extraction of a natural resource and secondary economic activities (B) involve the processing of raw materials into finished goods by manufacturing. Quaternary economic activities (D) deal with information and knowledge processing, and quinary economic activities (E) involve high-level decision making.

2. **D**—The Industrial Revolution began in Great Britain and diffused into Britain's colonies in North America first and then spread to Europe (A), (B), (C), and (E).

3. **E**—Commodity chains are centered around core markets for finish goods, not periphery markets. All of the other statements regarding commodity chains are true. They begin in periphery countries where the raw materials originate and labor is cheap (A), and reap the highest profits for core countries (B) since they are the ones to add the "finishing touches" and market the product. Commodity chains contain locations around the world (C), including locations near cheap sources of labor (D).

4. **D**—The locational interdependence theory was developed by Hotelling to explain what happens when competitors within a marketplace make locational decisions in an attempt to maximize their sales. Dependency theory (A) states that economic development is based on the periphery countries' dependence on core countries. The stages of economic development theory (B) was postulated by Rostow to explain the progression of economic development that a country goes through as it modernizes and becomes competitive in the global marketplace. World-systems theory (C) states there is a world system of core, periphery, and semi-periphery countries that serve as actors in operating the global economy. Capitalist countries in the core dominate the periphery states using their skilled labor force, technological advantage, and control of business, banking, and trade while the peripheral countries with their low-paid labor force suffers unequal development opportunities. The domino theory (E) is the notion from the Cold War Era that once a country falls to communism, neighboring countries are subject to falling to communism, too.

5. **E**—Climate is usually not an important factor in locating an industrial activity, but the cost of labor (A) and land on which to build (B) are very important. Generally, industries are located in a region where the market demand for the product (C) is high to minimize transportation and storage costs. Government policies (D) are always important in locating an industry. For example, areas with low taxes and trade tariffs attract industry.

CHAPTER 12

Cities and Urban Land Use

IN THIS CHAPTER

Summary: Cities perform important functions in their societies. Most cities throughout the world are growing at a rapid pace that exceeds population growth in their regions. Seventy-five percent of Americans now live in cities, and the proportion of Europeans, Russians, Australians, and Japanese who live in cities is almost as high. Even countries and regions with low urbanization rates have cities of sizeable populations. World cities, megacities, and supercities all play important roles in their respective regions. This chapter reviews the main functions of cities and the relationships within the city itself and between the city and its surrounding hinterland.

KEY IDEA

Key Terms

basic sector
bid-rent curve
central business district (CBD)
central place theory
concentric zone model
congregation
edge city
gateway city
gentrification
ghettoization
gravity model
Green Revolution
hinterlands

megacity
megalopolis
multiple nuclei model
multiplier effect
New Urbanism
non-basic sector
primate city
public housing
rank-size rule
rural-to-urban migration
sector model
segregation
site

situation   urbanization
suburbanization   urban renewal
supercity   urban sprawl
uneven development   world city

Introduction

Almost half of the world's population lives in cities, and the urban population is growing at a much higher rate than the rural population. With this massive migration into cities and urban areas, it is important to learn more about urban dynamics—it is the wave of the future.

Nature and Function of Cities

The city is the center of every advanced society and serves as the economic, political, and social hub of a geographic region or area. The larger the city becomes, the more activities it develops as it assumes more responsibilities and functions for the populations within its **hinterland** or surrounding trade area. All cities provide the following functions: retail and wholesale operations; manufacturing, political, transportation, communication, education, religious, medical, legal, and financial services; defense and safety, and entertainment.

A city is interconnected to other cities within the region and often possesses a specialized function, or purpose, within that region. All cities have a **site** or local setting and a **situation** or regional setting, which evolve and change over time. For example, Pittsburgh's site is at the confluence of the Monongahela and Allegheny Rivers. Long ago its situation was a strategic defensive position as a fort during the early colonial days. Then Pittsburgh's situation changed as it boomed as a major steel-producing city because of the transportation advantages of being situated on three rivers. The abundant raw materials from the region were transported down the rivers to the steel mills in Pittsburgh, and finished steel was shipped down the Ohio River to destinations all over the world.

Origin and Evolution of Cities

The first cities or urban settlements developed in the following approximate order in five regions of the world:

Mesopotamia (present-day Iraq)	3500 B.C.E.
Egypt	3100 B.C.E.
Indus River Valley (present-day Pakistan)	2500 B.C.E.
Northern China (Huang He River)	1800 B.C.E.
Meso-America (present-day Mexico)	1500 B.C.E.

A combination of factors is responsible for the development of cities: agricultural surpluses, hydrological factors, increasing population densities, defense needs, religious reasons, and trade requirements.

Urbanization spread from these areas of origin in an uneven fashion, often as the result of long-distance trade. An example of this is the ancient Silk Road—a trade route that stretched across Central Asia from China to Europe. The Greek city-states along the Mediterranean coastline evolved from their Mesopotamian hearth and served defense, trade, religious, and administrative functions. The Roman Empire displaced Greek dominance around 338 B.C.E., and the rapidly expanding Roman Empire with its well-connected transportation networks established cities across southern Europe by A.D. 200; the Western European city is based on their setup. During the Dark Ages in Europe, the urban centers in Arab regions, such as Baghdad and Mecca, thrived and prospered.

The increase in trade during the following medieval and Renaissance periods (fourteenth to eighteenth centuries) spurred urban revival in Europe. Beginning in the sixteenth century, European colonization of Latin America by Spain and Portugal created colonial cities with a focus on administration and military defense. **Gateway cities** were established worldwide as control centers for the colonial powers. The Industrial Revolution in England ensured that cities took on the function of manufacturing and production centers. From England, industrialization and urbanization spread into other parts of Europe.

Urbanization is the rapid growth of—and migration to—large cities. Today urbanization is taking place at a rapid rate in most LDCs. **Rural-to-urban migration** is the movement of people from the countryside to the city usually in search of economic opportunities (jobs) and a better life (both "pull" factors of migration). This increase in urban population causes rapid physical expansion of cities and greater urbanization of the society. Because of this rapid urbanization, cities in LDCs face the following problems: increased levels of pollution and traffic congestion, shortages of clean drinking water, insufficient sanitation services, lack of sufficient electrical power, lack of enough job opportunities, strained education and healthcare facilities, housing shortages, and increased problems with drugs, gangs, and violence. A **supercity** is a very large city, and a **megalopolis** is a group of supercities that have merged together into one large urban area.

Global Cities and Megacities

A **world city** (also called a global city) is a city that serves as an important linkage or connection point in the global economic system. These cities serve as banking and finance world leaders and headquarters for multinational corporations (MNCs). They are also world communication and transportation hubs and have the most international political influence. The top-10 world cities (2016) in order of rank, according to Forbes, are:

Rank	City
1.	London
2.	New York City
3.	Paris
4.	Singapore
5.	Tokyo
6.	Hong Kong
7.	Dubai
8.	Beijing – tied with #9
9.	Sydney
10.	Los Angeles

A **megacity** is a metropolitan area with a total population of over 10 million people according to the United Nations. A growing number of megacities are found in LDCs, and they share the common characteristics of high population density, poverty, and limited resources. Problems that are rampant in megacities are high infectious disease rates, vulnerability to terrorism, natural hazards, ecological disasters, war conditions, and food scarcity. Competition for scarce resources and jobs often fosters social unrest in these cities. Waste disposal and air pollution are problems in megacities in both DCs and LDCs. Megacities are indicators of social and economic change in their country and region. For example, Karachi generates 20 percent of Pakistan's GDP and provides 50 percent of the government's revenue. Often, these cities are the site of cultural and educational institutions that promote social development, too. Finally, megacities are large, new markets for both DCs and LDCs.

Suburbanization and Edge Cities

With rapid urbanization occurring in North America since the end of World War II (1945), **suburbanization**, or the movement of people from urban core areas to surrounding the outer edges of the cities became a dynamic force in American society. This rapid change in the distribution of the population was aided by the widespread availability of the automobile as families were no longer totally dependent on fixed-route public transit systems. The 40-hour work-week gave Americans the opportunity to live farther from their workplaces since they now had time to commute. The housing boom that followed World War II was fueled by the increased need for family housing as families grew and changes in the home loan structures made home mortgages affordable for middle-class families.

During the 1970s, suburbanization reached a frenzied pace as developers converted 200 acres of rural land into urban use every hour. As population shifted to the outskirts of cities, so did the purchasing power; strip malls and shopping centers sprang up everywhere to service the suburbs. Industry was also attracted to the suburbs because of the large parking capacity and room for plant growth. Service industries followed to provide services for the workers and suburban families. In the 1990s, urban sprawl was deemphasized, development became more intensive, and suburbs became more self-sufficient—complete cities in themselves. Industrial parks, apartment and condominium complexes, office parks, and gated communities became the "new suburbia." These new urban complexes are called **edge cities**, and they contain large nodes of office buildings and commercial operations with more workers than residents.

Systems of Urban Settlements

Geographer Mark Jefferson theorized the **primate city** is at least twice as large as the next largest city in the country and more than twice as significant. Capital cities are often, but not always, primate cities. However, not every country has a primate city. Examples of primate cities are Paris, London, and Mexico City. Paris, with 2.2 million in the city itself and a metropolitan area of almost 12 million, is definitely the focus of France, while the next-largest city of Marseilles has a population of only 800,000. London is the United Kingdom's primate city (6.9 million with a metropolitan area of over 12 million), while the second largest city, Birmingham, is home to only a million people. Mexico City, with 9.8 million in the city and 16.6 million in the metropolitan area, is a primate city, while the next-largest city, Guadalajara, has only 1.7 million. Many African cities show primacy because they were once colonial capitals and centers of administration and power.

In most countries, there are many more small cities than large ones. The **rank-size rule** proposed by Zipf states that if all cities in a country are placed in order from the largest to the smallest, the rate of decrease in size of each city's population is large at first but quickly slows. Zipf postulated that the second-largest city would have about half the population of the largest city, the third-largest city would have about a third of the population of the largest city, the fourth-largest city would have about one-quarter the population of the largest city, etc. The United States and Russia come closest to complying with Zipf's rank-size rule, but no country completely satisfies it.

Every city has an influence on its surrounding **hinterlands** (urban influence zone). Geographer Walter Christaller developed a **central place theory**, which states that cities exist for economic reasons and that people gather together in cities to share goods and ideas. Therefore, the central place exists chiefly to provide goods and services to its surrounding population and functions as a distribution center. The assumptions of this theory are that the countryside would be flat, presenting no barriers to the movement of people across it. In addition, Christaller stated that humans will always purchase goods from the closest place that offers the good, and when a high demand for a certain good exists, the good will be offered in close proximity to the population. When demand drops, so does the availability of the good.

Christaller's central place theory. Source: *http://4.bp.blogspot.com/-MZHqWiVGQkA/ UPuuVSpyjXI/AAAAAAAACuM/Z5Fw83G8M-s/s1600/centralplacestheoryk3.gif*

The threshold is the minimum number of people needed for a central place business or activity to thrive and stay prosperous. Christaller concluded that towns and cities in his model were interdependent. Consumers would be willing to travel further for luxury goods but not for simple basics like milk and butter.

The **gravity model** is a law of spatial interaction based on Newton's law of gravity. It states that larger places attract people, ideas, and goods more strongly than smaller places. It also asserts that places closer together have a greater attraction. The relative strength of a bond between two places is determined by multiplying the population of city A by the population of city B and then dividing the product by the distance between the two cities squared.

Newton's gravity model

The gravity model of spatial interaction says that the shorter the distance between two places and the greater the size of either or both places, the greater the gravitational pull between the places. In equation form, the gravity model looks like this:

$$\frac{\text{Population of City}_1 \times \text{Population of City}_2}{\text{Distance}^2}$$

Models of Urban Land Use in the United States

Several models of urban land use have been developed, but the **central business district (CBD)** is at the center of every urban land use model. The CBD is found at the center of every older central city and is the area of skyscrapers, business headquarters, large banks, and crowded streets. Fanning out from this intensive land use area is a fringe of wholesale and retail businesses, warehouses, bus and light rail terminals, and light industry. The residential area extends outward beyond this ring of activity. Several models attempt to depict urban land use spatially.

Sociologist Ernest Burgess developed the **concentric zone model** in the 1920s based on his studies of Chicago. The model is dynamic—as the city grows and expands, the inner rings invade the outer ones. This invasion and succession process occurs continually as the city grows and expands outward. Burgess's work is based on the **bid-rent curve**, which states that the concentric circles are based on the amount that people will pay for the land. The amount they will pay depends on the profits that are available from maintaining a business on that land. The CBD will have the highest number of customers so it is profitable for retail activities. Manufacturing will pay less for the land as they are only interested in the accessibility for workers and "goods in" and "goods out." Residential land use will take the land beyond these circles (see Fig. 12.1).

In 1939, economist Homer Hoyt developed the **sector model** in which urban growth creates a pie-shaped urban structure due, in large measure, to the improvement of transportation. For example, the electric trolley extended low-income areas from the CBD to the outer edge of the city (see Fig. 12.2).

The **multiple nuclei model** was developed by Chauncey Harris and Edward Ullman in 1945 (see Fig. 12.3). They claimed the CBD was no longer the only nucleus of the urban area, but that other separate nuclei become specialized and differentiated. They concluded that the following attributes determine where these multiple nuclei, or nodes, are located:

- **Differential accessibility.** Wholesale activities require ports and railroad terminals, while the retail sector requires maximum accessibility and parking.

Commuter zone ⬛ Residential zone ⬜⋮⋮
Working class zone ▨ Zone of transition ▧
Factory zone ▦ CBD ⬜

Figure 12.1 Burgess's concentric zone model.

⬛ 1 CBD
▨ 2 Wholesale and light manufacturing
▨ 3 Low-class residential
⬜ 4 Middle-class residential
▨ 5 High-class residential

Figure 12.2 Hoyt's sector model.

- **Land use compatibility.** Centripetal forces operate based on economies of agglomeration. Some activities interact powerfully with one another such as banking and financial institutions.
- **Land use incompatibility.** Some activities repel each other causing centrifugal forces to operate. Heavy industry repels high-end residential areas, for example.
- **Location suitability.** Some activities must locate at a suboptimal location because of cost factors.

To keep these three models straight, think of the following analogies if they help you remember:

- **Concentric zone model:** the growth rings of a tree
- **Sector model:** a pie cut in wedges
- **Multiple nuclei model:** a chocolate chip cookie with each nucleus a chocolate chip in the urban cookie

Figure 12.3   Harris and Ullman's multiple nuclei model.

Cities are experiencing changes in demographic and social structures. Social area analysis uses parts of each of the three models above to explain why people live where they live in urban areas. The models are too basic and oversimplified to adequately explain residential preferences, and they relate only to US cities between the two World Wars; however, when used in combination, certain valuable facts can be surmised about housing in US cities.

Models of Urban Land Use in Other World Regions

The concept of the city is universal, but the land-use structure of the city differs from one region to the next based in part on cultural and regional differences. A quick review of other regions of the world follows.

Canadian cities are more compact than US cities; they typically contain more multiple-family apartment buildings and higher population densities. Public mass transportation is preferred, and expressways are less expansive and less widely used in Canadian cities than in the United States. A higher foreign-born population and much less suburbanization has helped homogenize urban populations in Canada, too, allowing greater social stability and higher average incomes than in comparable US cities.

West European cities share a common history with traces of Roman and Renaissance architecture, street patterns, and spatial layout often evident. They are more compact than US cities and lack urban sprawl and suburbanization. As in Canadian cities, West European cities have higher residential densities and a heavy reliance on public transportation. Mixed retail, business, and residential zones keep work and home in close proximity. European cities often have energetic downtown areas with social life blending with worksites. The old, historic core is gentrified and home to middle- and upper-class families, while less affluent residential zones exist on the periphery along with recently established industry. Immigrants live on the fringes of the city, unlike the poor conditions of American inner-city slums.

European city model. Source: *https://fthmb.tqn.com/cqxuB7QgqlVmRl0WZJGMFsA ffFSM=/960x0/filters:no_upscale()/about/paris_1789._historicalatlas1911-56a402ec3d f78cf7728059c8.jpg*

This map depicts Paris on the eve of the French Revolution in 1789. Paris at this time was still a typical medieval city of narrow, twisting cobblestone streets stretching along both sides of the Seine River in a narrow band. Many European cities started out as centers of trade and commerce located along navigable rivers or on the coast. Today, Paris is noted for its many wide avenues (boulevards), formal parks, and squares.

Today, Paris is one of the most densely populated cities in the world! This map shows modern Paris with its many permanent street markets, museums, cafes, boutiques, churches, monuments, and neighborhoods. Busy commercial areas are intermixed with quiet residential streets and streets.

Land use in East European cities remains heavily influenced by the centrally administered planners of the communist era, with a large central square containing government and cultural buildings common to most cities. The communist government—not the market—controlled land use; however, like West European cities, East European cities are compact, have high residential densities, and heavily rely on public mass transportation. Residential areas contain their own retail and service facilities, and a large park or recreation area is always located near the central square.

Latin American cities focus heavily on the central section of the city with transportation systems leading to center city. City life is the cultural norm, and the well-to-do and middle-class populations live, work, shop, and attend cultural events there. The periphery is mostly reserved for the poor and less fortunate. Figure 12.4 depicts the important features of a central spine or avenue extending central city residential areas and retail shops outward to the periphery and a ring highway that encircles the city and separates high-income from low-income residential areas. Squatter encampments and slums (*favelas, barrios*) are generally located on the outermost rings of the city and not in the crumbling inner city of the US urban model.

Figure 12.4   Latin American urban model.

Sub-Saharan Africa is the most rapidly urbanizing region of the world with urban populations growing far more rapidly than urban economies. This has created a gross inability to provide even the most basic amenities, such as clean drinking water and rudimentary sanitation services, to most residents. Disease, high rates of infant mortality, and low life expectancies are serious problems.

African city model. Source: *https://fthmb.tqn.com/cqxuB7QgqlVmRl0WZJGMFsA fFSM=/960x0/filters:no_upscale()/about/paris_1789._historicalatlas1911-56a402ec3d f78cf7728059c8.jpg*

Cities in North Africa and the Middle East region suffer structural deterioration, massive overcrowding, and uncontrolled urban sprawl. Sanitation and other basic amenities are not provided for many residents, and high birth rates, high immigrant rates, and high unemployment provide major challenges to urban governments.

Asian cities, on the other hand, are riding the wave of economic prosperity with city growth unparalleled in Asian history. The number of Asian megacities (cities with over 10 million inhabitants) is predicted to reach nearly 20 by 2020. Mega-urban regions (huge, sprawling urban concentrations) link huge cities together in vast concentrations of humanity.

| A | Squatter areas | AC | Alien commercial zone |
| B | Suburbs | WC | Western commercial zone |

Southeast Asian city model. Source: *http://lewishistoricalsociety.com/wiki2011/article_image.php?image_type=article&id=90*

Cities in the developing world differ greatly between regions. However, there are some important commonalities. Virtually all cities in the developing world:

- Have a large, vigorous informal economic sector
- Receive large numbers of rural migrants
- Produce a major portion of their country's gross domestic income (GDI)
- Are surrounded by huge high-density areas of squatter settlements with few if any amenities

Other important things to remember about cities in the developing world include:

- Colonial impact heavily influences many cities in former colonies.
- Centrally planned land-use patterns influenced many Asian cities.
- Forward capitals are new cities recently built to serve a growing and changing country.
- Cities serving as religious centers are strongly influenced by religion.
- Traditional cities are crowded with a single major business district.
- Modernized cities take on Western characteristics (CBD, public transportation).
- The chief purpose of the city governs land-use patterns (ports, industrial, mining center, markets).

The Urban Economy

Cities employ workers in both the basic and non-basic sectors of the economy. Workers who produce goods and services for individuals *outside* the urban area work are in the **basic sector** and produce an income flow of new money *into* the city. The **non-basic sector** workers produce goods and services for people employed within the urban area—to make it safer, healthier, and a better place to live and work. These jobs do *not* generate an income flow into the city. Usually, more basic jobs create a healthier, more prosperous urban economic base because fresh money is generated.

The **multiplier effect** can provide insight as to how many non-basic jobs are created by one basic job. Usually at least two non-basic jobs are created for every new basic job. Non-basic jobs also create more non-basic jobs because service workers also require services themselves. Some cities are huge service centers with new service activities serving older service industries. An example of this would be where computer industries serve the financial and banking industries. The size of the multiplier effect for any given year can be expressed as:

$$\text{Base Multiplier} = \frac{\text{Total Employment}}{\text{Basic Employment}}$$

When the demand for goods and services produced by a city falls, the need for workers also decreases, although workers often hesitate to leave because of ties to families and the local community. In the United States, cities in both the South and West have grown in recent decades, while many of those in the Northeast and Midwest are experiencing declining populations.

Urban Housing

Many US cities are full of marked contrasts—rich and poor, black and white, Latino and Anglo, immigrant and nonimmigrant. **Uneven development** plagues US cities as some areas receive lots of investment dollars and other areas receive only token amounts. Stunning contrasts between wealthy mansions and low-income neighborhoods abound in the older industrial cities of the Northeast and Midwest. Recently, however, some cities have enjoyed an economic comeback. The investment dollars filter very slowly into low-income neighborhoods, while finding their way into the more affluent areas. The inequities of public investment in urban centers represent uneven development on a small scale and mimic what we have seen in the core-periphery global scale.

As central city populations decrease, the US suburban populations keep rising. In 1950, 40 percent of Americans lived in central cities and 40 percent lived in rural areas and small towns. In 2000, over half of all Americans resided in the suburbs with 30 percent living in central city neighborhoods and the remainder in small towns and rural areas. The inner city neighborhoods are deteriorating because the majority of the housing was built before 1940 and has fallen into disrepair. As middle-class families move out of deteriorating neighborhoods into areas further from the central city, lower-income residents move in and the tax base continues to erode. Services for these low-income residents are a heavy burden to the city government, which subsidizes low-income housing and services. The cutbacks in city services and amenities in these neighborhoods encourage middle-class families to continue out-migration.

Photo of gentrification. Source: *https://whosedowntown.files.wordpress.com/2013/06 /10125v.jpg?w=598&h=454*

The redevelopment of Chinatown in Washington, D.C., led to the demolition of many affordable housing units in favor of luxury condo developments. The photo shows some ethnic Chinese "hold-outs" during gentrification.

Segregation is the physical separation of two groups of a population; in the United States, it is usually based on race. The levels of black-white segregation have decreased somewhat in the last decade in the United States; however, racial segregation continues to be a prominent feature of the country's urban areas. Income also segregates neighborhoods spatially with different sides of a city settled by different income classes. In the United States, families with higher incomes seek residential neighborhoods with natural beauty and good schools, while cheaper, unattractive land near industrial areas and railroad yards provides inexpensive housing for lower-income residents.

Housing density decreases as you travel outward from the city center. The number of houses or dwellings per unit of land decreases as distance from the center city increases. The number of residents living in city centers has decreased over the years as population declines and old tenement housing is abandoned and condemned. Housing density on the periphery of the city, however, has increased as new apartment complexes and housing projects diffuse outward. After World War II, the system of housing development that became commonplace was based on the distinct separation of uses, rather than the creation of neighborhoods. For example, retail shopping was strictly separated into shopping centers and strip malls. Residential housing was the only type of use permitted in suburban housing developments. This separate-use system has become known as **urban sprawl** or conventional suburban development (CSD). The majority of the US population now lives in suburban communities built during the last 60 years. This sprawl creates more dependency on the automobile and less dependency on public transportation systems. Streetcar suburbs built in the late 1800s have a higher housing density and are located near a former streetcar stop or station. Commuters traveled by railroad and streetcar between home and work. After the automobile became a viable means of transportation for many, large-scale development of the suburbs became feasible and commuters could live farther from the city where they worked.

Landlords in cities are required by city code to keep houses and apartment buildings in good condition. Sometimes, landlords cannot afford or choose not to maintain properties and abandon them instead. When rent is insufficient to maintain the apartment, the building will soon deteriorate past the condition fit for human occupancy and even the poorest tenants will vacate the premises to move to less run-down structures. **Urban renewal** refers to the process of identifying properties in inner-city neighborhoods that are then acquired, cleared of residents and structures, and then handed over to private investors or public agencies for construction of parks, schools, or new housing. Critics of urban renewal claim it has reduced the supply of low-cost housing and destroyed the older neighborhoods' sense of community.

Public housing is government-constructed and regulated low-income housing. The US government no longer funds the construction of new public housing since the old structures are not maintained and have deteriorated into run-down, high-crime neighborhoods. In the United Kingdom, over one-fifth of all housing is government-owned with private landlords controlling a very small portion of the housing. In Western Europe, governments subsidize construction of much of the privately built low-income housing but do not own the housing. Church groups and nonprofit organizations usually build the low-cost housing.

Older neighborhoods near the city center are sometimes renovated by middle-class and higher-income families in a process called **gentrification**. These areas were often enclaves of the wealthy, and the houses are usually architecturally interesting, large, and well built, while also being fairly inexpensive. Critics claim government subsidies (tax breaks and low-interest loans) for gentrification have the effect of stealing low-income housing and funding and using it to pay for middle-class renovation.

Different ethnic groups often group in specific parts of the city in a process called **congregation**. Minority groups based on ethnicity, religion, culture, or lifestyle live closer together to support each other and minimize conflict with nonminority groups. When discrimination is the reason for congregation, segregation is the result. **Ghettoization** is the concentration of a certain group of residents to a certain area against their will through either legal means or practices of social discrimination.

The large and rapidly growing urban areas of the less-developed countries all share a common characteristic—outer rings of slums and shantytowns. A shantytown (called *favela* in Brazil) is a spontaneous settlement that is often built illegally on vacant land on the edge of a city or along roadsides. The residents live without the most basic amenities such as clean drinking water and sanitation services.

Urban Planning and Design

New Urbanism is an urban design movement that started in the United States in the early 1980s and is very influential in urban planning today. The main emphasis of this urban design is a return to earlier neighborhoods and a sense of community. Sidewalks and traditional neighborhood designs are thought to reduce traffic congestion, increase the amount of affordable housing, and stop urban sprawl. Neighborhoods are designed to be pedestrian-friendly with assorted shops, retailing, recreational areas, and other structures within easy access of residential areas. The overall emphasis is to reduce dependency on the automobile and promote safer, more environmentally friendly neighborhoods.

Green building (also known as green construction or sustainable building) is the practice of building structure using materials and processes that are environmentally safe and resource-efficient throughout a building's life cycle: design, construction, maintenance, renovation, and demolition. Green building tries to minimize the impacts of new buildings on the environment and human health while using energy-efficient, non-polluting, resource-conserving methods and materials. Use of renewable resources through passive

Figure 12.5   Installation of a green roof at the USDA in Washington, DC.

and active solar systems, photovoltaic techniques, and use of vegetation through green roofs (Fig. 12.5), rain gardens, and for reduction of rainwater runoff, are just a few techniques widely used in green building. The use of packed gravel and permeable concrete instead of conventional concrete or asphalt to assist in the replenishment of groundwater is another popular green building technique.

› Rapid Review

Urbanization is a global occurrence with the majority of the world's population now living in cities. Each city has specific functions to perform for its residents and surrounding hinterlands. City land use and social structures vary among regions of the world and even within a region sometimes. Several models help explain land-use patterns in the United States. Cities in LDCs are growing in size so rapidly they are unable to provide housing, jobs, or social services for most of the new residents.

> Review Questions

1. An edge city could have any of the following attributes EXCEPT

   (A) more jobs than bedrooms.
   (B) being commonly perceived as a single place.
   (C) 500,000 square feet of retail area.
   (D) 500,000 square feet of office area.
   (E) being urban for 30 years or more.

2. A crucial part of Christaller's central place theory is the fact that goods and services vary in range and

   (A) access.
   (B) quantity.
   (C) spatial distribution.
   (D) threshold.
   (E) quality.

3. If you commuted to work by automobile every day in the city, in which zone of Burgess's concentric zone model would you be most likely to live?

   (A) 1
   (B) 2
   (C) 3
   (D) 4
   (E) 5

4. The movement of middle-class residents into run-down urban center city neighborhoods is called

   (A) urban renewal.
   (B) urban sprawl.
   (C) urban revitalization.
   (D) gentrification.
   (E) multiplier effect.

5. Which one of the following characteristics does NOT apply to cities of the developing world?

   (A) Rapid population growth
   (B) An inability to provide basic services for population
   (C) A colonial heritage
   (D) A small informal economic sector
   (E) A land-use pattern strongly influenced by function of the city

> Answers and Explanations

1. **E**—Edge cities are a new phenomenon that developed in the 1990s when rapidly expanding suburban areas took on the functions and characteristics of a city themselves as industry and retail areas followed the population. Choices A through D are all true characteristics of edge cities.

2. **D**—The threshold is the size of the population needed to make it possible to supply the good or service, and the range is the average furthest distance the population would be willing to travel to obtain the good or service. The other answer choices are not applicable as central tenets to Christaller's central place theory.

3. **E**—You would live in the outermost concentric ring as a commuter—zone 5. Zone 1 (A) is the CBD. Zone 2 (B) is a transition zone that includes inner-city neighborhoods and ethnic ghettos on the edge of the CBD. Zone 3 (C) is a zone of independent working-class housing. These low-density residential suburbs were just evolving at the time Burgess developed this model. Zone 4 (D) is a zone of better residential housing composed of high-rent apartment complexes and single-family homes.

4. **D**—Gentrification is the process of middle-class and wealthy individuals buying and restoring once-stately and magnificent homes in older run-down areas near the CBD. Urban renewal (A) is the process of identifying properties in inner-city neighborhoods that are then purchased, cleared of residents and structures, and then handed over to private investors or public agencies for construction

of parks, schools, or new housing. Urban sprawl (B) is a pattern of urban expansion that is based on separate use of land for residential neighborhoods, retail shopping centers and strip malls, etc. Urban revitalization (C) is another way of saying urban renewal that is preferred by some people since urban renewal has taken on negative connotations. The multiplier effect (E) refers to the number of non-basic jobs created by each basic job in the city.

5. **D**—All cities of the developing world contain a large and vigorous informal economic sector employing many individuals in jobs such as street vendors, errand runners, trinket peddlers, etc., who are outside the mainstream economy of wage jobs. Thus statement D is the one that does not apply. Rapid population growth (A), a basic inability to provide even the most basic services such as clean drinking water and housing for residents (B), and a strong heritage from colonial days (C) are typical of cities in the developing world. In all cities, the land-use pattern is strongly influenced by the function of the city (port, trading center, etc.).

STEP 5

Build Your Test-Taking Confidence

Practice Exam 1
Practice Exam 2
Practice Exam 3

Practice Exam 1

IN THIS CHAPTER

Summary: This chapter contains a practice exam that is very similar to the actual AP Human Geography exam you will take in May. Taking this practice exam now will give you practice in pacing yourself so that you will be able to have enough time to thoughtfully complete each part of the exam.

How to Take the Practice Exam

Give yourself exactly 60 minutes to complete the 75 multiple-choice questions of Section I and 75 minutes to write the three free-response essays of Section II. Set a timer so that the timing is exact and you don't have to keep looking at a clock. Try to re-create the conditions of the actual exam as much as possible. Set aside a block of time when you won't be interrupted. Also, choose a quiet place such as a library where you won't be distracted or interrupted if possible.

Taking this practice exam gives you a good chance to learn how to pace yourself for the actual exam. For Section I, you will have less than one minute to complete each question. Work quickly but carefully; if you don't know an answer, eliminate choices you know are incorrect, guess among those remaining, and move on. You can mark the ones you want to come back to if you have more time. For Section II, give yourself 20 minutes to complete each question. This will give you 5 minutes to review each question and make changes or corrections as needed at the end.

After you have completed both sections of this practice exam, check your answers. Review the explanations for both sections, and make sure you jot down the concepts or terms that you are unsure of or could not remember, for further review.

Practice Exam 1

ANSWER SHEET FOR SECTION I

1 (A) (B) (C) (D) (E)	26 (A) (B) (C) (D) (E)	51 (A) (B) (C) (D) (E)
2 (A) (B) (C) (D) (E)	27 (A) (B) (C) (D) (E)	52 (A) (B) (C) (D) (E)
3 (A) (B) (C) (D) (E)	28 (A) (B) (C) (D) (E)	53 (A) (B) (C) (D) (E)
4 (A) (B) (C) (D) (E)	29 (A) (B) (C) (D) (E)	54 (A) (B) (C) (D) (E)
5 (A) (B) (C) (D) (E)	30 (A) (B) (C) (D) (E)	55 (A) (B) (C) (D) (E)
6 (A) (B) (C) (D) (E)	31 (A) (B) (C) (D) (E)	56 (A) (B) (C) (D) (E)
7 (A) (B) (C) (D) (E)	32 (A) (B) (C) (D) (E)	57 (A) (B) (C) (D) (E)
8 (A) (B) (C) (D) (E)	33 (A) (B) (C) (D) (E)	58 (A) (B) (C) (D) (E)
9 (A) (B) (C) (D) (E)	34 (A) (B) (C) (D) (E)	59 (A) (B) (C) (D) (E)
10 (A) (B) (C) (D) (E)	35 (A) (B) (C) (D) (E)	60 (A) (B) (C) (D) (E)
11 (A) (B) (C) (D) (E)	36 (A) (B) (C) (D) (E)	61 (A) (B) (C) (D) (E)
12 (A) (B) (C) (D) (E)	37 (A) (B) (C) (D) (E)	62 (A) (B) (C) (D) (E)
13 (A) (B) (C) (D) (E)	38 (A) (B) (C) (D) (E)	63 (A) (B) (C) (D) (E)
14 (A) (B) (C) (D) (E)	39 (A) (B) (C) (D) (E)	64 (A) (B) (C) (D) (E)
15 (A) (B) (C) (D) (E)	40 (A) (B) (C) (D) (E)	65 (A) (B) (C) (D) (E)
16 (A) (B) (C) (D) (E)	41 (A) (B) (C) (D) (E)	66 (A) (B) (C) (D) (E)
17 (A) (B) (C) (D) (E)	42 (A) (B) (C) (D) (E)	67 (A) (B) (C) (D) (E)
18 (A) (B) (C) (D) (E)	43 (A) (B) (C) (D) (E)	68 (A) (B) (C) (D) (E)
19 (A) (B) (C) (D) (E)	44 (A) (B) (C) (D) (E)	69 (A) (B) (C) (D) (E)
20 (A) (B) (C) (D) (E)	45 (A) (B) (C) (D) (E)	70 (A) (B) (C) (D) (E)
21 (A) (B) (C) (D) (E)	46 (A) (B) (C) (D) (E)	71 (A) (B) (C) (D) (E)
22 (A) (B) (C) (D) (E)	47 (A) (B) (C) (D) (E)	72 (A) (B) (C) (D) (E)
23 (A) (B) (C) (D) (E)	48 (A) (B) (C) (D) (E)	73 (A) (B) (C) (D) (E)
24 (A) (B) (C) (D) (E)	49 (A) (B) (C) (D) (E)	74 (A) (B) (C) (D) (E)
25 (A) (B) (C) (D) (E)	50 (A) (B) (C) (D) (E)	75 (A) (B) (C) (D) (E)

Section I: Multiple-Choice Questions

Time: 60 Minutes

Section I Comprises 50 Percent of Total AP Score

Directions: Each of the following questions is followed by five answer choices. Choose the one answer choice that best answers the question or completes the statement.

1. The distance north and south of the equator is the

   (A) global grid system.
   (B) Prime Meridian
   (C) latitude.
   (D) longitude.
   (E) scale.

2. Which type of transportation system created the star-shaped city pattern?

   (A) Highways to airports that link cities
   (B) Interstate highways that link cities
   (C) Beltways around cities
   (D) Sidewalks in the CBD
   (E) Streetcar and trolley lines extending from the CBD

3. The concentration of production activities and people spatially to benefit everyone is called

   (A) the substitution principle.
   (B) deglomeration.
   (C) agglomeration.
   (D) infrastructure.
   (E) the multiplier effect.

4. Which form of migration below are farm workers from another country most likely to be practicing during the year?

   (A) Chain migration
   (B) Cluster migration
   (C) Circular migration
   (D) International migration
   (E) International travel

5. Of these, the map using the smallest map scale would be the map of

   (A) the world.
   (B) Atlanta, Georgia.
   (C) Main Street, Small Town, Ohio.
   (D) Pennsylvania.
   (E) South America.

6. All of the following are reasons major cities attract young people in Latin America EXCEPT

   (A) the availability of jobs.
   (B) the potential for decent housing.
   (C) educational opportunities.
   (D) their families live there already.
   (E) the urban lifestyle.

7. The attempt by core countries to stimulate increased agricultural production in the periphery through use of technology, hybrid seed, and fertilizers is called the

   (A) First Agricultural Revolution.
   (B) Second Agricultural Revolution.
   (C) Third Agricultural Revolution.
   (D) Fourth Agricultural Revolution.
   (E) Green Revolution.

8. Which country below is best represented by a population pyramid with a broad base that slopes quickly to a narrow top?

   (A) France
   (B) Russia
   (C) Austria
   (D) Uganda
   (E) Italy

9. The use and spread of English in nineteenth-century India is an example of what type of diffusion?

   (A) Stimulus
   (B) Contagious
   (C) Hierarchal
   (D) Relocation
   (E) Migratory

10. The outlying area serviced by a urban center is referred to as a

    (A) redline area.
    (B) threshold.
    (C) range.
    (D) hinterland.
    (E) sphere of influence.

11. World population tends to be concentrated

    (A) in continental interiors.
    (B) on continental margins.
    (C) in the desert.
    (D) in the tropical lowlands and river valleys.
    (E) at higher elevations.

12. Boundary problems along the United States–Mexico border are caused by which type of issue below?

    (A) Ownership of fertile ground
    (B) Land use
    (C) Irredentism
    (D) Document interpretation
    (E) Immigration

13. Which of the following countries does NOT have a well-known example of a relict boundary?

    (A) Vietnam
    (B) United Kingdom
    (C) Germany
    (D) China
    (E) Bolivia

14. What monotheistic religion is based on the life and teachings of Jesus Christ of Nazareth?

    (A) Islam
    (B) Christianity
    (C) Hinduism
    (D) Buddhism
    (E) Judaism

15. The "melting pot" theory of combining several immigrant groups into one mainstream culture is called

    (A) amalgamation theory.
    (B) acculturation.
    (C) ethnic islands.
    (D) ethnic clustering.
    (E) cluster migration.

16. The birth of an urban industrial workforce in Europe contributed to the start of the

    (A) First Agricultural Revolution.
    (B) Second Agricultural Revolution.
    (C) Third Agricultural Revolution.
    (D) Fourth Agricultural Revolution.
    (E) Green Revolution.

17. Which of the following world regions is NOT considered one of the world's most densely populated regions?

    (A) South Asia
    (B) Europe
    (C) South America
    (D) Northeast United States
    (E) East Asia

18. Which language family contains Italian, Spanish, Portuguese, and Romanian?

    (A) European
    (B) Slavic
    (C) Germanic
    (D) Romance
    (E) Celtic

19. What is the most widespread primary economic activity in the world?

    (A) Mining
    (B) Hunting and gathering
    (C) Fishing
    (D) Agriculture
    (E) Forestry

20. Which one of the following is NOT a centripetal force in a state?

    (A) A high level of confidence in central government
    (B) The existence of strong separatist groups
    (C) The existence of national transportation networks
    (D) The national anthem
    (E) The national flag

21. The global lingua franca is

 (A) Chinese.
 (B) English.
 (C) French.
 (D) Arabic.
 (E) Hindi.

22. Historically, the world's major languages have spread by all of the following methods EXCEPT

 (A) Sanskrit records.
 (B) migration.
 (C) trade.
 (D) conquest.
 (E) expanding populations.

23. Which urban model theorizes that high-rent residential areas grow outward from the center of the city along major highways with lower-rent inhabitants taking over sequentially?

 (A) Concentric zone model
 (B) Central place model
 (C) Urban realms model
 (D) Sector model
 (E) Multiple-nuclei model

24. Which one of the following is NOT an advantage of urban agriculture?

 (A) Helping to solve the problem of solid waste disposal
 (B) Fresh produce for sale to others
 (C) Beautification of a dingy urban area
 (D) Low transportation and storage costs for food
 (E) Renewed or purified water supplies

25. What is the most rapidly growing religion in the United States today?

 (A) Islam
 (B) Christianity
 (C) Hinduism
 (D) Buddhism
 (E) Judaism

26. What is the population statistic that tells us the level of fertility at which a population will have just enough births to replace parents and compensate for early deaths?

 (A) Crude birth rate
 (B) Replacement level
 (C) Mortality rate
 (D) Total fertility rate
 (E) Crude death rate

27. Which of the following statements regarding historical North American migration streams is NOT correct?

 (A) Canada's first major migration came from France.
 (B) Canada's second major migration stream originated in the British Isles.
 (C) Canada's third major migration stream came from Latin America.
 (D) The first major migration wave to the United States originated in Europe.
 (E) The last major wave of immigration to the United States came from Latin America and Asia.

28. The main factor preventing subsistence economies from advancing economically is the lack of

 (A) a currency.
 (B) a well-connected transportation infrastructure.
 (C) government activity.
 (D) a banking service.
 (E) a market surplus.

29. Ankara, Turkey and Islamabad, Pakistan are both examples of

 (A) desert cities.
 (B) forward-thrust capitals.
 (C) old colonial capitals.
 (D) rival cities.
 (E) low-latitude capital cities.

30. What are the two major branches of Islam?

 (A) Sunni and Shinto
 (B) Shinto and Shiite
 (C) Sunni and Shiite
 (D) Shamanism and Shiite
 (E) Shamanism and Sunni

31. Which type of economic activity is most closely tied to the physical environment?

 (A) Primary
 (B) Secondary
 (C) Tertiary
 (D) Quaternary
 (E) Quinary

32. A map that presents a single class of statistics is called a

    (A) general purpose map.
    (B) thematic map.
    (C) reference map.
    (D) mental map.
    (E) location map.

33. Which of the following is a centrifugal force in a country?

    (A) Religious differences
    (B) A national holiday
    (C) An attack by another country
    (D) A charismatic national leader
    (E) Effective national government

34. In which country does language pose a centrifugal force?

    (A) Canada
    (B) United States
    (C) Brazil
    (D) Norway
    (E) Thailand

35. According to the map below showing US farmland, which grouping of states has roughly half its land area in farms?

    (A) Pennsylvania, West Virginia, New York
    (B) Louisiana, Mississippi, Georgia
    (C) Illinois, Indiana, Ohio
    (D) Maine, New Hampshire, Vermont
    (E) Nevada, Utah, Oregon

36. Which one of the following North American associations is NOT correct?

    (A) Southeast—African Americans
    (B) Oklahoma and the Southwest—Native Americans
    (C) Quebec and northern Maine—French Americans and French Canadians
    (D) Southern California—Hispanic Americans
    (E) Southern prairie provinces—African Americans

37. Which one of the following groups is excluded from the caste system of Hinduism?

    (A) Scholar-priests
    (B) Warrior-landowners
    (C) Businessmen and farmers
    (D) Servants
    (E) Untouchables

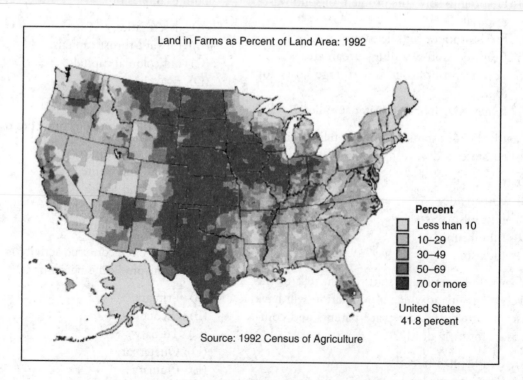

Land in Farms as Percent of Land Area: 1992

Percent
Less than 10
10–29
30–49
50–69
70 or more

United States
41.8 percent

Source: 1992 Census of Agriculture

Source: *United States Department of Agriculture (USDA).*

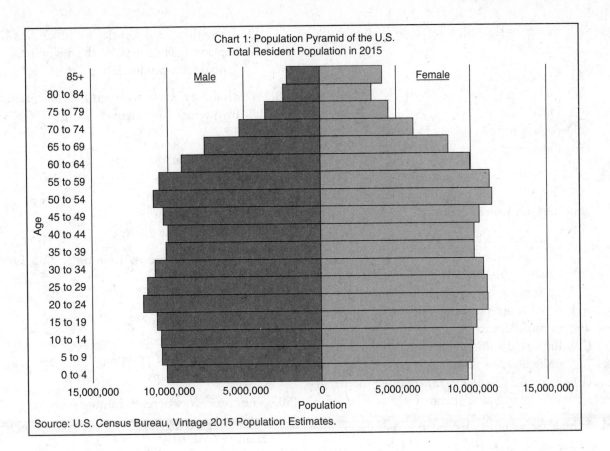

Chart 1: Population Pyramid of the U.S.
Total Resident Population in 2015

United States Population, 2000. Source: *US Census Bureau.*

38. Which one of the following is NOT a factor in creating the Third Agricultural Revolution?

(A) Use of chemical fertilizers
(B) Use of chemical pesticides and herbicides
(C) Mechanization
(D) The processing and packaging of agricultural products
(E) The use of field drainage systems

39. In which urban US setting below would you expect to find planned communities?

(A) Ghettos
(B) Suburbs
(C) CBDs
(D) Transition zones
(E) Barrios

40. Which of the following factors has little or no impact on mortality rates in the developing countries?

(A) New medicines
(B) Improved birth control methods
(C) Pesticides
(D) Famine relief
(E) Improved vaccines

41. The Rhine River is an example of which type of boundary?

(A) Geometric
(B) Artificial
(C) Natural
(D) Relict
(E) Subsequent

42. According to the population pyramid above, which one of the following statements is correct?

(A) The death rate exceeds the birth rate.
(B) The economically active and productive population is too small to support the youth and old-age population.
(C) Gender numbers are nearly identical until the older-age cohort is reached.
(D) The population is experiencing a rapid growth rate.
(E) The population is experiencing a high mortality rate.

43. Which one of the following items is an example of nonmaterial culture?

    (A) Dove soap
    (B) Dove candy bar
    (C) Dove symbol
    (D) A dove (bird)
    (E) Dove stew

44. Which of the following statements does NOT describe a factor that contributed to suburbanization in the United States?

    (A) A shorter workweek made time for a commute possible.
    (B) Changes in the housing mortgage regulations made home ownership easier.
    (C) Fixed-route public transit routes increased in importance.
    (D) Improved automobiles made transportation easier and less limited.
    (E) Increased demands for housing occurred after World War II ended.

45. Which factor in the last quarter century greatly destabilized Eastern Europe and led to ethnic conflict?

    (A) The introduction of new languages
    (B) The end of the Cold War
    (C) The invasion by the Soviets
    (D) The acceptance of many Eastern European countries into the EU
    (E) The adoption of the euro

46. The sacred book of the Hindu is called the

    (A) Talmud.
    (B) Bible.
    (C) Torah.
    (D) Veda.
    (E) Koran.

47. Urban agriculture can benefit urban society in all of the following ways EXCEPT

    (A) create sustainable food systems in urban areas.
    (B) provide jobs for women and children.
    (C) turn urban waste into a resource when utilized in safe manner.

    (D) strengthen food security for urban families.
    (E) replace agribusiness as the main focus of global food production.

48. Which theory below was used as justification for US involvement in Vietnam in the 1960s and 1970s?

    (A) Devolution
    (B) Colonialism
    (C) Heartland theory
    (D) Rimland theory
    (E) Containment theory

49. The Basques, Bretons, Kashmiris, and Tamils are all examples of

    (A) regionalist groups.
    (B) separatist groups.
    (C) terrorist groups.
    (D) interventionist groups.
    (E) religious groups.

50. The process whereby immigrants learn the values, language, and customs of their new country is called

    (A) assimilation.
    (B) acculturation.
    (C) adaptation.
    (D) amalgamation.
    (E) dispersion.

51. Which of the following jobs is in the non-basic employment sector?

    (A) Software engineer
    (B) F-10 pickup truck assembly-line worker
    (C) Oil refinery worker
    (D) Warehouse guard
    (E) Parking lot attendant

52. Variations in vocabulary, pronunciation, and rhythm in a spoken language are called

    (A) syntax.
    (B) isoglosses.
    (C) lingua francas.
    (D) creoles.
    (E) dialects.

53. The map shown above is the following type of map:

(A) statistical map.
(B) topographic map.
(C) general-purpose map.
(D) dot-distribution map.
(E) graduated circle map.

54. The intensive agricultural practice of planting and harvesting the same crop more than once a year is called

(A) swidden.
(B) double cropping.
(C) pastorialism.
(D) intertillage.
(E) shifting agriculture.

55. A large node of office and commercial land use outside the central city with more jobs than residents is a(n)

(A) suburb.
(B) primate city.
(C) town.
(D) edge city.
(E) gated community.

56. Which one of the following statements does NOT correctly describe the Green Revolution?

(A) It changed centuries-old methods of farming.
(B) It was an attempt to feed a growing world population.
(C) It centered on increased rice, wheat, and maize yields.
(D) It greatly improved crop yields in sub-Saharan Africa.
(E) It required use of new seeds and lots of fertilizer, pesticides, and water.

57. The theory that whoever controlled the landmass of Europe would rule the world is called the

(A) devolution theory.
(B) domino theory.
(C) heartland theory.
(D) rimland theory.
(E) containment theory.

58. Which of the following is a distinct characteristic of an East European city?

(A) A central park
(B) Prominent religious buildings
(C) A large central square surrounded by government and administrative buildings
(D) Luxury apartment buildings
(E) A well-developed retail sector

59. Which religion below is a universalizing religion?

(A) Taoism
(B) Islam
(C) Shintoism
(D) Confucianism
(E) Judaism

60. What is the most abundant fossil fuel?

(A) Phosphate
(B) Oil
(C) Petroleum
(D) Natural gas
(E) Coal

61. The majority of Kurds are found in which country?

(A) Iran
(B) Iraq
(C) Turkey
(D) Egypt
(E) Pakistan

62. According to Alfred Weber's least-cost theory, which one of the following costs of production is the most important factor in locating an industry?

(A) Labor
(B) Transport
(C) Raw materials
(D) Agglomeration costs
(E) Rent

63. Which one of the following demographic factors characterizes stages 4 and 5 in the demographic transition model?

    (A) Zero population growth
    (B) High mortality rates
    (C) High birth rates
    (D) High sex ratios
    (E) Overpopulation

64. The purpose for the creation of NATO was to

    (A) defend North America and Western Europe against the threat of communism.
    (B) form an economic alliance for trade between Europe and North America.
    (C) defend Europe against a second Nazi invasion.
    (D) defend northern Europe against Chinese missiles.
    (E) form a binding peace treaty for all Europe.

65. The way of life based on breeding and herding of animals that are used as a source of food, shelter, and clothing is called

    (A) swidden.
    (B) subsistence farming.
    (C) pastorialism.
    (D) hunting and gathering.
    (E) domestication.

66. State-sponsored terrorism has occurred recently in which of the following countries?

    (A) Rwanda
    (B) United States
    (C) Canada
    (D) Spain
    (E) Bahrain

67. Which type of city model contains a distinct residential spine proceeding outward from center city along the main boulevard?

    (A) European
    (B) Muslim
    (C) Sub-Saharan African
    (D) Asian
    (E) Latin American

68. With what religion is the architecture shown above associated?

    (A) Roman Catholicism
    (B) Russian Orthodox
    (C) Hinduism
    (D) Judaism
    (E) Buddhism

69. Which of the following is a major concern in countries with a large and rapidly aging population?

    (A) Immunization
    (B) Adequate schools
    (C) Daycare facilities
    (D) Birth control
    (E) Health care

70. Which of the following capital cities is located OUTSIDE the central core area of the country?

    (A) Abuja, Nigeria
    (B) Paris, France
    (C) London, United Kingdom
    (D) Cairo, Egypt
    (E) Moscow, Russia

71. The language with the largest number of "speakers" is

    (A) English.
    (B) Russian.
    (C) Spanish.
    (D) Mandarin Chinese.
    (E) Hindi/Urdu.

72. An earlier boundary formed before meticulous geographic knowledge and mapping was available is known as

    (A) an antecedent boundary.
    (B) a geometric boundary.
    (C) a relict boundary.
    (D) a subsequent boundary.
    (E) a natural boundary.

73. Which of the following religions developed first?

    (A) Buddhism
    (B) Christianity
    (C) Islam
    (D) Judaism
    (E) Hinduism

74. If you wanted to find the global distribution of coal, you would use a

    (A) reference map.
    (B) topographic map.
    (C) thematic map.
    (D) location map.
    (E) general-purpose map.

75. The practice of drawing the boundaries of voting districts to give an unfair advantage to one political party is called

    (A) separatism.
    (B) gerrymandering.
    (C) containment.
    (D) domino theory.
    (E) redistricting.

END OF SECTION I

Section II: Free-Response Questions

Time: 75 minutes

Section II Comprises 50 Percent of Total AP Score

Directions: Answer each of the three questions below in the allotted time of 75 minutes. You should spend approximately 25 minutes on each question. Answers must be in essay form, not a list of facts or thoughts, although a formal essay (with an introduction and conclusion) is not required. Use substantive examples where appropriate. Make sure you answer all parts of each question and label each part of your answer to correspond with the part of the question you are answering. Feel free to make a short outline first to capture your thoughts, but only the essay will be scored.

1. Folk culture and pop culture are both important defining elements of American society today.
   (A) Define folk culture and pop culture in the United States today.
   (B) Give one example of folk culture and one example of pop culture in the United States today.
   (C) Explain how folk culture and pop culture can both unify and divide a society.

2. (A) Define a central place.
   (B) Identify and discuss one function of a central place.
   (C) Explain why towns of the same size that perform the same function in a central place system will be the same distance from each other.

3. (A) Define the term "world city."
   (B) Identify two examples of a world city and explain how each of these cities fits your definition.
   (C) Discuss the role of a world city in the international scene and explain why a world city is not just a very large city.

END OF SECTION II

Answer Key: Section I (Multiple-Choice Questions)

1. C	39. B
2. E	40. B
3. C	41. C
4. C	42. C
5. A	43. C
6. D	44. C
7. E	45. B
8. D	46. D
9. C	47. E
10. D	48. E
11. B	49. B
12. E	50. B
13. E	51. E
14. B	52. E
15. A	53. B
16. B	54. B
17. C	55. D
18. D	56. D
19. D	57. C
20. B	58. C
21. B	59. B
22. A	60. E
23. D	61. C
24. E	62. B
25. A	63. A
26. B	64. A
27. C	65. C
28. B	66. A
29. B	67. E
30. C	68. E
31. A	69. E
32. B	70. A
33. A	71. D
34. A	72. A
35. C	73. E
36. E	74. C
37. E	75. B
38. E	

Explanations for Section I (Multiple-Choice Questions)

1. **C**—Latitude is measured in degrees north and south of the equator (0 degrees). The global grid system (A) is the global reference system using both latitude and longitude. Longitude (D) refers to distance east and west of the Prime Meridian (B), which is the 0 degrees line that passes through the North and South Poles and Greenwich, England.

2. **E**—Horse-drawn streetcars in the 1860s and electric ones starting in 1890 encouraged city residents to live along the trolley lines in a star-shaped pattern that radiated out from the CBD like spokes on a wheel.

3. **C**—Agglomeration refers to the grouping of activities and people to gain economic advantage by sharing services and resources. The substitution principle (A) is the replacement of one economic input with another. Deglomeration (B) refers to the locating of an industry away from an agglomeration to avoid higher costs of traffic congestion or competition. Infrastructure (D) refers to all the facilities and services required to support economic development.

4. **C**—Circular migration is a type of temporary migration associated with agricultural work where the migrant follows the harvest of various crops, moving from one place to another each time. This is common in agriculture in the United States (Mexican farm workers) and in Western Europe (Eastern European farm workers). Chain migration (A) is the practice of relatives and friends moving to a location based on the good reports of already established family members. Cluster migration (B) is seen in regions dominated by one particular ethnic group. International migration (D) is the permanent movement and relocation of people from one country to another country. International travel (E) is the temporary travel between countries for work or vacation.

5. **A**—The smaller the map scale, the larger the area being represented on the map. A map of the entire world represents the largest area from these choices.

6. **D**—In Latin America, most young people migrating to the city leave their families behind; the families do not already live in the city. The other answer choices all list factors why young people in Latin America are drawn to the city. The availability of jobs (A) and the potential for decent housing (B), educational opportunities (C), and urban lifestyle, including its nightlife (E) are all reasons for the in-migration of many persons to the large cities of this region.

7. **E**—The Green Revolution started in the late 1960s as the core countries exported new hybrid seeds and fertilizers to periphery countries to help stimulate greater food harvests. The other answer choices refer to earlier agricultural revolutions that occurred at different times in different regions of the world.

8. **D**—Uganda (D) as well as the majority of sub-Saharan African states, have very young populations with roughly 50 percent of the population 15 years of age or younger. European states such as France (A), Austria (C), and Italy (E), along with Russia, (B) have population pyramids that reflect lower birth and total fertility rates.

9. **C**—During the British colonial period in nineteenth-century India, language was a very important part of the administrative and judicial systems of the country. English was required in schools, trade, commerce, and government and it became the language of power and a higher station in life. Its use gradually diffused downward into Indian society. Stimulus diffusion (A) occurs when a cultural trait from one culture causes a change in the culture of another society. Contagious diffusion (B) is the spread of a cultural trait from one person to another like catching a cold. Relocation diffusion (D) is the process of taking a cultural trait or innovation from one geographic location to another by immigrants or traders. There is no diffusion type called migratory (E).

10. **D**—The hinterland is the outlying region served by an urban center. Redline (A) refers to the illegal

practice of refusing mortgage loans to persons buying houses in a minority-dominated neighborhood on the excuse they would likely default on their loans. Threshold (B) is the minimum number of people needed for a particular economic function to be performed in a central place according to Christaller's central place model. The more unique and specialized the economic function, the higher the threshold for it to exist, and the more common and mundane its function, the lower the threshold or number of customers it would need in order to operate. Range (C) is the maximum distance a customer is willing to travel to purchase a good or service in Christaller's central place model. The sphere of influence (E) of an urban center is the area it serves for a particular economic function. The larger an urban center is, the greater its sphere of influence is likely to be because it has a wider range of services and functions to draw people to go there.

11. **B**—Continental margins have always drawn the largest settlement of people. Approximately 60 percent of the world's population lives within 60 miles of the ocean. Continental interiors (A) are not generally much more sparsely settled than seacoasts. Aridity (deserts) (C) and high elevation (mountains) (E) usually create harsher living conditions that limit human habitation. Population is more concentrated in lowlands and river valleys (D), but not particularly in tropical river valleys and lowlands.

12. **E**—Illegal aliens crossing the United States–Mexico border has been an ongoing source of conflict and a continuing boundary problem between the two countries. The other answer choices list types of boundary disputes that do not apply to the United States–Mexico border. Ownership of fertile ground (A) and land use (B) are resources issues. Irredentism (C) involves a territorial conflict and document interpretation (D) is a boundary disagreement based on differing interpretations of how the boundary was defined in writing.

13. **E**—Bolivia does not have a well-known example of a relict boundary. Since Vietnam's reunification in 1976 (A), the old boundary between North and South Vietnam has been a relict

boundary. The United Kingdom (B) contains the relict boundary between England and Wales as evidenced by the abandoned castles on the old frontier. The old border between East and West Germany, now within a reunited Germany (C), is an example of a relict boundary. The Great Wall of China, now within China, served at one time as a boundary between China (D) and the warring nomadic tribes from the north.

14. **B**—Christianity is the monotheistic religion based on the teachings of Jesus Christ, and the Bible is its main document of faith. Islam (A) and Judaism (E) regard Jesus Christ as a prophet. Hinduism (C) and Buddhism (D) are polytheistic religions that worship a pantheon of gods.

15. **A**—Amalgamation theory refers to the traditional theory of blending diverse immigrant groups into the host country's mainstream culture. In today's climate of ethnic conflicts, this theory is no longer a realistic expectation. Acculturation (B) refers to the embracing of the host country's culture and values by the immigrant. Ethnic islands (C) are regions of ethnic concentration scattered among the dominant cultural realm. Ethnic clustering (D) is the process of immigrants grouping in communities in the host country. Cluster migration (E) refers to the process of immigrants of a certain ethnicity grouping in a particular region.

16. **B**—The demands for more food by a swelling urban workforce combined with the ability to produce larger harvests due to the use of horse-drawn farm equipment birthed the Second Agricultural Revolution. The other answer choices refer to more recent changes in agricultural methods and technologies.

17. **C**—South America is *not* one of the top four regions of population density in the world while South Asia (A), Europe (B), Northeast United States (D), and East Asia (E) are the most densely populated regions of the world.

18. **D**—The Romance language family is part of the large Indo-European language tree and traces its beginnings to the Latin protolanguage. European languages (A) are not a valid linguistic classification. Slavic languages (B) are part of the Balto-Slavic

branch of the Indo-European language tree. The Germanic languages (C) are also part of the Indo-European family tree but trace back to a northern European Germanic proto-language. The Celtic languages (E) are Welsh, Irish, Gaelic, and Breton and form a separate branch of the Indo-European language tree.

19. **D**—Agriculture (raising crops and livestock) is the most widespread economic activity in the world today. One-third of all land area is now used for some form of agricultural activity. The other primary economic activities—mining (A), hunting and gathering (B), fishing (C), and forestry (E) are important, too, but are based on the uneven distribution of natural resources. This means they are not practiced as universally as agriculture throughout the world.

20. **B**—Separatists groups are not a unifying, or centripetal force, in a country. They usually lead to division and strife. The other answer choices are generally all unifying, centripetal forces that serve to bind a country together.

21. **B**—English is the global lingua franca or language of global trade, commerce, and communication. Although some of the other languages listed serve as regional lingua francas, none of them has the global dominance that English has.

22. **A**—Sanskrit records have not contributed to the spread of world languages. All the other answer choices indicate ways languages have spread. For example, migration (A) carried Spanish to the Americas and trade (C) carried Hindi/Urdu to the countries of Southeast and East Asia. The Roman conquests (D) spread Latin into Europe and replaced the widespread use of the Celtic languages there. Driven by a growing Bantu population, the Bantu language spread southward, replacing traditional languages.

23. **D**—The sector model views urban housing like spokes radiating from a central hub on a wheel. It states that new housing for the wealthy extends outward on its original axes from the city as it grows, middle-income housing extends in the same way to higher-income sector, and lower-income housing fills in the gaps. The concentric

zone model (A) depicts the city as a set of rings radiating out from the CBD and was developed to explain the social patterns of American cities in the 1920s. The central place model (B) was developed by German geographer Walter Christaller in 1933 to explain the patterns and distributions of settlements as they are interconnected with their surrounding hinterlands. The urban realms model (C) is an economic model that states an urban resident's life is mainly lived in one realm within the urban environment. The multiple-nuclei model (E) states that large cities spread out from several nodes of growth rather than just one.

24. **E**—Urban agriculture often diverts valuable urban water supplies, and animal waste, pesticides, and fertilizer can leak into and contaminate a city's drinking water supplies. All the other answer choices are positive factors when urban agriculture is practiced in the world's cities.

25. **A**—Islam is the fastest growing religion in the United States today. Over six million Muslims live in the United States. The increase is the result of Americans converting to Islam, as well as from immigration.

26. **B**—The replacement level of 2.1 is the fertility level that allows a population to replace itself. The crude birth rate (A) is the number of live births per 1000 every year. The mortality rate (C) and the crude death rate (E) both refer to the number of deaths per 1000 of a population. The total fertility rate (D) refers to the average number of children a woman of childbearing age is expected to produce.

27. **C**—Canada's third major wave of migration came from Europe, not Latin America. All the other answer choices correctly describe migration streams to the United States and Canada.

28. **B**—Subsistence economies usually lack adequate transportation infrastructure. Currency (A), government activity (C), banking services (D), and market surplus (E) are all nice to have, but transportation is the key to economic advancement.

29. **B**—Ankara and Islamabad are both forward-thrust capital cities built to encourage more even

development and move the seat of government away from the coastal margin and into a more inland and central position within the country. (A) They are not desert cities nor are they rival cities (D). Both cities are newer cities and not old colonial capitals and both are located in the mid-latitudes (between 23 and 66 degrees north or south of the equator)(E).

30. **C**—The two major branches of Islam are Sunni and Shiite. Shintoism is the historic Japanese worship of gods in shrines and combines elements of animism or shamanism with later-arriving elements of Buddhism. Shamanism is part of many traditional native religions found in the Americas, Asia, and Africa. A shaman is a spiritual healer or person who is thought to be able to make the connection between the spiritual world and the "real" world to get guidance, healing, etc. for others in the group.

31. **A**—Primary economic activities are dependent on natural resources that are randomly distributed in the natural environment. All the other economic activities can occur in almost any location and are not as dependent on the physical environment.

32. **B**—Thematic maps show a particular category of information such as persons per square mile or annual corn production in the United States. General-purpose maps (A), reference maps (C), and location maps (E) are maps which show both natural and man-made features without any analysis. A mental map (D) is the map-like image a person carries in his mind of an area.

33. **A**—Religious differences often divide a country, creating a centrifugal force. All the other choices are centripetal forces that serve to promote unity and strength in a country.

34. **A**—Canada has had a continuing centrifugal force at work—language. Quebec, a large French-speaking province in chiefly English-speaking Canada, periodically seeks independence from Canada through public referendums. All the other answer choices are countries unified by one, clearly dominant national language.

35. **C**—All three of these states—Illinois, Indiana, and Ohio—have far more than half their land

area in farms. The other choices all show combined land use categories that total less than half in farms.

36. **E**—The southern prairie provinces of Canada (Alberta, Saskatchewan, Manitoba) have large ethnic distributions of Native Americans (called First Nation people in Canada). African Americans (A) are found in large numbers in the Southeast, Native Americans (B) are located in the Southwest and in Oklahoma, and Franco Americans and French Canadians (C) are well distributed in Quebec Province and northern Maine. (E) Hispanic Americans are found in concentrations along the United States–Mexico border from southern California through Texas.

37. **E**—The untouchables of India are outside the Hindu caste system and considered to be of such low status in Hindu society that the nastiest, dirtiest jobs are reserved for them. The other answer choices list occupations, each of which has a separate caste in the Hindu caste system.

38. **E**—Field drainage systems are most closely associated with the Second Agricultural Revolution when it became common to drain fields and add fertilizers. All the other answer choices describe activities associated with the Third Agricultural Revolution.

39. **B**—Planned communities (American suburbs are a general example) are neighborhoods that are typically built at the same time by a developer according to a master plan. The modern planned community has evolved to include shopping, parks, similar architecture throughout, and includes other well-chosen amenities. Planned cities take this concept to a larger scale and include Canberra, Australia; Abuja, Nigeria; Ottawa, Canada; and New Delhi, India to name a few. Ghettos (A) are poverty zones in urban areas. CBDs (central business districts) (C) are the original cores of economic activity in cities. Transition zones (D) are areas on the outskirts of the CBD that are always in a state of change because of invasion and succession patterns that keep it destabilized for development and settlement. In the United States, barrios (E) are Spanish-speaking enclaves in a city.

40. **B**—Birth control methods (B) have very little, if any, impact on mortality rates in developing countries. New and better medicines (A), vaccines (E), pesticides (C), and famine relief in the form of adequate food supplies (D) have all led historically to reduced mortality rates in developing countries.

41. **C**—The Rhine River is an example of a natural, or physical, boundary. Mountains, deserts, lakes, and rivers are all types of natural boundaries that are often used as political boundaries. A geometric boundary (A) is an artificial boundary, often a parallel of latitude or a meridian of longitude. An artificial boundary (B) is the same as a geometric boundary and often used when precise geographic information is lacking. A relict boundary (D) is an old boundary that is no longer used. Examples of relict boundaries are the Berlin Wall, the Great Wall of China, and the abandoned castles on the old border between England and Wales. A subsequent boundary (E) is one put into place after the people and settlement have already modified the cultural landscape. The imposed political borders of the Berlin Conference on the cultural landscape of Africa are an example of a subsequent boundary.

42. **C**—There are fairly equal numbers of males and females in all cohorts until 80 years of age and older, then women outlive men in the United States. In the United States, the birth rate actually exceeds the death rate (A). In regards to choice B, the working-age-population middle cohort consisting of ages 15 to 64 is large enough to comfortably provide the goods and services required by the dependent sectors of the population (the very young and the older folks). The problem lies in the future when the huge middle cohort of Baby Boomers advances into their "golden years" when it will be required that their needs and services to be met by a much smaller middle cohort. The country is not experiencing a rapid growth rate (D) or a high mortality (death) rate (E).

43. **C**—The symbol of a dove is used in several cultures and is an example of nonmaterial culture. The Dove soap, Dove candy, and dove stew are all tangible articles that are examples of material culture. The bird itself is not a creation of human culture but a part of nature.

44. **C**—Streetcar and trolley lines decreased in importance as the automobile was perfected and came into wider use, freeing residents from the necessity of only shopping, working, and living along public transit routes. The other choices all describe changes that contributed to suburbanization in the United States.

45. **B**—The Cold War ended in 1991 when the Soviet Union collapsed. Communism was a strong centripetal force holding people of many ethnicities together; when it collapsed, ethnic conflicts naturally arose that destabilized or split many countries of Eastern Europe. No new languages were introduced (A) and there was no Soviet invasion (C). The acceptance of many formerly communist countries into the EU (D) was a stabilizing force rather than a destabilizing force. The euro (E) has not yet become the currency of any formerly communist countries other than tiny Slovenia.

46. **D**—The Veda is the sacred book of Hinduism. The Talmud (A) is the ultimate book of Jewish law. The Bible (B) is the sacred book of Christianity. The Torah (C) consists of the books of Jewish scriptures and holy writings. The Koran (E) is the teachings of the Muslim prophet Mohammad.

47. **E**—Urban agriculture is a secondary system of food production that enhances, but cannot take the place of, modern commercial agriculture in the world. The other answer choices all describe ways that urban agriculture helps urban residents.

48. **E**—The containment theory, from which was derived the US foreign policy of blocking the expansion of the Soviet Union's area of control, was used as a basis for US involvement in Vietnam in the 1960s and 1970s. Devolution (A) refers to the transfer of powers from a central authority to a regional one. Colonialism (B) is a system in which a country declares control over a territory or people outside its own boundaries, usually for economic purposes. The English geographer Halford Mackinder theorized that the greatest world power would be situated

in Eurasia, in the "heartland" of the landmass with Eastern Europe at its core (C). Nicholas Spykman theorized that the densest populations, richest resources, and best strategic position overall lay in the peripheries of continents so his "rimland" theory (D) claimed the coastal areas of Eurasia would have more power and wealth.

49. **B**—These groups are all separatists groups fighting for greater autonomy or total separation from the country in which they live. The Basques of Spain, the Bretons of France, the Kashmiris in India, and the Tamils in Sri Lanka all identify more closely with their regional ethnic group than with their political state, a fact which often causes great conflict and tension.

50. **B**—Acculturation describes the process through which new immigrants adopt the cultural traits of their new host country. Assimilation (A) occurs when the newcomers blend into the host culture, completely losing their own original culture. Adaptation (C) is the process of adapting one's culture to a new environment. Amalgamation (D) refers to the theory that societies characterized by diversity form a fusion of the cultural traits of their separate ethnic groups. Dispersion (E) is the spread of something over a spatial area.

51. **E**—Non-basic jobs provide services to the city dwellers and do not usually generate "new" income for the city. The other answer choices are all basic jobs that produce goods for "export" out of the city and generate an inflow of revenue.

52. **E**—Dialects are different spoken regional versions of the same language. They usually vary in pronunciation, rhythm, and speed. Syntax (A) refers to how words are arranged in a sentence. An isogloss (B) is the geographic boundary of a linguistic feature such as the sound given to a vowel. A lingua franca (C) is the language of business and trade among groups of people who normally speak different languages. A creole (D) is a language that began as a pidgin language and graduated to a permanent language.

53. **B**—A topographical map gives a detailed representation of the shape and elevation of an area by using contour lines. A statistical map (A) is a map that shows the actual number of an item per unit or location. A general-purpose map (C) shows both natural and manmade features without analysis. A dot-distribution map (D) shows the distribution, dispersion, and spatial pattern of a feature. A graduated circle map (E) is a map that uses circles of increasing size to show the frequency of occurrence of something.

54. **B**—Double cropping is an intensive land use widely practiced in milder climates where it is possible to plant and harvest two crops in one year. Swidden (A) is land that has been cleared off and burned to prepare it for planting. Pastoralism (C) is a subsistence lifestyle revolving around breeding and herding animals for livelihood. Intertillage (D) is the practice of planting several different plants in the swidden to minimize the impact of crop failure and enhance the farmer's diet. Shifting agriculture (E) is based on growing crops in different fields on a rotating basis.

55. **D**—An edge city is a large collection of office and retail activities on the outskirts of an urban center. A suburb (A) is a residential and retail area outside of the central city. A primate city (B) is a city that is far more than twice as large as any other city in the country. A town (C) is an urban center that is larger than a village but smaller than a city. A gated community (E) is a planned residential community that is surrounded by walls or fences with a security guard and limited access.

56. **D**—Poor soils and insufficient water supplies in sub-Saharan Africa combined with lack of research in the main food grains of the region—millet and sorghum—made the Green Revolution a poor fit for this region. Crop yields were not measurably increased. All the other statements correctly describe the Green Revolution.

57. **C**—The English geographer Halford Mackinder theorized that the greatest world power would be situated in Eurasia, in the "heartland" of the landmass with Eastern Europe at its core. Devolution (A) refers to the transfer of powers from a central authority to a regional one. The domino theory (B) was the theory that if one country in a region became communist, communism would then easily spread to neighboring countries. Nicholas

Spykman theorized that the densest populations, richest resources, and best strategic position overall lay in the peripheries of continents, so his "rimland" theory (D) claimed the coastal areas of Eurasia would have more power and wealth. Containment theory (E) refers to the US foreign policy of surrounding the Soviet Union with military alliances to hold communism in check—a position based on the rimland theory.

58. **C**—Eastern European cities generally contain reminders of the Soviet communist era in East Europe in a large central square lined with government and administrative buildings. Due to the historical communist influence, the cities are not generally characterized by prominent religious structures (B), luxury apartment buildings (D), or commercial buildings (E).

59. **B**—Islam is a universalizing religion since its adherents believe their religion is applicable to all people. The other answer choices are ethnic religions that do not actively try to gain new members or converts.

60. **E**—Coal, the first important fossil fuel to be exploited, is still the most abundant, although it is unevenly distributed. Phosphate (A) is not a fossil fuel formed from hydrocarbon compounds in sedimentary rocks. It is a mineral widely used to produce fertilizer. Oil or petroleum (C) and natural gas (D) are also unevenly distributed. Although their reserves are not as easily predicted, it is apparent that they are less abundant than coal.

61. **C**—Approximately 55 percent of the world's Kurdish population lives in Turkey. Kurds constitute the largest ethnic minority in both Turkey and Iraq (B), and there are smaller Kurdish minorities in Iran (A), Egypt (D), and Pakistan (E).

62. **B**—Weber's theory stated that the best location for a manufacturing business would be where the costs of transporting raw materials to the factory and the finished product to the market are the lowest. Labor (A), the cost of raw materials (C), agglomeration costs (D), and rent (E) are all important costs to any industry making location decisions, but transportation is the most important cost consideration.

63. **A**—In stages 4 and 5 of the demographic model, there is zero growth in a population. New births are equal to deaths, and the population experiences no growth. There is a low birth rate (C) and a low mortality rate (B). In regard to choice D, there is no way to predict the sex ratio without knowing more demographic characteristics and economic characteristics of the population. Overpopulation (E) is highly unlikely in this scenario as there is no population growth at all.

64. **A**—NATO was created to defend North America and Western Europe against the threat of communism, particularly an attack by the Soviet Union. The other answer choices are not reasons for the formation of NATO.

65. **C**—Pastoralism is a subsistence lifestyle based on the breeding and herding of animals used as a source of food, shelter, and clothing. It is practiced in marginal lands such as deserts, steppes, and savannas where the climate is generally unfavorable for farming. Swidden (A) is land cleared for planting by slash-and-burn methods. In subsistence farming (B), produce is consumed by the farmer and his family rather than sold for consumption by others. Hunting and gathering (D) is a way of life that involves a diet of meat obtained by hunting and killing wild animals and of roots, nuts, berries, and fruits that are gathered. (E) Domestication is the transforming of a plant or animal species into a tame condition that is dependent on humans.

66. **A**—Rwanda's government carried out genocidal state-sponsored terrorist acts against its own citizens, the Tutsi minority, in 1994. None of the other countries listed have engaged in state-sponsored terrorism.

67. **E**—Latin American cities generally have a spine that begins in the center city and proceeds outward along a wide boulevard. High- and middle-income residential housing in the form of apartments and town houses is situated along this spine.

68. **E**—This is the temple (pagoda) used in Buddhist worship. This temple holds an image or relic of Buddha, the Enlightened One and founder of Buddhism.

69. **E**—Health care and social security support systems are a major need in country's with a large number of older adults (E). Immunizations (A), adequate schools (B), daycare facilities (C), and birth control (D) are things needed in countries with a younger population.

70. **A**—Abuja, Nigeria is located in the center of the country and away from the core economic area of the Niger River delta and the coast. All of the other capital cities are located in the national cores of their respective countries.

71. **D**—Mandarin Chinese is spoken by well over a billion people (as native and second-language speakers). English (A) is the second most-spoken language. Hindi/Urdu (E), or Hindustani, is the third most spoken. Spanish (D) is fourth on the list and Russian (C) is fifth.

72. **A**—An antecedent boundary is an earlier boundary put in place before the region was mapped and populated. A geometric boundary (B) is an artificial boundary, often a parallel of latitude or a meridian of longitude. An example of this is the 49th parallel separating the United States and Canada. A relict boundary (C) is an old boundary that is no longer used. A subsequent boundary (D) is one put into place after the people and settlement have already modified the cultural landscape. A natural boundary (E) is one formed by a feature of the physical landscape such as a mountain range or a river.

73. **E**—Hinduism emerged about 4000 B.C.E. in the lowlands of the Indian subcontinent as the first of the Indo-Gangetic religions. Buddhism (A) evolved from Hinduism in 500 B.C.E.; Judaism (D), Christianity (B), and Islam (C) emerged in the Middle East, and are all related. Judaism is the oldest of these and was the first monotheistic religion. Christianity followed, and Islam is the most recent.

74. **C**—A thematic map shows a specific spatial allocation of something such as coal, Democrats, or people who grow sweet potatoes for a living. Reference maps (A), location maps (D), and general-purpose maps (E) are maps that simply display an assortment of both natural and man-made features without providing any analysis or explanation. A topographical map (B) is a map that gives a detailed representation of the shape and elevation of an area by using contour lines.

75. **B**—Gerrymandering is a practice of drawing voting district boundaries to give an unfair advantage to one political party over another. Separatism (A) refers to the attempt of a minority group to govern themselves or obtain greater autonomy. Containment theory (C) refers to the US foreign policy of surrounding the Soviet Union with military alliances to hold communism in check. The domino theory (D) is the theory that if one country in a region becomes communist, communism would then easily spread to neighboring countries too. Redistricting (E) is the process in the United States of redrawing the boundaries of voting districts based on the latest census results.

Explanations for Section II (Free-Response Questions)

Question 1 (6 points total)

1A. (2 points)
Folk culture is the sum total of institutions, customs, traditions, dress, music, etc. of a fairly isolated, homogenous ethnic group that is self-sufficient and not reliant on mainstream society. Pop culture is the constantly changing material and nonmaterial cultural elements that influence mainstream society via the mass media.

1B. (2 points)

Folk culture example: any cultural element relating to the Amish, Mennonite, Hutterite, aborigine, Appalachian, or other rural, isolated group. Correct answers would include Amish clothing, Appalachian medicinal healing herbs, aboriginal artwork, etc.

Pop culture example: anything pertaining to the culture of the mainstream society as promoted by mass media. Correct answers would include types of clothing, fast food, housing, sports, social customs, etc.

1C. (2 points)

Folk culture can unify a society by proving that distinct cultural groups can hold onto their unique cultural identities while living peacefully within a larger society of people who hold a different set of beliefs. This has happened in the United States with the Amish and Mennonite folk cultures. They peacefully coexist within the larger mainstream culture without giving up their cultural practices.

Pop culture unifies a society by providing cultural artifacts that are widely accepted and used by the majority of the population. For example, McDonald's, Michael Jackson, and Levi's jeans are elements of pop culture that the majority recognize and hold in common.

Folk and pop cultures can also divide a society. The aborigines of Australia had to fight for their culture when mainstream settlers tried to wrest their land away from them and force them to conform with their cultural ways. Some societies cannot accept cultural differences and constantly try to force the minority folk culture to assimilate into their culture. Pop culture has a subtler divisive influence. Television shows, movies, and books that depict the Amish as old-fashioned and strange or the Appalachian mountain folk as inbred hillbillies serve to propagate negative stereotypes that are divisive.

Question 2 (6 points total)

2A. (2 points)

A central place is an urban center or settlement that serves as a distribution center for the supply of goods and services to the surrounding area. Central places can be large cities, small towns, or tiny villages—wherever residents go to obtain goods and services. A central place is much more than just a distribution point; it involves a pattern of similar-sized distribution areas that provide basically the same functions to their surrounding areas. Central places are not grouped together with each other but are distributed in a regular pattern with central places spaced equal distances from each other.

2B. (2 points—1 for identifying one function and 1 point for the discussion of it.)

The functions of a central place are to provide goods to local market area (pizza, groceries, gasoline, birdseed, specialty goods like Harley-Davidson motorcycles, designer clothing, jewelry, exotic plants, etc.) or to provide services to a local market area (dental, pharmacy, doctor, medical, school or education, firefighting, ambulance, police, water and sanitation, etc.).

The discussion can include examples such as:

- Pizza shops are found in every small neighborhood strip mall or as freestanding stores.
- Grocery stores are found in every small neighborhood and service small noncompeting market areas.
- Specialty stores, such as Harley-Davidson motorcycles, floral shops specializing in exotic plants, high-priced designer clothing stores like Burberry's and Tommy Hilfiger, etc. are spaced farther apart, usually in retail malls.
- Big-box retail—Walmart, Kmart, Target, etc.—are found on the outer perimeter of the local market areas and often service more than one central place.

2C. (2 points)
Customers generally buy their good or service from the nearest supplier, which would usually be the store or supplier of the service in their central place. If people wanted pizza for supper, they would drive to the nearest pizza place to purchase the pizza, usually a neighborhood pizza shop. If they need to get their winter coats cleaned, they would drop them off at a neighborhood drycleaner. In central place theory, customers go to the closest central place to obtain everyday items such as milk and bread. For luxury items like Mercedes-Benz automobiles or fur coats, they would be willing to travel further. These market areas of demand each contain a central place in the center and form a system of hexagonal patterns that gives us a hierarchy of central places with cities and towns of similar size grouped into several classes.

Question 3 (6 points total)

3A. (2 points)
A world city is a large urban center that is a command-and-control center in the global economy. It is also called a world center or alpha city and serves as a node in the world's economic system. It is a hub for banking, finance, and trade.

3B. (2 points—1 point for identifying two cities and 1 point for the explanation)
New York City, London, and Tokyo are the top three world cities. Also acceptable are Hong Kong, Paris, Singapore, Sydney, Milan, Shanghai, etc. from the secondary tier of world cities.

An explanation for New York City could include the following information: New York City is the top international air passenger gateway to the United States. The area is served by three major airports, John F. Kennedy International, Newark Liberty International and LaGuardia, with plans for a fourth airport. It is the headquarters of the United Nations. New York is the only global city that has a subway system running 24/7.

An explanation for London could include the following information: London has five international airports that offer numerous direct flights to every conceivable international destination. The London Internet Exchange (LINX) is the world's largest Internet hub, and it is the transit point for much of Europe's Internet traffic. The London Stock Exchange is the world's largest international exchange with a $1470 billion yearly turnover of foreign equities—more than New York and Tokyo combined. It was once the head of a vast empire and has kept the vitality and power of that connection with the world.

An explanation for Tokyo could include the following information: Tokyo has the largest metropolitan economy in the world. According to a study conducted by PricewaterhouseCoopers, the Tokyo urban area (35.2 million people) had a total GDP of US $1.479 trillion in 2008 (at purchasing power parity). Tokyo is a major international finance center and houses the headquarters of several of the world's largest investment banks and insurance companies.

3C. (2 points)
A world city is much more than just a large international city. Some cities count as world-class not just because of their size but because of their importance in business, finance and government, or all three. World-class business cities are those where strategic and tactical decisions are made on everything from new plant investment to developing new markets and products. They are the cities others watch and react to. World-class business cities are not guaranteed exclusivity in producing the next wave of influential products, technologies, or companies, but they are a likely incubator for them. And those products, technologies and companies are where new jobs come from.

Practice Exam 2

IN THIS CHAPTER

Summary: This chapter contains a practice exam that is very similar to the actual AP Human Geography exam you will take in May. Taking this practice exam now will give you practice in pacing yourself so that you will be able to have enough time to thoughtfully complete each part of the exam.

How to Take the Practice Exam

Give yourself exactly 60 minutes to complete the 75 multiple-choice questions of Section I and 75 minutes to write the three free-response essays of Section II. Set a timer so that the timing is exact and you don't have to keep looking at a clock. Try to re-create the conditions of the actual exam as much as possible. Set aside a block of time when you won't be interrupted. Also, choose a quiet place such as a library where you won't be distracted or interrupted if possible.

Taking this practice exam gives you a good chance to learn how to pace yourself for the actual exam. For Section I, you will have less than one minute to complete each question.

Work quickly but carefully; if you don't know an answer, eliminate choices you know are incorrect, guess among those remaining, and move on. You can mark the ones you want to come back to if you have more time. For Section II, give yourself 20 minutes to complete each question. This will give you 5 minutes to review each question and make changes or corrections as needed at the end.

After you have completed both sections of this practice exam, check your answers. Review the explanations for both sections, and make sure you jot down the concepts or terms that you are unsure of or could not remember, for further review.

Practice Exam 2

ANSWER SHEET FOR SECTION I

1 (A) (B) (C) (D) (E) 26 (A) (B) (C) (D) (E) 51 (A) (B) (C) (D) (E)
2 (A) (B) (C) (D) (E) 27 (A) (B) (C) (D) (E) 52 (A) (B) (C) (D) (E)
3 (A) (B) (C) (D) (E) 28 (A) (B) (C) (D) (E) 53 (A) (B) (C) (D) (E)
4 (A) (B) (C) (D) (E) 29 (A) (B) (C) (D) (E) 54 (A) (B) (C) (D) (E)
5 (A) (B) (C) (D) (E) 30 (A) (B) (C) (D) (E) 55 (A) (B) (C) (D) (E)
6 (A) (B) (C) (D) (E) 31 (A) (B) (C) (D) (E) 56 (A) (B) (C) (D) (E)
7 (A) (B) (C) (D) (E) 32 (A) (B) (C) (D) (E) 57 (A) (B) (C) (D) (E)
8 (A) (B) (C) (D) (E) 33 (A) (B) (C) (D) (E) 58 (A) (B) (C) (D) (E)
9 (A) (B) (C) (D) (E) 34 (A) (B) (C) (D) (E) 59 (A) (B) (C) (D) (E)
10 (A) (B) (C) (D) (E) 35 (A) (B) (C) (D) (E) 60 (A) (B) (C) (D) (E)
11 (A) (B) (C) (D) (E) 36 (A) (B) (C) (D) (E) 61 (A) (B) (C) (D) (E)
12 (A) (B) (C) (D) (E) 37 (A) (B) (C) (D) (E) 62 (A) (B) (C) (D) (E)
13 (A) (B) (C) (D) (E) 38 (A) (B) (C) (D) (E) 63 (A) (B) (C) (D) (E)
14 (A) (B) (C) (D) (E) 39 (A) (B) (C) (D) (E) 64 (A) (B) (C) (D) (E)
15 (A) (B) (C) (D) (E) 40 (A) (B) (C) (D) (E) 65 (A) (B) (C) (D) (E)
16 (A) (B) (C) (D) (E) 41 (A) (B) (C) (D) (E) 66 (A) (B) (C) (D) (E)
17 (A) (B) (C) (D) (E) 42 (A) (B) (C) (D) (E) 67 (A) (B) (C) (D) (E)
18 (A) (B) (C) (D) (E) 43 (A) (B) (C) (D) (E) 68 (A) (B) (C) (D) (E)
19 (A) (B) (C) (D) (E) 44 (A) (B) (C) (D) (E) 69 (A) (B) (C) (D) (E)
20 (A) (B) (C) (D) (E) 45 (A) (B) (C) (D) (E) 70 (A) (B) (C) (D) (E)
21 (A) (B) (C) (D) (E) 46 (A) (B) (C) (D) (E) 71 (A) (B) (C) (D) (E)
22 (A) (B) (C) (D) (E) 47 (A) (B) (C) (D) (E) 72 (A) (B) (C) (D) (E)
23 (A) (B) (C) (D) (E) 48 (A) (B) (C) (D) (E) 73 (A) (B) (C) (D) (E)
24 (A) (B) (C) (D) (E) 49 (A) (B) (C) (D) (E) 74 (A) (B) (C) (D) (E)
25 (A) (B) (C) (D) (E) 50 (A) (B) (C) (D) (E) 75 (A) (B) (C) (D) (E)

Section I: Multiple-Choice Questions

Time: 60 Minutes

Section I Comprises 50 Percent of Total AP Score

Directions: Each of the following questions is followed by five answer choices. Choose the one answer choice that best answers the question or completes the statement.

1. Which of the following items below is an absolute location?

   (A) 10 miles east of Pittsburgh
   (B) Washington
   (C) 3 degrees south
   (D) 479 Elm Street, Muncie, Indiana
   (E) Prime Meridian

2. China and Vietnam's dispute over the Spratley Islands is

   (A) a positional dispute.
   (B) a territorial dispute.
   (C) a resource dispute.
   (D) a functional dispute.
   (E) a religious dispute.

3. Every country with a seacoast has an exclusive economic zone (EEZ) under the UN Convention on the Law of the Sea. Which one of the following statements regarding the Law of the Sea and the EEZ is NOT correct?

   (A) The EEZ extends up to 200 nautical miles (370 km) from the coastline.
   (B) Countries have the right to exploit natural resources in their EEZ.
   (C) Countries can exploit resources on the continental shelf extending up to 350 nautical miles (560 km) beyond their EEZ.
   (D) A country does not have the right to exploit living resources in its EEZ.
   (E) A country has the right to exploit nonliving resources in its EEZ.

4. A person who practices the Hindu religion would be most likely to

   (A) visit a shrine built on the shore of a lake.
   (B) pray five times a day.
   (C) bathe in the Ganges River.
   (D) make a pilgrimage to Jerusalem.
   (E) make a pilgrimage to Mecca.

5. Which of the following is MOST likely to experience population pressure?

   (A) An industrial society with abundant natural resources and large imports of food
   (B) A society with a highly mechanized agricultural sector
   (C) A non-ecumene
   (D) A society that uses fertilizers, biocides, and irrigation extensively
   (E) A slash-and-burn agricultural society

6. The voluntary association of three or more countries willing to give up some measure of sovereignty is called

   (A) nationalism.
   (B) devolution.
   (C) supranationalism.
   (D) complementarity.
   (E) transferability.

7. The idea that people, and not their environment, are the forces that create cultural development is called

   (A) possibilism.
   (B) animism.
   (C) environmental determinism.
   (D) cultural ecology.
   (E) syncretism.

Use the map above to answer questions 8–9.

8. Which region of China has the largest number of Tibeto-Burman speakers?

   (A) A
   (B) B
   (C) C
   (D) D
   (E) E

9. Which religion is practiced by most inhabitants of Region A?

   (A) Buddhism
   (B) Shintoism
   (C) Catholicism
   (D) Hinduism
   (E) Islam

10. Which one of the following statements does NOT correctly describe transnational companies (TNCs)?

    (A) Many TNCs operate in areas of electronics, chemicals, pharmaceuticals and petroleum.
    (B) Most TNCs produce and sell manufactured goods.
    (C) Most TNCs are headquartered in the United States, Japan, and the European Union.
    (D) TNCs actively make use of the principle of comparative advantage.
    (E) TNCs are generally controlled by foreign governments.

11. Which one of the statements below correctly describes immigrants living in Europe?

    (A) Most find citizenship easy to get in host countries.
    (B) Muslims immigrants from North Africa are well integrated in France.
    (C) Immigrants to European cities rarely bring their families.
    (D) They are usually restricted to certain neighborhoods.
    (E) They enjoy the same treatment as received by immigrants to the United States.

12. A strong movement away from all religions is called

    (A) secularism.
    (B) heathenism.
    (C) sacrilege.
    (D) nationalism.
    (E) communism.

13. Which of the following is NOT a characteristic of a city in the developing world?

    (A) Contains modern centers of commerce
    (B) Has a well-developed infrastructure
    (C) Experiences large in-migrations of rural people into the city
    (D) Produces a large share of its country's GDI
    (E) Is surrounded by high-density squatter settlements

14. Shifting cultivation is most often practiced in

    (A) alpine tundra.
    (B) tropical forests.
    (C) flood plains.
    (D) deserts.
    (E) boreal forests.

15. A rejection of or indifference to religion in a country is called

    (A) polytheism.
    (B) animism.
    (C) secularism.
    (D) monotheism.
    (E) heathenism.

16. The first stage of the demographic transition exhibits

    (A) high birth rates with high but fluctuating death rates.
    (B) declining birth rates with continuing high death rates.
    (C) low birth rates with continuing high death rates.
    (D) high birth rates with declining death rates.
    (E) high birth rates with low and stable death rates.

17. Which continent has the highest total fertility rates?

    (A) Africa
    (B) Asia
    (C) South America
    (D) Europe
    (E) Australia

18. With what religion is the architecture shown in the picture on this page associated?

    (A) Buddhism
    (B) Judaism
    (C) Christianity
    (D) Hinduism
    (E) Islam

19. The Philippines and Indonesia are each an example of

    (A) a perforated state.
    (B) a fragmented state.
    (C) an elongated state.
    (D) a prorupt state.
    (E) a compact state.

20. The increasing interconnectedness of different parts of the world through economic, political, and cultural interaction is called

    (A) culture.
    (B) core-periphery.
    (C) globalization.
    (D) development.
    (E) diffusion.

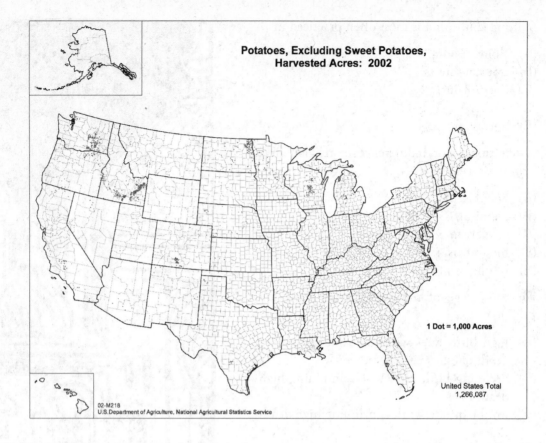

Potatoes, Excluding Sweet Potatoes, Harvested Acres: 2002

1 Dot = 1,000 Acres

United States Total
1,266,087

02-M218
U.S. Department of Agriculture, National Agricultural Statistics Service

21. Which of the following associations linking a US region to an industrial base is NOT correct?

(A) Gulf Coast of Texas—petroleum and natural gas
(B) United States–Mexico border—gold and silver mining
(C) Silicon Valley (San Francisco Bay area)—high-tech industries
(D) Southeast United States—textiles, tobacco, and furniture
(E) Ohio River Valley/Monongahela River Valley (Pittsburgh area)—advanced material processing and high-tech industries

22. Which one of the following statements is best supported by the map above?

(A) Potatoes are grown mostly in the Midwest.
(B) Potatoes are not grown in the Southwest because of a cultural preference for corn.
(C) Potatoes would be in the first ring of von Thünen's model of agricultural location.
(D) Potatoes are most profitable when grown in cooler climates.
(E) Potatoes have overtaken bread as the staple of American life.

23. Which term describes the forces that unify and strengthen a country?

(A) Diffusion
(B) Centrifugal
(C) Centripetal
(D) Ethnocentric
(E) Naturalizing

24. The European Union (EU) replaced which of the following organizations?

(A) NATO
(B) EEC
(C) UN
(D) ASEAN
(E) NAFTA

25. A chief factor that contributed to the Second Agricultural Revolution was

(A) the Industrial Revolution.
(B) World War I.
(C) World War II.
(D) the discovery of the plow.
(E) the domestication of plants and animals.

26. Which stage of the demographic transition model is characterized by high birth rates and high variable death rates?

(A) Stage 1
(B) Stage 2
(C) Stage 3
(D) Stage 4
(E) Stage 5

27. The largest Hindu temple complex ever constructed is found in

(A) Calcutta.
(B) Bombay.
(C) Cambodia.
(D) Bali.
(E) New York City.

28. Which country faces a serious trade disadvantage due to its location?

(A) Singapore
(B) Italy
(C) Spain
(D) Argentina
(E) Mongolia

29. A city that is more than twice as large as the next largest city in a country is called a

(A) global city.
(B) world leader city.
(C) megalopolis.
(D) primate city.
(E) metropolis.

30. Which one of the following statements best describes an application of the S-curve?

(A) Graph of the Bantu migration
(B) Graph of the growth of human populations since their first appearance on Earth
(C) The chart showing how cities associate with one another based on their population sizes
(D) A model showing the decrease in population growth for several countries after they industrialize
(E) A case study explaining how countries gain stability and a sense of "openness" over time

31. Which one of the following organizations is NOT a supranational organization?

(A) UN
(B) NATO
(C) ASEAN
(D) NAFTA
(E) PLO

32. Which of the following is NOT used by geographers to determine absolute location?

(A) Longitude
(B) Latitude
(C) Equator
(D) Prime Meridian
(E) Distance to the nearest city

33. Which of the following is NOT a problem Europe currently faces today?

(A) Rising immigration
(B) Lack of population growth
(C) Environmental apathy
(D) Urban ethnic ghettos on the rise
(E) Lack of cultural activities

34. The most rapidly urbanizing area of the world is:

(A) Europe
(B) East Asia
(C) Sub-Saharan Africa
(D) South Asia
(E) Latin America

35. Which of the following supranational organizations is not an economic union?

(A) EU
(B) CARICOM
(C) NAFTA
(D) NATO
(E) MERCOSUR

36. In what country are the most Basque speakers found?

(A) Denmark
(B) Finland
(C) Luxembourg
(D) Spain
(E) Germany

37. Opponents of genetically modified organisms (GMOs) in food are afraid that the GMOs

(A) will hinder global trade.
(B) make plants more resistant to disease.
(C) may cause irreversible changes in humans.
(D) make plants more resistant to drought.
(E) help clean up the environment.

38. Which one of the following is NOT a characteristic of world cities?

(A) World cities contain the headquarters of many transnational corporations.

(B) World cities are well connected to secondary-level world cities.

(C) World cities contain many offices of multinational organizations.

(D) World cities are found only in the northern and western hemispheres.

(E) World cities contain a concentration of legal, banking, and marketing services.

39. Which theorist(s) tried to explain the prices of farm products as they relate to patterns of land use?

(A) Rostow

(B) Ravenstein

(C) Von Thünen

(D) Burgess

(E) Harris and Ullmann

40. Regions share all of these characteristics EXCEPT

(A) boundaries.

(B) common features.

(C) relative location.

(D) easily defined.

(E) spatial extent.

41. The rehabilitation of old, rundown inner-city neighborhoods by middle- and high-income people is called

(A) urbanization.

(B) gentrification.

(C) suburbanization.

(D) multiplier effect.

(E) home improvements.

42. Which term below best describes a religion that uses missionaries to spread its faith?

(A) Ethnic

(B) Universalizing

(C) Monotheistic

(D) Polytheistic

(E) Animistic

43. Which crop began the Third Agricultural Revolution?

(A) Rice

(B) Wheat

(C) Barley

(D) Millet

(E) Sorghum

44. The idea that you identify with, and give allegiance, to a nation-state is

(A) regionalism.

(B) diffusion.

(C) iconography.

(D) ethnocentrism.

(E) nationalism.

45. The theory that most migration occurs over a short distance and in steps is attributed to

(A) Rostow.

(B) Ravenstein.

(C) von Thünen.

(D) Burgess.

(E) Harris and Ullmann.

46. The largest exporter of agricultural goods in the world is

(A) China.

(B) Mexico.

(C) Chile.

(D) France.

(E) the United States.

47. The multiplier effect is

(A) the addition of non-basic workers to an urban economy that has added more basic workers.

(B) a ratio of urban to rural workers in an economy.

(C) the ratio of city workers to farm workers in an economy.

(D) the addition of rural jobs created by the urban economy.

(E) the multiple jobs eliminated by foreign workers.

48. Which geographer viewed the US urban community of the 1920s as a set of concentric rings radiating outward from a central core?

(A) Rostow

(B) Ravenstein

(C) Von Thünen

(D) Burgess

(E) Harris and Ullmann

49. Which of the following is NOT a key milestone reached by the EU?

   (A) The introduction of a common currency used by many EU countries
   (B) A customs union
   (C) A single market
   (D) A common European language
   (E) Broad support of the Kyoto Protocol

50. Which pair of religions below share a long-held tradition of cremating their dead?

   (A) Hindu and Buddhist
   (B) Hindu and Muslim
   (C) Muslim and Jewish
   (D) Christian and Buddhist
   (E) Christian and Jewish

51. Part of the boundary between the United States and Mexico is the Rio Grande, an example of

   (A) a water divider.
   (B) a watercourse.
   (C) an artificial boundary.
   (D) a natural boundary.
   (E) a relict boundary.

52. Which of the following is NOT an important environmental factor influencing a country's agriculture?

   (A) Number of frost-free days per year
   (B) Availability of sufficient rainfall
   (C) Reliability of sufficient rainfall
   (D) Amount of fertilizer produced in the country
   (E) Existence of a 90-day-or-longer growing season

53. The key factor Thomas Malthus failed to recognize in his population theory was

   (A) population is limited by their means of subsistence.
   (B) all populations have the potential to increase more than the actual rate of increase.
   (C) wars and famine inhibit population's reproductive capacity.
   (D) populations will always increase if the means of subsistence increase.
   (E) technology's ability to raise the Earth's carrying capacity.

54. What family do most European languages belong to?

   (A) Ural-Altaic
   (B) Basque
   (C) Indo-European
   (D) Phoenician
   (E) Sino-Tibetan

55. The latitude and longitude coordinates of a place are an example of

   (A) a formal region.
   (B) a functional region.
   (C) an absolute location.
   (D) a relative location.
   (E) a perceptual region.

56. All of the following are non-basic jobs in the city EXCEPT

   (A) city firefighter.
   (B) social worker.
   (C) dry cleaner.
   (D) waitress.
   (E) garment factory worker.

57. The theory that cities grow outward from a core utilizing several nodes of growth was proposed by

   (A) Rostow.
   (B) Ravenstein.
   (C) von Thünen.
   (D) Burgess.
   (E) Harris and Ullmann.

58. What was the primary reason the Green Revolution did NOT help Africa much?

   (A) It targeted crops Africans don't grow and eat.
   (B) It required sophisticated machinery.
   (C) Population growth has fallen so drastically that Africans don't need the increased food production.
   (D) African agricultural production went up without its help.
   (E) Africans refused to use the Green Revolution's farming techniques.

59. You are planning to move from your hometown to Pittsburgh. Along the way, you stop in Columbus, Ohio to visit a relative and fall in love with the city! You decide to stay and make Columbus your new home. This is an example of

(A) intervening opportunity.
(B) distance decay.
(C) involuntary migration.
(D) push-pull factors.
(E) transhumance.

60. What type of countries generally possesses a greater variety of climates and resources than other countries?

(A) Perforated states
(B) Fragmented states
(C) Elongated states
(D) Prorupt states
(E) Compact states

61. Which one of the following statements is NOT true of the "core" countries?

(A) They are technologically advanced.
(B) They are wealthy.
(C) They are powerful.
(D) They are less developed.
(E) They are more developed.

62. Which of the following statements best describes the United Nations?

(A) The UN operates a worldwide police force.
(B) Member states surrender sovereignty to the UN.
(C) World laws are enforced by the UN.
(D) UN membership includes all countries.
(E) The UN often practices interventionism in world conflicts.

63. Which pair of religions are both universalizing religions?

(A) Islam and Judaism
(B) Judaism and Buddhism
(C) Hinduism and Buddhism
(D) Christianity and Buddhism
(E) Islam and Hinduism

64. Olives, grapes, and chickpeas are staple crops of which type of farming?

(A) Pastoral nomadism
(B) Subsistence
(C) Plantation
(D) Mediterranean
(E) Commercial

65. Which one of the statements below is characteristic of most African cities?

(A) They have thriving, clean residential areas.
(B) There are jobs for most rural-to-urban migrants.
(C) They have three separate business districts.
(D) They have a well-developed infrastructure.
(E) They offer an adequate social welfare system.

66. The theory that every society develops economically according to a five-stage pattern of growth is attributed to

(A) Rostow.
(B) Ravenstein.
(C) von Thünen.
(D) Burgess.
(E) Harris and Ullmann.

67. A society in which two or more population groups coexist while maintaining their unique culture demonstrates

(A) racial segregation.
(B) miscegenation.
(C) cultural pluralism.
(D) cultural segregation.
(E) cultural integration.

68. In which of the following Asian countries would one find special economic zones (SEZs)?

(A) Japan
(B) South Korea
(C) China
(D) Vietnam
(E) North Vietnam

69. The practice of hiring a foreign third-party service provider to run an operation is called

    (A) outsourcing.
    (B) offshoring.
    (C) maquiladoras.
    (D) locational interdependence.
    (E) Fordism.

70. The theory that the main purpose of a settlement or market town is to furnish goods and services to the surrounding market area is called the

    (A) urban hierarchy theory.
    (B) central place theory.
    (C) concentric zone model.
    (D) multiplier effect.
    (E) rank-size rule.

71. When a country combines its religion with its government, it is called a

    (A) dictatorship.
    (B) theocracy.
    (C) democracy.
    (D) autocracy.
    (E) oligarchy.

72. Which structure(s) traditionally occupies the center of a historic Asian city?

    (A) A central market
    (B) High-density housing
    (C) A religious building
    (D) Government office buildings
    (E) Commercial buildings

73. Which of the following is a push factor?

    (A) Dissatisfaction with current jobs
    (B) Higher-paying jobs elsewhere
    (C) An attractive retirement community elsewhere
    (D) A pleasant climate
    (E) Safer communities elsewhere

74. The influence of neo-Malthusianism can be seen in

    (A) government programs for birth control and planning.
    (B) famine relief.
    (C) increased spending in social welfare programs.
    (D) increased total fertility rates.
    (E) pro-natalist policies.

75. What is the chief religion practiced in Europe?

    (A) Christianity
    (B) Islam
    (C) Hinduism
    (D) Animism
    (E) Buddhism

END OF SECTION I

Section II: Free-Response Questions

Time: 75 minutes

Section II Comprises 50 Percent of Total AP Score

Directions: Answer each of the three questions below in the allotted time of 75 minutes. You should spend approximately 25 minutes on each question. Answers must be in essay form, not a list of facts or thoughts, although a formal essay (with an introduction and conclusion) is not required. Use substantive examples where appropriate. Make sure you answer all parts of each question and label each part of your answer to correspond with the part of the question you are answering. Feel free to make a short outline first to capture your thoughts, but only the essay will be scored.

1. (A) Define separatism.
   (B) Identify a separatist movement and explain the reason for this group's activity.
   (C) Discuss why this separatist movement operates on the periphery of the state and not within its national core.

2. (A) Define an ethnic enclave in an urban center.
   (B) Identify an example of an ethnic enclave in a European city and describe the probable relative location of this enclave within the urban center.
   (C) Discuss the problems of assimilation faced by residents of this ethnic enclave and explain why this assimilation process is problematic.

3. (A) Using the map above, identify the charter group in this location.
   (B) Identify the land survey pattern used by this charter group and explain why they used it wherever they settled.
   (C) Compare and contrast the land survey pattern used in this map with the metes-and-bounds pattern of land survey used by other charter groups in North America.

END OF SECTION II

Answer Key: Section I (Multiple-Choice Questions)

1.	D	39.	C
2.	C	40.	D
3.	D	41.	B
4.	C	42.	B
5.	E	43.	A
6.	C	44.	E
7.	A	45.	B
8.	E	46.	E
9.	E	47.	A
10.	E	48.	D
11.	D	49.	D
12.	A	50.	A
13.	B	51.	D
14.	B	52.	D
15.	C	53.	E
16.	A	54.	C
17.	A	55.	C
18.	E	56.	E
19.	B	57.	E
20.	C	58.	A
21.	B	59.	A
22.	D	60.	C
23.	C	61.	D
24.	B	62.	E
25.	A	63.	D
26.	A	64.	D
27.	C	65.	C
28.	E	66.	A
29.	D	67.	C
30.	D	68.	C
31.	E	69.	B
32.	E	70.	B
33.	C	71.	B
34.	C	72.	C
35.	D	73.	A
36.	D	74.	A
37.	C	75.	A
38.	D		

Explanations for Section I (Multiple-Choice Questions)

1. **D**—This address is the only one of its kind; it is an absolute location and marks a specific place in terms of latitude and longitude coordinates. Three degrees south (C) and the Prime Meridian (E) are lines that run around the Earth with multiple places along them. Ten miles east of Pittsburgh (A) changes depending on which part of Pittsburgh you depart from. Washington (B) is the name of several cities and a state.

2. **C**—This is a dispute caused primarily by the desire to harvest the oil and gas reserves beneath the sea surrounding the Spratley Islands in the South China Sea. Vietnam and China both claim ownership of the Spratly Islands, and the history of prior settlement, foreign invasions, and wars have made the oil and gas-rich islands and their watery surroundings a source of much dispute between the two countries. A positional dispute (A) occurs when two countries disagree over the interpretation of treaties or other documents that concern their boundaries. Latin America has several ongoing boundary disputes today, many as a result of old colonial treaties and documents. A territorial dispute (B) is a dispute over the ownership of a particular region such as the long-standing conflict between India and Pakistan over Kashmir. Irredentist forces in a country often fuel these territorial disputes. A functional dispute (D) is generally about regulations affecting the boundary between two political states. For example, there are often functional disputes in Europe between countries over such issues as water use and pollution regarding rivers (Danube, Rhine, etc.) that form natural boundaries between states. There is no religious dispute (E) between the two countries relating to the islands.

3. **D**—Under the UN Convention on the Law of the Sea, each country has the right to exploit all resources—both living and nonliving—within 200 nm of its coastline. This makes answer choice D an incorrect statement. All other choices are correct statements regarding EEZs and the Law of the Sea.

4. **C**—Hindus practice ritual bathing as a purification before undertaking a ritual activity such as worship. Bathing in the "Mother Ganges" is considered the ultimate in cleansing impurities of the inner being. Buddhists (A) or Shintoists would likely visit shrines by the river. Muslims would pray five times daily (B) as part of the Five Pillars of Islam and are required to take a pilgrimage to Mecca (E) at least once during their lifetime. Jerusalem (D) is a holy city for Christians and Jews and also for Muslims.

5. **E**—A society that does not have a high carrying capacity, such as a slash-and-burn society, will have a difficult time feeding a growing population. The societies described in answer choices A, B, and D have higher carrying capacities so they can support a greater number of people per square unit of arable land. A non-ecumene (C) is a very sparsely inhabited area not likely to feel population pressure any time soon.

6. **C**—Supranationalism is the idea that three or more separate political states each give up some measure of national sovereignty to work with the others to achieve a common goal. Nationalism (A) is identification with and feeling a strong allegiance to a nation. Devolution (B) is the transfer of some central government powers to the regional government. Complementarity (D) occurs when two places or regions each produce a good or service that the other needs and wants with the mutual exchange of goods as the result. Transferability (E) is the cost of moving a product or commodity relative to its ability to afford the cost of the move.

7. **A**—Possibilism is the theory that humans have a choice in how they think, act, and live within a range of available possibilities given them by their physical environment. Animism (B) is the religious belief that things in nature (rocks, trees, lakes) contain spirits that can interact with humans. Environmental determinism (C) is the belief that our environment influences and controls our actions, lifestyle, and culture. Cultural ecology (D) is the study of a culture and its environment. Syncretism (E) is the development of a new culture trait through the fusing of two or more separate forms of the trait.

8. **E**—Xizang Autonomous Region (Tibet) is the region of China that contains the largest number of speakers of the Tibeto-Burman dialect—a part of the Sino-Tibetan language family. Chinese is also part of this language family. The Sino-Tibetan language family is second only to the Indo-European languages in terms of the number of native speakers.

9. **E**—The majority of the inhabitants of Region A (Xinjiang Autonomous Region) are Muslims, and Islam has dominated the region since A.D. 984. The Uygur is the major ethnic group of the 47 ethnic groups calling this region home.

10. **E**—Most TNCs are private companies with branches in many nations. TNCs are common in the electronical, chemical, pharmaceutical, and petroleum industries (A). They are chiefly involved in making and selling manufactured goods (B). Nearly all TNCs are headquartered in the United States, Japan, or the EU (C). They use the principle of comparative advantage to ensure a high profit margin (D).

11. **D**—In practice, immigrants to Europe are often spatially restricted to certain neighborhoods and do not usually receive the same treatment as those coming to the United States (E). Citizenship (A) is very hard to obtain for an immigrant in Europe and most do not arrive in the host country expecting to permanently reside there. Most Muslim immigrants from North Africa (B) isolate themselves in bleak quarters on the outskirts of French cities. Many immigrants to Europe choose to bring their families with them (C).

12. **A**—Secularism (A) is dominant in Europe today as less than 21 percent claim to have an active belief in God. In the United States today, over 60 percent of Americans claim to have an active religious life and a strong belief in God. Heathenism (B) is a pre-Christian religion that comes under the umbrella religion of paganism. Sacrilege (C) is the intentional defamation of anything that is sacred. Nationalism (D) is the identification with a nation-state. Communism (E) is a system of government in which the state plans and controls the economy ruled by a single authoritarian political party that espouses that property and goods will be held equally by all.

13. **B**—A typical city in the developing world does not have adequate infrastructure to meet the demands of its rapidly growing population. The larger cities in the developing world have modern commercial areas (A) surrounded by large high-density areas of squatter settlements (E). The large numbers of rural migrants coming into the cities for jobs (C) overwhelm the social services and aging infrastructures of most cities in the Third World. A large share of a developing country's GDI (gross domestic income) is generally produced in its cities (E). For example, Sao Paulo, Brazil, contributes 37 percent of Brazil's GDI and Mumbai generates one-sixth of India's GDI.

14. **B**—Shifting cultivation in which farmers rotate fields is mostly practiced in tropical rain forests where the heavy constant rainfalls and climate conditions produce soils that do not hold their fertility. The other answer choices are biomes where other forms of agriculture are more prevalent.

15. **C**—Secularism is a movement away from religion that either rejects religion or holds it to be of little importance. A polytheistic religion (A) involves the worship of many gods. An animistic religion (B) holds that rocks, rivers, mountains, animals, etc. all possess a soul and have the ability to help or hurt humans in life. Followers of a monotheistic religion (D) worship one supreme being that is the creator of all life. Heathenism (E) is a pre-Christian religion that comes under the umbrella religion of paganism.

16. **A**—During the first phase (which is not found in any country now), birth rates are high but high death rates prevent the population from growing. Diseases, wars, and famines cause death rates to fluctuate. As causes of early death are eradicated, death rates drop while birth rates remain high, and the population shoots forward in a growth spurt into the second phase of the demographic transition (D).

17. **A**—Africa continues to have the highest fertility rates in the world, but they are slowly declining. Population control pressures from the government and NGOs have also communicated a

message that is starting to be heard by more Africans: "Fewer children are desirable now. Can you really afford to raise more children?"

18. **E**—The structures shown are minarets, or towers of a mosque from which the faithful are called to pray five times a day in the Muslim faith.

19. **B**—Fragmented states such as the Philippines and Indonesia have part or all of their territory represented by islands. A perforated state (A) is broken up by the existence of an independent country within its national boundaries; for example, the Republic of South Africa completely surrounds the independent country of Lesotho. An elongated state (C) is a long, narrow country like Chile or Vietnam. A prorupt state (D) is almost totally compact but also has an extension protruding from it; Myanmar and Thailand are both examples of a prorupt state. Compact states (E), such as Uruguay and Poland, are roughly circular in shape.

20. **C**—Globalization is the interconnectedness of various parts of the world through many avenues—communication, trade, supranational organizations, and culture. Culture (A) is the patterns of socialization, behavior, understandings, and beliefs of a people that are passed down from one generation to the next. Core-periphery (B) refers to a model of the global economic system in which underdeveloped countries and regions on the periphery are dependent on the countries of the central and dominant core region. Development (D) is the process of economic growth and expansion. Diffusion (E) refers to the spread of a culture trait such as new religion, idea, or technology over space or through time.

21. **B**—The United States–Mexico border region is the fastest-growing industrial zone in North America. It is noted for diversified assembly and manufacturing plants called maquiladoras, not gold and silver mining. The Gulf Coast of Texas (A) is home to a large petrochemical industry based on large oil and gas reserves. The Silicon Valley area around San Francisco (C) is home to a high-tech industrial cluster centered on the electronics and computer industries. The US Southeast (D) has an industrial base centered on

agriculture—textiles, tobacco, and the harvesting of forests for furniture and wood products. The old steel-based industries of the Ohio/Mongahela River Valleys (Pittsburgh area) have diversified into fabrication and high-tech manufacturing (E).

22. **D**—This map shows where potatoes are raised for the wholesale food markets. The vast majority of potatoes raised in the United States are grown in Idaho, but nearby Washington State comes in second. Potatoes thrive in their hot days, cool nights, and rich volcanic soil. Significant areas of potato production are found in other northern states, which supports the statement that potatoes are best grown in cooler climates. Although potatoes are commercially grown in northern parts of the Midwest (A), this is not the chief potato-growing region of the United States. The map does not contain information about cultural preferences, but in fact, potatoes are not extensively farmed in the Southwest (B) because climate and soil conditions do not make their production economically feasible—not because of cultural preferences. Potatoes would be grown in the fifth ring of von Thünen's model (C)—the extensive farming ring—because they can be stored easily and do not need to be grown close to market. The map does not contain information regarding American food consumption, but in fact, bread is still the chief staple of the American diet and throughout most of the world.

23. **C**—Centripetal forces unite the residents of a political state. A national school system, national religious institutions, and the armed forces are centripetal forces, as well as a strong, centralized national government and well-developed transportation and communication systems. Diffusion (A) refers to the spread of a culture trait such as a new religion, idea, or technology over space or through time. Centrifugal forces (B) are forces, such as religious conflicts and the struggle for autonomy by an ethnic minority, that pull the political state apart and cause strife and unrest. Ethnocentric (D) refers to the idea that one's own race or ethnicity is superior to all others. Naturalizing (E) refers to the process of obtaining citizenship in a country by a person who was not a citizen of that country when he or she was born.

24. **B**—The European Union developed out of the EEC, or European Economic Community, as its interests and areas of power extended beyond purely economic matters.

25. **A**—The Industrial Revolution in England and Western Europe greatly increased the demand for food and spurred on the Second Agricultural Revolution, which had already begun. World Wars I and II (B and C) came in the twentieth century after the Second Agricultural Revolution. It was during the First Agricultural Revolution that the use of the plow (D) and the domestication of cereal grains and animals (E) replaced hunting and gathering as a way of life.

26. **A**—Stage 1 of the demographic transition model assumes both birth rates and death rates of a society will be high. Stage 2 (B), Stage 3 (C), Stage 4 (D), and Stage 5 (E) are the later stages that are marked by falling birth rates and/or death rates.

27. **C**—Angkor Wat, constructed by the Khmer Civilization in the twelfth century , is the largest Hindu temple complex ever constructed. In fact, the temple, located in northwestern Cambodia, is still the largest religious structure in the world (now serving as a Buddhist temple). Hindu temples are found in India, Bali, and the countries of Southeast Asia where Hinduism eventually spread.

28. **E**—Mongolia is located in the interior of a continent—landlocked, and far from any coastal areas and port facilities. This is a huge locational disadvantage in terms of trade, communication of new ideas, and interconnections in the global economy. Singapore (A) has a superb shipping and trade advantage because of its location on the Straits of Malacca. Italy (B) and Spain (C) are both peninsular countries with ample opportunities for trade and communication. Argentina (D) has a long extensive coast on the Atlantic Ocean and has excellent port facilities for trading with other countries.

29. **D**—A primate city is a city that is more than twice as large as any other city in the country. A global city (A), also called a world-leader city (B), is a city which sits at an intersection of financial, banking, and commercial markets. Megalopolis (C) is an almost 600-mile-long conurbation stretching from southern Maine to southern Virginia. A metropolis (E) is a large urban center.

30. **D**—The S-curve depicts the world's population during the four stages of the demographic transition model. After a slow start, population levels expand dramatically and then slow down as scarce resources provide a natural "brake" on the process. Populations may even decrease at this time giving the model its name, S-curve. Choice C refers to the gravity model and choice E reflects the J-curve model.

31. **E**—The Palestinian Liberation Organization (PLO) is a political movement involving Palestinian Arabs who are fighting to create an independent state of Palestine. The PLO is made up of individuals supportive of this goal, not countries. The UN (United Nations) (A), NATO (North American Treaty Organization) (B), ASEAN (Association of Southeast Asian Nations) (C), and NAFTA (North American Free Trade Alliance) (D) are all supranational organizations whose members are countries that have united under a common mission or set of goals.

32. **E**—Distance to the nearest city is not a part of determining an absolute location on the global grid. The other answer choices are all used in finding the intersection of lines of latitude and longitude.

33. **C**—Environmental apathy does not characterize Europe today. Europe is actively pursuing environmental awareness, especially in the member states of the EU Comenius, a teacher training and educational partnership program of the EU, stresses environmental education starting in the lower grades. All the other answer choices describe problems Europe faces.

34. **C**—Sub-Saharan Africa is the world's fastest-urbanizing region, and the majority of its population is predicted to live in urban centers by 2030. Sadly, economic growth is not keeping up with the rapid urban expansion and rates of natural increase found in most countries in this region.

35. **D**—NATO is a defensive alliance including the United States and a number of European countries that agree to stand united in the event of military aggression against any of NATO's members. NATO has nothing to do with economics. All the other choices are economic unions. The EU (A) consists of European nations, CARICOM (B) is composed of Caribbean nations, NAFTA (C) includes North American nations (United States, Canada, and Mexico), and MERCOSUR (E) includes several South American nations.

36. **D**—The Basque language is spoken in the ethnic Basque region of the Pyrenees Mountains of Spain. Spain now permits the regional language to be taught in Basque schools. A smaller population of Basques is found in the adjacent part of France.

37. **C**—Research is continuing into the health effects of genetically modified foods. Opponents fear GMOs may cause developmental problems in children or harmful mutations in humans. Positive effects of GMOs are the stimulation of world trade in food commodities (A) and the increase in plant resistance to disease (B) and drought (D). The use of GMOs is not intended to clean up the environment (E) and it is unclear whether the net effect of GMOs on the environment will be positive or negative (E).

38. **D**—World cities are also found in the southern and eastern hemispheres, not just in the northern or western hemispheres. Sydney, Australia; Djakarta, Indonesia; and Johannesburg, South Africa are examples of world cities neither in the western or northern hemispheres. The other answer choices correctly describe characteristics for world cities.

39. **C**—Von Thünen proposed a model of agricultural land use that takes into account market prices as well as production and transportation costs. Farm products that were more costly to transport were grown closer to the central market and commanded a higher price, which caused this land to be more expensive. Those farm products that could be transported at lower cost were grown on less-expensive land farther from the central market. W. W. Rostow (A) developed a theory in 1960 that claims societies develop economically in a five-stage progression from take-off to postindustrial. E. G. Ravenstein (B) developed seven "laws of migration" in the late nineteenth century. Two of the laws are that most migrants only move a short distance and do it in a step-by-step fashion. Burgess's concentric zone model (D) attempted to explain residential zone patterns of US cities in the 1920s. It details the invasion and succession movement that is ongoing as one zone stretches and invades the next outer zone. Harris and Ullman (E) developed an urban land-use model; they claimed that, instead of a single central business district, there are several CBDs. From these multiple nodes, growth occurs in a pattern that does not conform to the concentric or sector patterns of the other models.

40. **D**—Regions are not easily defined, but there are patterns of spatial similarities that help us generalize and group places into regions. All regions have the following characteristics of boundaries (A), common features (B) such as shared physical or cultural characteristics, a relative location (C), and spatial extent (an amount of space a region occupies) (E).

41. **B**—Gentrification is the process whereby middle- and upper-income residents move into older, rundown urban neighborhoods and renovate them. Urbanization (A) is the process of creation and expansion of cities. Suburbanization (C) is the growth of residential areas on the outskirts of cities and the process through which city residents move out into these areas. The multiplier effect (D) means that for every basic worker the city employs, several new non-basic jobs will also be created as additional workers are needed to provide services such as parking, food preparation, drycleaning, etc. services for the basic worker. Home improvements (E) are improvements made by homeowners on their houses.

42. **B**—Followers of a universalizing religion believe it is designed for all mankind so they proselytize and actively seek new converts. One way to do this is by sending missionaries into other countries to convert others. An ethnic religion (A) is a religion practiced by an ethnic group; adherents

of this type of religion usually do not seek converts. A monotheistic religion (C) is based on the worship of one supreme being that is the creator of all life, and a polytheistic religion (D) involves the worship of many gods, but these beliefs are unrelated to whether or not missionaries are used to spread the religion. An animistic religion (E) believes rocks, rivers, mountains, animals, etc. all possess a soul and have the ability to help or hurt humans in life, and adherents of this type of religion generally do not use missionaries to seek converts.

43. **A**—Rice was developed in the 1960s for growth in drier climates, making it able to be grown in a wider variety of climates for a larger world harvest.

44. **E**—Nationalism is the idea of identifying with a particular people or nation-state. Regionalism (A) occurs when a minority group identifies with—and gives its allegiance to—a region more than the nation as a whole. Most separatist movements occur when ethnic groups owe more allegiance to their ethnic region than to the country as a whole. Devolution (B) is the transfer of some central government powers to the regional government. Iconography (C) refers to the study of symbols that unite people. Examples of these symbols include a national sports team, flag, or national holiday. Ethnocentrism (D) is the belief that one's own race or ethnicity is superior to all others.

45. **B**—E. G. Ravenstein developed seven "laws of migration" in the late nineteenth century. Two of the laws are that most migrants only move a short distance and do it in a step-by-step fashion. W. W. Rostow (A) developed a theory in 1960 that claims societies develop economically in a five-stage progression from take-off to postindustrial. Von Thünen (C) suggested a model of agricultural land use based on concentric circles of crops radiating outward from an urban central market. Burgess's concentric zone model (D) attempted to explain residential zone patterns of US cities in the 1920s. It details the invasion and succession movement that is ongoing as one zone stretches and invades the next outer zone. Harris and Ullman (E) developed an urban land-use model that claimed that, instead of a single

central business district, there are several CBDs. From these multiple nodes, growth occurs in a pattern that does not conform to the concentric or sector patterns of the other models.

46. **E**—The United States exports more food than any other country in the world. It is also the largest exporter of foods produced from genetically modified organisms (GMOs).

47. **A**—The multiplier effect means that for every basic worker employed in a city's economy, several new non-basic jobs will also be created as additional workers are needed to provide services such as parking, food preparation, dry cleaning, etc. for the basic worker. In other words, added basic jobs "multiply" the number of jobs in the urban economy.

48. **D**—Burgess's concentric zone model attempted to explain residential zone patterns of US cities in the 1920s. It details the invasion and succession movement that is ongoing as one zone stretches and invades the next outer zone. W. W. Rostow (A) developed a theory in 1960 that holds that societies develop economically in a five-stage progression from take-off to postindustrial. E. G. Ravenstein (B) developed seven "laws of migration" in the late nineteenth century. Two of the laws are that most migrants only move a short distance and that they do it in a step-by-step fashion. Von Thünen (C) proposed a model of agricultural land use based on concentric circles of crops radiating outward from an urban central market. Harris and Ullman (E) developed an urban land-use model, but they held that, instead of a single central business district, there are several CBDs. From these multiple nodes, growth occurs in a pattern that does not conform to the concentric or sector patterns of the other models.

49. **D**—A common language is not being considered as a key milestone, or goal, of the European Union (EU). All the other responses are key milestones, which have already been achieved to some degree.

50. **A**—Both Hindu and Buddhist faiths cremate their dead and do not bury the deceased in graveyards or

cemeteries. Muslim (B), Jewish (C), Christian (D), and most animists (E) bury their dead in graveyards and cemeteries laid aside for that purpose.

51. **D**—A natural boundary is a physical feature of the landscape such as a river that is used to mark a boundary between political states. However, since they often change course, rivers are usually not good choices as boundaries. Water divider (A) and watercourse (B) are not valid geographical terms used to describe boundaries. An artificial boundary (C), also called a geometric boundary, is usually a parallel of latitude or a meridian of longitude that is used because detailed geographic knowledge of the area being outlined is limited. A relict boundary (E) is an abandoned boundary that is no longer used as a boundary.

52. **D**—The amount of fertilizer produced in a country is not an environmental variable (something that is part of the natural environment such as average amount of annual rainfall or average yearly temperatures). The other answer choices are all environmental factors that have a direct impact on the agricultural sector of an economy.

53. **E**—Generally, advancing technology has improved the Earth's ability to sustain larger populations. All the other answer choices are all important factors mentioned in Malthus's thesis.

54. **C**—The Indo-European language family is the largest of world language families. Approximately one-half of the world speaks languages from this family. Most European languages and many Asian languages are part of the Indo-European family.

55. **C**—Absolute location is the unique location of a place. Latitudinal and longitudinal coordinates are often used to represent absolute location. A formal region (A) is a region that is uniform in one or more physical or cultural specifics. The Corn Belt is a formal region that shows the states producing the required amount of corn to be included in the definition of a Corn Belt state. A functional region (B) has a core and a periphery and all parts are connected and func-

tion together as a unit. Relative location (D) is the position of a place spatially as it relates to other places nearby. If you described the relative location of your home, you would probably talk about its proximity to your school, the store, and perhaps a nearby park. A perceptual region (E) is a region defined by feelings and prejudices that may or may not be true.

56. **E**—A garment factory worker performs a basic economic function because he or she produces a product that generates an income flow into the city. The other responses are all non-basic jobs that provide services to the city workers but do not generate an income flow into the city.

57. **E**—Harris and Ullman developed an urban land-use model that states that, instead of a single central business district, there are several CBDs. From these multiple nodes, growth occurs in a pattern that does not conform to the concentric or sector patterns of the other models. W. W. Rostow (A) developed a theory in 1960 that claims societies develop economically in a five-stage progression from take-off to postindustrial. E. G. Ravenstein (B) developed seven "laws of migration" in the late nineteenth century. Two of the laws are that most migrants only move a short distance and do it in a step-by-step fashion. Von Thünen (C) proposed a model of agricultural land use based on concentric circles of crops radiating outward from a urban central market. Burgess's concentric zone model (D) attempted to explain residential zone patterns of US cities in the 1920s. It details the invasion and succession movement that is ongoing as one zone stretches and invades the next outer zone.

58. **A**—The Green Revolution revolutionized rice, maize, and wheat farming primarily in Asia during the latter part of the twentieth century. This "high-input/high-yield" agriculture emphasized the use of hybrid seeds developed to grow faster and produce higher yields (if given lots of water and expensive fertilizer and treated with expensive pesticides). However, Africa's chief cereal crops—millet, sorghum, peanuts, yams, and cassava—were crops not addressed in the Green Revolution. Answer choice B is not the chief reason why the Green Revolution failed

the African farmer, although poor African farmers are unable to afford the expensive inputs required for raising hybrid crops successfully and lack the money for the expensive machinery required for commercial monoculture. The population of Africa is increasing rapidly, not falling (C). Farm production cannot meet the demands of Africa's growing population (D). Willingness to participate (E) was not an issue; the Green Revolution simply focused on crops African farmers did not grow. Even if it had focused on millet and sorghum, most African farmers could not afford to participate.

59. **A**—You have responded to an intervening opportunity when you stop in Columbus and fall in love with the amenities of this new place. Distance decay (B) refers to the drop-off of an activity the farther it gets from its place of origin. Involuntary migration (C) is the forced movement of individuals without their consent from one location to another. Push-pull factors (D) of migration are the forces that either "pull" people to a new place or "push" them from their old place. Transhumance (E) is the movements of herds and flocks to new pastures based on the location of the best pastures for each season of the year.

60. **C**—An elongated state usually spans more climate zones giving it the ability to raise a more diverse array of crops and livestock and exploit more resources. A perforated state (A) is broken up by the existence of an independent country within its national boundaries; for example, the Republic of South Africa completely surrounds the independent country of Lesotho. Fragmented states (B) such as the Philippines and Indonesia have part or all of their territory represented by islands. A prorupt state (D), such as Thailand, is almost totally compact but also has an extension protruding from it. Compact states (E), such as Uruguay and Poland, are roughly circular in shape.

61. **D**—The core countries are the more developed countries (E) that are more technologically advanced (A), wealthy (B), and powerful (C).

62. **E**—The UN increasingly intervenes in situations where human rights are blatantly violated by sovereign states or conflicts erupt within or between states. None of the other answer choices are true statements about the United Nations. There is no worldwide police force operated by the UN (A), and member states retain their sovereignty (B). The UN does not make or enforce world laws (C), although it often encourages countries to negotiate treaties and work together to solve international problems. A few countries, such as Switzerland, have chosen not to join the UN (D).

63. **D**—Both Christianity and Buddhism actively seek converts and thus are universalizing religions. Both religions believe they are applicable to all humans. Islam is also universalizing, but all the other answer choices contain a non-universalizing religion, which makes those selections incorrect.

64. **D**—The climate around the Mediterranean Sea with its hot, dry summers and its mild, rainy winters is ideal for the production of olives, grapes, and chickpeas. Pastoral nomadism (A) is the continual movement of people with their herds in search of pastures. Subsistence farming (B) is a system of agriculture where everything that is produced is consumed by the farmer. Plantation farming (C) is growing a single specialty crop, such as pineapples or sugar for the market. Commercial farming (E) is a system of farming where farmers produce products chiefly for the market.

65. **C**—African cities often have three central business districts (CBDs). The CBD established in the colonial era served as the headquarters for the colonial administration. Banks and other commercial ventures are found in the traditional CBD, and the third CBD serves as a lively market zone with buying and selling taking place. Most African cities include many residents living in grave poverty in slums and squatter settlements that lack even the most basic amenities (A). Rural migrants flock to the urban centers in search of work but many do not find jobs and add to the underground economy to survive the best they can (B). Infrastructure in many cities is an antiquated remnant of the colonial past and government spending on roads and adequate

water and sanitation systems is sadly lacking (D). Social welfare systems (E) are also under-funded and depend heavily on non-governmental organizations (NGOs) and religious groups to assist their residents.

66. **A**—W. W. Rostow developed a theory in 1960 which holds that societies develop economically in a five-stage progression from take-off to postindustrial. E. G. Ravenstein (B) developed seven "laws of migration" in the late nineteenth century. Two of the laws are that most migrants only move a short distance and do it in a step-by-step fashion. Von Thünen (C) proposed a model of agricultural land use based on concentric circles of crops radiating outward from an urban central market. Burgess's concentric zone model (D) attempted to explain residential zone patterns of US cities in the 1920s. It details the invasion and succession movement that is ongoing as one zone stretches and invades the next outer zone. Harris and Ullman (E) also developed an urban land-use model, but they stated that, instead of a single central business district, there are several CBDs. From these multiple nodes, growth occurs in a pattern that does not conform to the concentric or sector patterns of the other models.

67. **C**—Cultural pluralism is the condition in which two or more distinct cultural groups exist together in a country while maintaining their distinct cultural identities. The United States is a country in which cultural pluralism exists. Racial segregation (A) is the practice of separating people by race in their use of space, housing, schools, etc. Miscegenation (B) is the marriage of people from two different races. In some countries this racial mixing is culturally taboo, or forbidden, and in some cases even illegal. Misegenation was against the law in several US states until 1967. Cultural segregation (D) is the separation of people based on their culture. Cultural integration (E) is the blending of cultural traits. Sometimes this creates something new such as happened with Buddhism. Buddhism was birthed in India but spread throughout Asia, merging with elements of animism, shamanism, Confucianism, and Shintoism to form a new version of Buddhism. Today there are not many Buddhists living in India, but elements of Buddhism have merged with Hinduism.

68. **C**—China established four special economic zones (SEZs) along its eastern coast in 1979 and added Hainan island in 1988. These SEZs fueled China's economy by welcoming foreign dollars for investment. China provided inexpensive labor, tax breaks, low export tariffs, and other economic incentives to spur foreign investment in products for export.

69. **B**—Offshoring involves contracting with a foreign company to provide products or services formerly produced domestically. Outsourcing (A) is the practice of hiring an outside company—domestic or foreign—to produce products or services formerly produced by the company itself. A maquiladora (C) is a foreign-owned (usually US) plant in Mexico. Locational interdependence (D) is the situation in which a company's locational decisions are based on the location of its competition. Fordism (E) is the concept of assembly-line mass production and mass consumption of goods named for its chief innovator, Henry Ford.

70. **B**—Central place theory was developed by German geographer Walter Christaller in 1933 to explain the patterns and distributions of settlements as they are interconnected with their surrounding hinterlands. Urban hierarchy (A) is a ranking of cities based on size and function. The concentric zone model (C) depicts the city as a set of rings radiating out to form the CBD; it was developed to explain the social patterns of American cities in the 1920s. The multiplier effect (D) refers to the fact that, for every basic worker the city employs, several new non-basic jobs will also be created as additional workers are needed to provide services such as parking, food preparation, drycleaning, etc., for the basic worker. The rank-size rule (E) states that the nth largest city will be $1/n$ the size of the largest city in a political state or national system of cities.

71. **B**—A theocracy incorporates its religious laws and rules into its government structure. An example is Iran, which is a Shi'ite theocracy and ruled by Islamic clerics, or mullahs. A dictatorship (A) is an autocratic form of government (D) in which a state is ruled by one person who has absolute power and control. A democracy (C) is a form of government in which citizens

are governed by their elected representatives. An oligarchy (E) is a form of government in which a small select group of people (usually the wealthy, powerful, or royalty) rule the state.

72. C—Traditionally, Asian cities have some type of religious monument in their urban center instead of the government and commercial buildings most often found in other world regions, although this is changing as Asian cities modernize.

73. A—Push factors are situations that help to cause a person to move from a location. They could be dissatisfaction with a job, rising crime in the neighborhood, or even a war. If higher paying jobs (B), more attractive retirement communities (C), a more pleasant climate (D), or a safer community environment (E) can be found elsewhere, these are all pull factors that draw, or pull, a person to another location.

74. A—Generally, the neo-Malthusians believe that improved living standards for each person without reducing capital investment is only feasible by reducing the number of persons. Famine relief (B), increased total fertility rates (D), and policies that encourage childbearing (E) usually result in increased fertility rates and growing populations. More spending on social welfare programs (C) diverts important scarce resources away from capital investment.

75. A—Christianity is Europe's main religion today, but Islam is growing rapidly there due to immigration and high birth rates.

Explanations for Section II (Free-Response Questions)

Question 1 (6 points total)

1A. (2 points)
Separatism is the goal of a minority group to separate from the country or state in which it resides. Separatism is synonymous with autonomous nationalism or regional autonomy.

1B. (2 points)
There are a number of separatist movements that can be named in a response to 1B, including:

- Quebec has continually threatened to secede from Canada and become a separate country in an effort to protect and develop its strong French cultural identity.
- The Basques of north central Spain have a unique language and culture. A Basque separatist movement has existed for many years with the goal of creating a separate Basque nation.
- Some Bretons of Brittany (northwest France) desire to separate from France and become an independent nation. Historically, Brittany has had a different language and culture than France and struggled to maintain a separate identity.
- Religious, linguistic, and cultural differences separate the Hindu Tamil-speaking residents of northern Sri Lanka from the Buddhist Sinhalese-speaking majority which dominates the state. A long civil war ended in 2009 with the defeat of separatist Tamil military forces; however, separatist sentiment remains strong among many Tamils.
- The Moros of the Philippines are a Muslim minority in the predominantly Christian nation of the Philippines. A Moro separatist movement seeks to form a separate nation in southern areas of the Philippines in which Moros comprise a majority.
- A separatist movement of Sikhs in the Punjab region of India seeks the creation of a separate Punjabi-speaking, Sikh-majority state in the western region of India bordering on Pakistan. The Sikhs' religion is a mix of Islam and Hinduism.

1C. (2 points)

Note: Your answer must specifically discuss the separatist group you have identified. The discussion below is not intended to be an answer but only to provide a general starting point for your response.

Separatist movements often operate on the periphery of a country because they are usually isolated minority groups living in rural parts of the country. Because of the distance from the national core and its strong governmental influence, separatist groups feel disenfranchised and alienated, excluded from the rest of the country. The dominant group in a country is viewed as exploitive and ready to steal the separatist group's language, religious freedom, power to govern, and economic resources.

Question 2 (6 points total)

2A. (2 points)

An ethnic enclave in an urban area is a neighborhood or small area that is occupied by an ethnic minority group.

2B. (2 points)

Some examples of ethnic enclaves in European cities and of their location within the urban center include:

- **Enclaves of Caribbean and Asian ethnic minorities in London:** There is a deep divide between whites and Caribbean and Asian ethnic minorities who live in racially segregated enclaves in the old, inner-city areas that are run-down and decrepit.
- **Enclaves of Muslim minorities from North Africa in Paris and most other French cities:** Muslim minorities live in poor ethnic neighborhoods on the distant outskirts of the city while existing on the periphery of the mainstream Western culture of the city.
- **Ethnic enclaves of Muslims from Turkey in German cities:** Muslims from Turkey choose to stay to themselves in densely clustered residential areas of German cities. These ethnic enclaves are usually found in the old working-class neighborhoods and are limited to certain districts within the city. Most Muslims from Turkey isolate themselves from the mainstream German society due to a rejection of Western culture and religion. They do not want to acculturate, or assimilate, and are there to work only. It is extremely difficult for them to become citizens and even their German-born children are considered aliens.

2C. (2 points)

Note: Your answer must specifically discuss the ethnic enclave you have identified. The discussion below is not intended to be an answer but only to provide a general starting point for consideration of your response.

Assimilation is generally affected by both external controls such as the charter group's attitudes towards the ethnic minority and internal controls such as the ethnic minority's rejection of mainstream culture, chain migration, voluntary and involuntary residential segregation, and a strong sense of immigrant ethnic self-identity. Many problems of assimilation are a result of an ethnic community's self-segregation, which is based on cultural norms that differ from those of the receiving culture (for example, prohibitions of equality for women, drinking, and freedom of expression). In addition, many European countries impose severe restrictions on immigrants' abilities to become citizens, participate in government, access higher quality housing, etc.

Question 3 (6 points total)

3A. (2 points)
The French were the charter group to settle the area shown in the map.

3B. (2 points)
The French settlers usually used the long-lot system of land survey because it was easy and inexpensive to use. It gave each farm access to the river or road, as well as equal amounts of each kind of soil on the floodplain of the river or lake. Each family could live on its own farm but still be close to neighbors.

3C. (2 points)
The metes-and-bounds pattern of land survey was used by the English charter groups in Pennsylvania and other eastern US states where land was obtained by royal land grant. This survey method utilized features in the natural landscape (mountains, rivers, large trees, etc.) to mark and define property boundaries in an allotment of otherwise unsurveyed land. Because of the topography, this system led to lots of boundary disputes as rivers changed course, trees were cut down, and other changes occurred to these natural boundary markers. The French long-lot survey system was more exact, but boundary disputes often arose in the bends of rivers where lots became spatially distorted. Also, as the French (who had large families) subdivided their family landholdings, the long lots became extremely narrow and difficult to farm.

Practice Exam 3

IN THIS CHAPTER

Summary: This chapter contains a practice exam that is very similar to the actual AP Human Geography exam you will take in May. Taking this practice exam now will give you practice in pacing yourself so that you will be able to have enough time to thoughtfully complete each part of the exam.

How to Take the Practice Exam

Give yourself exactly 60 minutes to complete the 75 multiple-choice questions of Section I and 75 minutes to write the three free-response essays of Section II. Set a timer so that the timing is exact and you don't have to keep looking at a clock. Try to re-create the conditions of the actual exam as much as possible. Set aside a block of time when you won't be interrupted. Also, choose a quiet place such as a library where you won't be distracted or interrupted if possible.

Taking this practice exam gives you a good chance to learn how to pace yourself for the actual exam. For Section I, you will have less than one minute to complete each question. Work quickly but carefully; if you don't know an answer, eliminate choices you know are incorrect, guess among those remaining, and move on. You can mark the ones you want to come back to if you have more time. For Section II, give yourself 20 minutes to complete each question. This will give you 5 minutes to review each question and make changes or corrections as needed at the end.

After you have completed both sections of this practice exam, check your answers. Review the explanations for both sections, and make sure you jot down the concepts or terms that you are unsure of or could not remember, for further review.

Practice Exam 3

ANSWER SHEET FOR SECTION I

1 Ⓐ Ⓑ Ⓒ Ⓓ Ⓔ	26 Ⓐ Ⓑ Ⓒ Ⓓ Ⓔ	51 Ⓐ Ⓑ Ⓒ Ⓓ Ⓔ
2 Ⓐ Ⓑ Ⓒ Ⓓ Ⓔ	27 Ⓐ Ⓑ Ⓒ Ⓓ Ⓔ	52 Ⓐ Ⓑ Ⓒ Ⓓ Ⓔ
3 Ⓐ Ⓑ Ⓒ Ⓓ Ⓔ	28 Ⓐ Ⓑ Ⓒ Ⓓ Ⓔ	53 Ⓐ Ⓑ Ⓒ Ⓓ Ⓔ
4 Ⓐ Ⓑ Ⓒ Ⓓ Ⓔ	29 Ⓐ Ⓑ Ⓒ Ⓓ Ⓔ	54 Ⓐ Ⓑ Ⓒ Ⓓ Ⓔ
5 Ⓐ Ⓑ Ⓒ Ⓓ Ⓔ	30 Ⓐ Ⓑ Ⓒ Ⓓ Ⓔ	55 Ⓐ Ⓑ Ⓒ Ⓓ Ⓔ
6 Ⓐ Ⓑ Ⓒ Ⓓ Ⓔ	31 Ⓐ Ⓑ Ⓒ Ⓓ Ⓔ	56 Ⓐ Ⓑ Ⓒ Ⓓ Ⓔ
7 Ⓐ Ⓑ Ⓒ Ⓓ Ⓔ	32 Ⓐ Ⓑ Ⓒ Ⓓ Ⓔ	57 Ⓐ Ⓑ Ⓒ Ⓓ Ⓔ
8 Ⓐ Ⓑ Ⓒ Ⓓ Ⓔ	33 Ⓐ Ⓑ Ⓒ Ⓓ Ⓔ	58 Ⓐ Ⓑ Ⓒ Ⓓ Ⓔ
9 Ⓐ Ⓑ Ⓒ Ⓓ Ⓔ	34 Ⓐ Ⓑ Ⓒ Ⓓ Ⓔ	59 Ⓐ Ⓑ Ⓒ Ⓓ Ⓔ
10 Ⓐ Ⓑ Ⓒ Ⓓ Ⓔ	35 Ⓐ Ⓑ Ⓒ Ⓓ Ⓔ	60 Ⓐ Ⓑ Ⓒ Ⓓ Ⓔ
11 Ⓐ Ⓑ Ⓒ Ⓓ Ⓔ	36 Ⓐ Ⓑ Ⓒ Ⓓ Ⓔ	61 Ⓐ Ⓑ Ⓒ Ⓓ Ⓔ
12 Ⓐ Ⓑ Ⓒ Ⓓ Ⓔ	37 Ⓐ Ⓑ Ⓒ Ⓓ Ⓔ	62 Ⓐ Ⓑ Ⓒ Ⓓ Ⓔ
13 Ⓐ Ⓑ Ⓒ Ⓓ Ⓔ	38 Ⓐ Ⓑ Ⓒ Ⓓ Ⓔ	63 Ⓐ Ⓑ Ⓒ Ⓓ Ⓔ
14 Ⓐ Ⓑ Ⓒ Ⓓ Ⓔ	39 Ⓐ Ⓑ Ⓒ Ⓓ Ⓔ	64 Ⓐ Ⓑ Ⓒ Ⓓ Ⓔ
15 Ⓐ Ⓑ Ⓒ Ⓓ Ⓔ	40 Ⓐ Ⓑ Ⓒ Ⓓ Ⓔ	65 Ⓐ Ⓑ Ⓒ Ⓓ Ⓔ
16 Ⓐ Ⓑ Ⓒ Ⓓ Ⓔ	41 Ⓐ Ⓑ Ⓒ Ⓓ Ⓔ	66 Ⓐ Ⓑ Ⓒ Ⓓ Ⓔ
17 Ⓐ Ⓑ Ⓒ Ⓓ Ⓔ	42 Ⓐ Ⓑ Ⓒ Ⓓ Ⓔ	67 Ⓐ Ⓑ Ⓒ Ⓓ Ⓔ
18 Ⓐ Ⓑ Ⓒ Ⓓ Ⓔ	43 Ⓐ Ⓑ Ⓒ Ⓓ Ⓔ	68 Ⓐ Ⓑ Ⓒ Ⓓ Ⓔ
19 Ⓐ Ⓑ Ⓒ Ⓓ Ⓔ	44 Ⓐ Ⓑ Ⓒ Ⓓ Ⓔ	69 Ⓐ Ⓑ Ⓒ Ⓓ Ⓔ
20 Ⓐ Ⓑ Ⓒ Ⓓ Ⓔ	45 Ⓐ Ⓑ Ⓒ Ⓓ Ⓔ	70 Ⓐ Ⓑ Ⓒ Ⓓ Ⓔ
21 Ⓐ Ⓑ Ⓒ Ⓓ Ⓔ	46 Ⓐ Ⓑ Ⓒ Ⓓ Ⓔ	71 Ⓐ Ⓑ Ⓒ Ⓓ Ⓔ
22 Ⓐ Ⓑ Ⓒ Ⓓ Ⓔ	47 Ⓐ Ⓑ Ⓒ Ⓓ Ⓔ	72 Ⓐ Ⓑ Ⓒ Ⓓ Ⓔ
23 Ⓐ Ⓑ Ⓒ Ⓓ Ⓔ	48 Ⓐ Ⓑ Ⓒ Ⓓ Ⓔ	73 Ⓐ Ⓑ Ⓒ Ⓓ Ⓔ
24 Ⓐ Ⓑ Ⓒ Ⓓ Ⓔ	49 Ⓐ Ⓑ Ⓒ Ⓓ Ⓔ	74 Ⓐ Ⓑ Ⓒ Ⓓ Ⓔ
25 Ⓐ Ⓑ Ⓒ Ⓓ Ⓔ	50 Ⓐ Ⓑ Ⓒ Ⓓ Ⓔ	75 Ⓐ Ⓑ Ⓒ Ⓓ Ⓔ

Section I: Multiple-Choice Questions

Time: 60 Minutes

Section I Comprises 50 Percent of Total AP Score

Directions: Each of the following questions is followed by five answer choices. Choose the one answer choice that best answers the question or completes the statement.

1. Which of the following is a formal region?

   (A) Dixie
   (B) Pennsylvania
   (C) The market area of Winn-Dixie
   (D) The Pacific Northwest
   (E) Pizza Hut delivery area

2. An immigrant learning English in the United States is an example of

   (A) structural assimilation.
   (B) amalgamation theory.
   (C) acculturation.
   (D) adaptation.
   (E) multiculturalism.

3. Which of the following U.S. **main** immigration flow associations is NOT correct?

   (A) Pioneer settlement to 1870—Germans, British, Scotch-Irish, Africans
   (B) 1870–1914—Asians
   (C) 1870–1914—Eastern and southern Europeans
   (D) 1965–present—Hispanics
   (E) 1914–1965—Northern and western Europeans

4. Which of the following factors would be considered a "pull" factor for Riva when considering a move from India to the United States?

   (A) Abject poverty
   (B) Better job and higher wages
   (C) India's caste system
   (D) Violence in her neighborhood
   (E) Bride dowry practices

5. Which of the following is an example of a bulk-gaining industry?

   (A) Steel
   (B) Bottled orange juice
   (C) Paper
   (D) Copper
   (E) Meat-packing

6. If I wanted to ship a small piece of very valuable jewelry to my aunt who lives in Poughkeepsie, which mode of transportation makes the most sense?

   (A) Truck
   (B) Air
   (C) Ship
   (D) Railroad
   (E) Passenger pigeon

7. Which of the following industries does NOT need to be close to its markets?

   (A) Dairy foods
   (B) Bulk-gaining products
   (C) Single-market products
   (D) Bulk-reducing products
   (E) Fresh seafood

8. A primate city is

   (A) a large city located on the periphery of the country.
   (B) the most important city in a country.
   (C) when the largest city in a country is more than twice the size of the next largest city.
   (D) the largest city in a country.
   (E) the largest city located in the central region of a country.

9. The best definition of an urban area is

   (A) the central city and its developed areas.
   (B) the central city and its surrounding suburbs.
   (C) the central city and its hinterlands.
   (D) the central city and the adjacent counties.
   (E) the CBD.

10. Johnny and Susie are moving to Scotland to renovate and live in the family castle. What makes their move a migration?

   (A) They are crossing another country's borders.
   (B) They are not taking anything with them.
   (C) They are moving permanently.
   (D) They will be gone more than one year.
   (E) They will be gone less than one year

11. When we talk about diffusion of a cultural trait, what do we mean by "hearth"?

   (A) Destination
   (B) Origin point
   (C) All locations along the diffusion path
   (D) Axis point
   (E) Midway point

12. The process of invasion and succession is a process involving migration and is best described as when

   (A) new residents tear down and rebuild housing units.
   (B) new residents live peacefully with old residents.
   (C) new residents assimilate with old residents completely.
   (D) new residents move into areas occupied by older resident groups.
   (E) new residents take over old neighborhoods with military force.

13. Which of the following statements is TRUE concerning women in the labor force?

   (A) Most women work in agriculture
   (B) The percentage of women economically active in the labor force declined worldwide
   (C) The percentage of women in the total labor force declined
   (D) Women spend more hours per day working than men in all regions except Anglo America and Australia
   (E) Attitudes towards women in the workplace are less favorable that ever

14. What is the oldest, biggest, and most widely distributed language family from the Hudson Bay to Tierra del Fuego?

   (A) Amerindian
   (B) Malayo-Polynesian
   (C) Austronesian
   (D) Eskimo-Aleut
   (E) Sino-Tibetan

15. Which language family is most widely spoken in North America and Europe and includes Baltic, Celtic, Germanic, and Greek?

   (A) Dravidian
   (B) Uralic-Altaic
   (C) Sino-Tibetan
   (D) Amerindian
   (E) Indo-European

16. Which group represents the Persian (Iranian) variation of Islam and believes in the infallibility and divine right to authority of the Imams descended from Ali?

   (A) Sunni
   (B) Shiite
   (C) Imam
   (D) Untouchables
   (E) Shintoists

17. Which of the following is an example of a state-less nation?

    (A) Germany
    (B) Israel
    (C) Palestine
    (D) Romania
    (E) North Korea

18. The world systems theory divides the world into

    (A) core, periphery, and semi-periphery.
    (B) rich and poor.
    (C) developed and undeveloped.
    (D) haves and have-nots.
    (E) First World and Third World.

19. The process of devolution involves

    (A) the change of government from a democracy to a communist dictatorship.
    (B) the movement of power from the central government to regional governments in the country.
    (C) the movement of power from a monarchy to a military dictatorship.
    (D) the movement of power from regional governments to central governments.
    (E) the movement of power from dictatorship to democracy.

20. Which description best describes the urban hierarchy model in which the population of a city is inversely proportional to its rank in the hierarchy?

    (A) Multiplier effect
    (B) Rank-size rule
    (C) Central place theory
    (D) Burgess's sector model
    (E) Megalopolis

21. The photo below shows which of the following concepts in action?

Source: *https://farm8.staticflickr.com/7688/16765145 843_8af3280bf3_z.jpg*.

    (A) Growth poles
    (B) Spread effects
    (C) Agglomeration effects
    (D) Backwash effects
    (E) Creative destruction

22. Which of the following is NOT a problem for cities in LDCs?

    (A) Lack of jobs
    (B) Shortage of electricity
    (C) High levels of pollution
    (D) Housing shortages
    (E) Abundance of drinking water

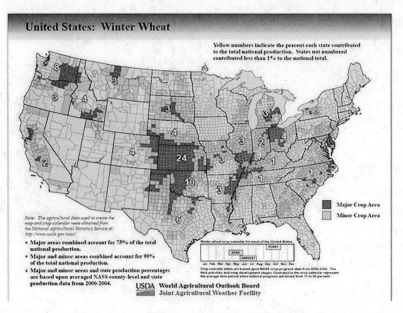

Source: *https://farm3.staticflickr.com/2412/1800188972_f647b1a96e.jpg*.

23. The map above best exemplifies which type of farming?

(A) Specialty farming
(B) Truck farming
(C) Plantation
(D) Monoculture
(E) Polyculture

24. The majority of workers in periphery countries are probably employed in which type of activities?

(A) Primary
(B) Secondary
(C) Tertiary
(D) Quaternary
(E) Quinary

25. Which of the following countries is actively trying to preserve the purity of their native language from contamination by English or other languages?

(A) Italy
(B) Russia
(C) Japan
(D) Brazil
(E) Canada

26. Which of the following languages is NOT an example of a *creole* language in use today?

(A) Haitian Creole
(B) Bazaar Malay
(C) Swahili
(D) Afrikaans
(E) Hindi

27. Ralph purchases garden fertilizer at the nearby garden shop rather than drive 50 miles to the neighboring town for the same product. This reflects which type of spatial interaction?

(A) Transferability
(B) Complementarity
(C) Intervening opportunity
(D) Territoriality
(E) Distance decay

28. Change in any culture is introduced through all the following processes EXCEPT

(A) innovation.
(B) diffusion.
(C) acculturation.
(D) invention.
(E) gravity.

29. Which of the following entities is a state?

    (A) Antarctica
    (B) American Samoa
    (C) Egypt
    (D) Marshall Islands
    (E) Puerto Rico

30. Which of the following items is NOT a challenge to the state?

    (A) Transnational corporations
    (B) EU
    (C) World Trade Organization
    (D) Separatist movements
    (E) Good transportation network

31. Which of the following is a characteristic of a developed country?

    (A) Over 50% of workforce engaged in agriculture
    (B) Women held in inferior place in society
    (C) Main disease related to age and lifestyle
    (D) High birth and death rates
    (E) Primary industries as main drivers of national economy

32. Which of the following factors does NOT play a role in gender relationships in a culture or society?

    (A) Biology
    (B) Advancements in technological development
    (C) Religion
    (D) Custom
    (E) Agricultural advances

33. Which group enacted the first effective settlement in the eastern United States?

    (A) French
    (B) British (English, Scotch-Irish, Welsh, Scottish)
    (C) Russian
    (D) Chinese
    (E) Swiss

34. Which of the following activities are NOT secondary economic activities?

    (A) Assembling automotive parts
    (B) Sewing shirts
    (C) Mining copper
    (D) Binding books
    (E) Stamping out toy soldiers

35. Which of the following statements is true concerning folklore?

    (A) It is the written tradition of a group.
    (B) It encourages changing the old values and customs.
    (C) It serves to blend all cultures into one.
    (D) It expresses in words the shared values of a group by expressing their ideals.
    (E) It cannot be shared among various cultural groups.

36. The rectangular land survey system is based on all of the following EXCEPT

    (A) block pattern of land survey.
    (B) rural road patterns.
    (C) dispersed pattern of isolated farmsteads.
    (D) French and Spanish settlement patterns.
    (E) homesteading.

37. The rate of natural increase of a population is found by subtracting the

    (A) crude death rate from the crude birth date.
    (B) crude birth rate from the crude death rate.
    (C) doubling time from the crude birth rate.
    (D) fertility rate from the crude death rate.
    (E) fertility rate from the crude birth rate.

38. During the third stage of the demographic transition model, which of the following is true?

(A) Birth rates increase and population growth rate is less rapid.
(B) Birth rates decline and population growth rate is less rapid.
(C) Birth rates increase and population growth rate increases.
(D) Birth rates decrease and population growth rate increases.
(E) Birth rates stay the same and population growth rate decreases.

39. Which of the following is NOT a feature of an export processing zone (EPZ)?

(A) Tariff reductions on exports
(B) Raw materials imported duty-free
(C) Exemption from customs duties
(D) Strict pollution regulations
(E) Top-notch infrastructure

40. Transnational corporations distribute their operations

(A) manufacturing goods where production costs are the highest.
(B) conducting accounting and research services where economical.
(C) based on comparative advantage.
(D) with headquarters located in LDCs.
(E) with headquarters located in MDCs.

41. Which of the following statements is NOT part of Gunnar Myrdal's theory of cumulative causation?

(A) Developing and developed regions share similarly in wealth through trade.
(B) The core will always dominate the periphery.
(C) Growth and prosperity of the core exists at the expense of the periphery.
(D) Regions with initial advantage keep and expand it as they attract labor, capital, and trade.
(E) Economic improvement in one area will trigger an economic decline in other areas.

42. Which zone contains low-income slums, ethnic ghettos, and general deterioration in Burgess's concentric zone model of urban form?

(A) First
(B) Second
(C) Third
(D) Fourth
(E) Fifth

43. In which zone of Burgess's concentric zone model would one find better houses, single-family homes, and higher-rent apartments?

(A) First
(B) Second
(C) Third
(D) Fourth
(E) Fifth

Transport artery
1 CBD
2 Manufacturing
3 Poor housing
4 Medium housing
5 Superior housing

Source: *http://imgarcade.com/sector-model-city.html.*

44. In the above urban model, what could be said is the main theme dictating residential land use?

(A) The areas of industrialization
(B) The size of the CBD
(C) The proximity of rich to poor housing
(D) Transportation arteries
(E) Circular expansion of the city

45. National sports teams, flags, national anthems, and national holidays all promote

(A) nationalism.
(B) sectarianism.
(C) political unrest.
(D) functional disputes.
(E) resource disputes.

46. What condition occurs when the people of one state want to annex a territory whose population is ethnically related to that state's population but now under the rule of another state?

(A) Nationalism
(B) Resource dispute
(C) Irredentism
(D) Positional dispute
(E) Functional dispute

47. Which of the following statements is NOT accurate regarding the services provided by local governments in the United States?

(A) Duplication of efforts occurs often.
(B) Social problems of the central city spill over into the surrounding residential suburbs.
(C) Inefficiency in providing services occurs often.
(D) One neighborhood's efforts to reduce pollution are always supported by neighboring communities.
(E) Land zoned for a shopping mall in one municipality may conflict with the wishes of a neighboring municipality.

48. Which of the following is NOT usually a possible reason for migration?

(A) Educational opportunities
(B) Environmental appeals or dislikes
(C) Changes in life cycle
(D) Political party affiliation
(E) Retirement comforts

49. All the following factors can be considered pull factors of migration EXCEPT

(A) safety.
(B) better climate.
(C) better schools.
(D) job opportunities.
(E) overcrowding.

50. Which of the following items below is NOT considered a barrier to the diffusion of an innovation?

(A) Internet
(B) Distance
(C) Cultural obstacles
(D) Government interference
(E) Rough terrain and oceans

51. Which of the following is NOT an example of syncretism?

    (A) Halloween
    (B) Foreign cuisine changed to suit American tastes
    (C) Hasidic Judaism
    (D) Catholicism in Louisiana
    (E) Mahayana Buddhism

52. College students who live in dormitories near the college cafeteria are more likely to eat in the cafeteria. This is an example of

    (A) gravity concept.
    (B) distance decay.
    (C) complementarity.
    (D) transferability.
    (E) movement bias.

53. New stores opening around a large shopping mall reflect which concept?

    (A) Gravity concept
    (B) Distance decay
    (C) Complementarity
    (D) Transferability
    (E) Movement bias

Source: *http://cdn-6.freeclipartnow.com/d/21727-1/Iowa.jpg.*

54. In the above map of Iowa, which of the following land survey methods has been used?

    (A) Long lots
    (B) New England village
    (C) Metes and bounds
    (D) Rectangular
    (E) Agricultural village

55. A systematic way of transferring a spherical surface to a flat map is called a(n)

    (A) map scale.
    (B) map projection.
    (C) legend.
    (D) aggregation.
    (E) simplification.

56. What object in the photo below is the most distinctive expression of regional identity?

Source: *https://tse2.mm.bing.net/th?id=OIP.VsU1 sIpTk60tvE5kcnNDgwEsDh&pid=15.1&P=0& w=240&h=181.*

(A) Tree in the courtyard
(B) Lights by the front door
(C) Adobe construction of the houses
(D) Cross by the front door
(E) Mountains in the background

57. The tendency for migration to decrease with distance is called

(A) push factors.
(B) pull factors.
(C) distance decay.
(D) migration selectivity.
(E) migration stream.

58. Zero population growth (ZPG) is achieved when

(A) CBR – CDR = 2.
(B) Births + immigration = deaths + emigration.
(C) Total fertility = 3.
(D) Replacement fertility is achieved.
(E) TFR = 2.5.

59. The tendency for a population to continue to grow long after replacement fertility has been achieved is called

(A) zero population growth.
(B) rapid growth rate.
(C) homeostatic plateau.
(D) demographic momentum.
(E) overpopulation.

60. Which of the following is NOT a spread effect in the core-periphery model of development?

(A) Congestion in the core
(B) High cost of labor in the core
(C) High density in the core
(D) Environmental decay in the core
(E) More infrastructure in the core

61. Which of the following could be considered a higher-order central place function?

(A) Winn-Dixie grocery store
(B) Mercedes-Benz dealership
(C) Shoe store
(D) Family doctor
(E) Medical clinic

62. How do city planners separate discordant land uses such as housing and sewage plants?

(A) Malls
(B) Fences
(C) Zoning
(D) Tunnels
(E) Rivers

63. The construction of freeways leads to all but which of the following results?

(A) Urban sprawl
(B) Traffic increase
(C) Traffic congestion
(D) Decreased dependency on cars
(E) Need for more freeways

64. What do the terms *apartheid*, *ethnic cleansing*, and *integration* all have in common?

    (A) They all occurred in Nazi Germany during World War I.
    (B) They are all forms of residential segregation.
    (C) They are all ways to integrate different ethnic populations in neighborhoods.
    (D) They are different expressions for the same concept.
    (E) They are all forms of community bonding.

65. Which of the following countries is NOT a federal state?

    (A) Canada
    (B) United States
    (C) France
    (D) People's Republic of China
    (E) Brazil

66. Which of the following situations does NOT occur in a federal state?

    (A) Central government possesses a two-level system of government.
    (B) Central government governs country as a single unit.
    (C) It often possesses a written constitution.
    (D) Lower-level divisions have unique powers.
    (E) Lower-level divisions have their own government and budget.

67. Quebec is a strong example of which of the following situations?

    (A) Irredentism
    (B) Secession
    (C) Ethnonationalism
    (D) A colony
    (E) A nation-state

68. Which of the following characteristics is NOT true of a state?

    (A) Independent territory
    (B) Internationally recognized
    (C) Boundaries
    (D) Full sovereignty over land of the inhabitants
    (E) A national language

69. Mary lives in a neighborhood with stores, offices, and restaurants so close that she does not need to own a car; however, she feels she has very little privacy. This is an example of a(n)

    (A) win-win.
    (B) trade-off.
    (C) infill.
    (D) leapfrog development.
    (E) ecologically sensitive space.

70. In a postindustrial economy, which of the following resources is considered most important to increase productivity?

    (A) Energy
    (B) Labor
    (C) Information
    (D) Specialization
    (E) Mechanization

71. Which of the following would NOT be considered a barrier to diffusion of a cultural trait?

    (A) Language
    (B) Religion
    (C) Oceans
    (D) Economic factors
    (E) Tolerant complaisant citizens

72. Which of the following is a functional region?

    (A) Dixie
    (B) Pennsylvania
    (C) The market area of Winn-Dixie
    (D) The Pacific Northwest
    (E) The Bible Belt.

73. To get to school in the morning, we ALL use this as our guide:

    (A) Rand-McNally Road Atlas.
    (B) world globe.
    (C) road map.
    (D) GIS.
    (E) mental map.

74. A population pyramid, or age-sex structure, displays all the following information about a country's population EXCEPT

    (A) future social spending needs of the population.
    (B) the impact of "baby booms" on the population.
    (C) the impact of wars on the population.
    (D) a quick visual depiction of the country's demographics.
    (E) the country's actual population in numbers.

75. Which of the following statements about East Asia's industrial regions is true?

    (A) Japan has a rich natural resource base.
    (B) China lacks natural resources but has a massive labor force.
    (C) China is industrializing rapidly.
    (D) Taiwan lacks industrial enterprise and an educated workforce.
    (E) Singapore is still considered a developing industrialized state.

END OF SECTION I

Section II: Free-Response Questions

Time: 75 minutes

Section II Comprises 50 Percent of Total AP Score

Directions: Answer each of the three questions below in the allotted time of 75 minutes. You should spend approximately 25 minutes on each question. Answers must be in essay form, not a list of facts or thoughts, although a formal essay (with an introduction and conclusion) is not required. Use substantive examples where appropriate. Make sure you answer all parts of each question and label each part of your answer to correspond with the part of the question you are answering. Feel free to make a short outline first to capture your thoughts, but only the essay will be scored.

1. (A) Define popular culture and folk culture.
   (B) Give an example of each—popular and folk-culture in the "built" environment.
   (C) Describe a negative impact of each culture—pop and folk—on the physical environment.

2. (A) Define spatially variable costs of manufacturing.
   (B) Give two examples of spatially variable costs and describe how each influences a company's choice of plant location.
   (C) Explain how spatially variable costs contribute to profit maximization in a firm.

3. (A) Define land survey.
   (B) Identify two types of land surveys used to allocate property in North America and give an example of each.
   (C) Give an example of a land survey system and how it affected settlement patterns.

END OF SECTION II

Answer Key: Section I (Multiple-Choice Questions)

1. B		39. D	
2. C		40. C	
3. B		41. A	
4. B		42. A	
5. B		43. C	
6. B		44. D	
7. D		45. A	
8. C		46. C	
9. B		47. D	
10. C		48. D	
11. B		49. E	
12. D		50. A	
13. D		51. C	
14. A		52. B	
15. E		53. E	
16. B		54. D	
17. C		55. B	
18. A		56. C	
19. B		57. C	
20. B		58. B	
21. C		59. D	
22. E		60. E	
23. D		61. B	
24. A		62. C	
25. C		63. D	
26. E		64. B	
27. C		65. C	
28. E		66. B	
29. C		67. C	
30. E		68. E	
31. C		69. B	
32. A		70. C	
33. B		71. E	
34. C		72. C	
35. D		73. E	
36. D		74. B	
37. A		75. C	
38. B			

Explanations for Section I (Multiple-Choice Questions)

1. **B**—A formal region has political boundaries, and everyone living in it must follow the same laws and regulations. Dixie (A) and the Pacific Northwest (D) are perceptual or vernacular regions, which reflect how people view their spatial world. The market area of Winn-Dixie (C) and the delivery area of Pizza Hut (E) are functional or nodal regions, with spatially based interactions.

2. **C**—Acculturation is the change that happens when an immigrant adopts the traits such as language of the dominant, or host, society. Structural assimilation (A) is the spreading of immigrants throughout the host society without a complete assimilation into the society. Amalgamation theory (B) is the idea that societies comprised of many ethnic groups become a composite of all their culture traits. Adaptation (D) is the process immigrants and their families go through as they adjust and adapt to their new homes. Multiculturalism (E) is the presence of several distinct cultures within a society in which they share equal rights and privileges.

3. **B**—The time period 1870–1914 saw a major inflow of immigrants from southern and eastern Europe—not Asia—to work in the growing steel mills and coal mines of the United States. The other main immigration flows are correct.

4. **B**—A pull factor of migration is a draw or factor that makes a move attractive. (A), (C), (D), and (E) would be "push" factors that would motivate—or push—Riva to leave India.

5. **B**—Bottled orange juice is a bulk-gaining industry because the final product (bottle of juice) weighs more than the inputs (juice, water, and bottle). Steel (A), paper (C), copper (D), and meat-packing (E) are bulk-reducing industries where the final product is of less weight and bulk than the original input due to refining, processing, etc.

6. **B**—Air is the best way to ship small valuable items. Trucks (B), ships (C), and railroads (D) are best for large, bulky products that do not have to be delivered quickly. Sadly, passenger pigeons (E) are extinct.

7. **D**—Bulk-reducing industries, such as copper, steel, meat-packing products, etc., are located near the input and not the market, because the input weighs more than the output. Perishable products (A) such as dairy with a limited shelf-life need to be situated close to their markets. Bulk-gaining products (B) such as Coca-Cola need to be close to their markets since they increase in weight. (C) Single-market products supply only one or two markets so it makes sense for them to locate near those markets. Thanks to refrigeration and airplanes, fresh seafood can be shipped almost anywhere (E) to any market.

8. **C**—A primate city is the chief city of a country and one that is much larger and far more complex in function than any other city in the country. It is not just the largest city in a country (D), nor is it a large city located on the periphery (A), as it could be located anywhere including, but not just, in the center of the country (E). It is not necessarily the most important city in the country (B), because arguably the capital city could be designated as such.

9. **B**—An urban area is the central city and its adjoining towns, suburbs, and cities. Developed areas (A) do not necessarily adjoin the central city, and hinterlands (C) are the outlying market areas served by the central city but not necessarily part of the urban area. Adjacent counties (D) are not connected to the central city, and the central business district (CBD) is synonymous with the central city but does not constitute an urban area by itself.

10. **C**—A migration is a permanent move from one location to another with the goal of taking up permanent residency. The crossing of borders (A), amount of baggage they are taking (B), and

time period (D) and (E) are of secondary importance and make the movement more of a visit than a migration.

11. **B**—The hearth of a culture trait is where it originated. Its destination (A) is the place where the culture trait was diffused and all locations along the diffusion path (C), as well as any point on the diffusion path (D) and (E) will be influenced by the culture trait as it spreads.

12. **D**—New residents move into the city's oldest neighborhoods near the city center and push earlier groups outward in a process depicted best in Burgess's concentric ring model. New residents do not tear down and rebuild (A), as they lack finances to do so, and they rarely live peacefully or assimilate completely with the older residents. New residents do not use military force to take over older neighborhoods.

13. **D**—Women spend more working hours each day than men in all world regions except the United States, Canada, and Australia. Since the agricultural revolutions, women no longer do the majority of farming, as men run the equipment such as plows, leaving women to work in the markets (A). The percentages of women in the total work force and economically active in the labor force have both increased worldwide (B) and (C). These days, women have gained favorable circumstances and benefits in the workplace compared to past times (E).

14. **A**—The Amerindian language family was composed of 300 or so North American and more than 70 Meso-American tongues when the Europeans first arrived. It is still the largest language family in the Americas. Malay-Polynesian (B), Austronesian (C), and Sino-Tibetan (E) are not found in this region, and the Eskimo-Aleut (D) tongue is part of the Amerindian language family and is found in the extreme northern part of the region.

15. **E**—The Indo-European language family is the language family most widely spoken in North America and Europe. Language types include Germanic, Romance, Slavic, Baltic, Celtic, Albanian, Greek, Armenian, and Indo-Iranian.

Dravidian (A) is spoken in southern India, and Uralic-Altaic (B) languages include Estonian, Finnish, and Hungarian and are not as widely spoken in Europe as the Indo-European family. Sino-Tibetan (C) is spoken in China, Tibet, and in Southeast Asian countries, and Amerindian (D) languages are spoken in the Americas.

16. **B**—The Shiite Muslims differ in leadership succession in the faith and split off from the majority group, the Sunni Muslims. Shiites are mainly found in Iran, Iraq, Bahrain, and Yemen. Sunni Muslims constitute the majority (80–85%) in all other countries with a Muslim population. An imam (C) is a worship leader in a mosque, and untouchables (D) are the very lowest caste individuals or those completely outside the caste system in Hindu society. Shintoists (E) are those who practice Shinto, an ancient Japanese ethnic religion that worships spirits and ancestors.

17. **C**—Palestine, the Kurds, Roma (gypsies), and Basques are other stateless nations—people without a territory to call their home. Germany (A), Israel (B), Romania (D), and North Korea (E) are all states with defined territories, full sovereign control over its affairs, and a permanent population of residents.

18. **A**—The world systems theory was developed by Immanuel Wallerstein to explain how the modern nation state fits into a larger world system of capitalism. The periphery are least developed states who are exploited by the developed core states for their resources, while the semi-periphery states are still being exploited but are beginning to also exploit peripheral areas, too. Rich and poor (B), developed and undeveloped (C), haves and have-nots (D), and first world and third world (E) are inadequate to explain the complexities of linkages that make up the world systems theory.

19. **B**—When a state devolves, some of the central power is transferred to a regional or local government as in the United Kingdom (Wales, Scotland, Northern Ireland) and Spain (Catelonia and Basque region). Devolution is not about changing the government structure from democracy (A) or movement of power from a monarchy (C) or

regional government back to central government (D) or from a dictatorship to democracy (E).

20. **B**—The rank-size rule says that the population of any town will be inversely proportional to its rank in the hierarchy. In other words, the fifth ranked city will be 1/5 the size of the largest city. The multiplier effect (A) shows the expected effect of nonbasic jobs added to an urban economy when basic jobs are added. Central place theory (C) is an attempt to explain the spatial arrangement, size, and number of settlements in an area. Burgess's concentric zone model (D) explains the distribution of social groups within urban areas using rings. Megalopolis (E) is the continuous urbanized northeastern coast of the United States from Maine to Virginia.

21. **C**—Agglomeration effects are shown because similar high-dollar retail stores locate near each other in this shopping plaza (Coach, J. Crew, etc.) to take advantage of shoppers desiring high-end designer merchandise. Growth poles (A) are cities where core industries cluster and attract more industries and jobs. Spread effects (B) are negative impacts, and backwash effects (D) are positive trickle-down effects caused by industry location decision. Creative destruction (E) is the reinvestment of funds in new, profitable ventures that were once used to fund older, less profitable ventures.

22. **E**—There is never enough clean safe drinking water in cities in LDCs! Problems for cities in LDCs include lack of jobs (A), electricity shortages (B), high levels of pollution (C), and housing shortages (D), to name just a few.

23. **D**—Winter wheat and other grain farming are a specialized agricultural activity where farmers grow one crop for commercial markets. Specialty farming (A) and truck farming (B) are forms of agriculture in which a variety of fruits and vegetables are grown for both small upscale consumer markets and large commercial processors. Plantation agriculture (C) is monocropping wherein a single crop is planted for profit and usually occurs in a former colonial setting. Polyculture (E) refers to the production of several crops.

24. **A**—In LDCs, over 2/3 of the population is involved in growing crops for food or in herding livestock. A very small segment of the population in LDCs is engaged in the other economic sectors (B), (C), (D), and (E).

25. **C**—Japan's Council on the Japanese Language is working to preserve the purity of the Japanese language from contamination by English as well as other foreign languages. Italy (A), Russia (B), Brazil (D), and Canada (E) do not have similar efforts underway and have multilingual populations.

26. **E**—Hindi is the Indo-European official language, but Haitian Creole (A), Bazaar Malay (B), Swahili (C), and Afrikaans (D) are all creole languages derived from their original pidgin forms.

27. **C**—Ralph takes advantage of the chance to buy his garden fertilizer nearby rather than drive 50 miles to purchase the same product by taking advantage of an intervening opportunity that saves him miles and money! Transferability (A) refers to the fact that spatial interaction occurs only when the time and money costs of moving an object are worthwhile and not too great. Complementarity (B) refers to the condition that interactions occur when one place has a supply of what another place wants and can afford to purchase and transport. Territoriality (D) refers to an attempt by an individual or group to identify and gain control over a clearly defined territory. Distance decay (E) is the decreasing intensity of an activity the farther it gets from it point of origin.

28. **E**—Gravity does not effect a direct change in culture; however, innovation (A), diffusion (B), acculturation (C), and invention (D) can all create major changes in a culture.

29. **C**—Egypt is a state but Antarctica (A) is a continent since it does not have permanent residents or belong to a country. American Samoa (B) and the Marshall Islands (D) are territories of the United States, and Puerto Rico (E) is a commonwealth of the United States.

30. **E**—A good transportation network is a blessing to the state as it helps facilitate the flow of people, goods, and services within a country. All of the other items – transnational corporations (A), the EU (B), the World Trade Organization (C), and separatist movements (D) are centrifugal factors in a state and serve to tear it apart.

31. **C**—In a developed country, the main diseases such as heart attacks and cancer are related to age and a lifestyle of overeating, consumption of harmful substances, and lack of physical activity. All the other answers are characteristics of lesser developed countries and are not found in developed ones.

32. **A**—Gender in a culture refers to the socially created differences between feminine and masculine and has little to do with biology. Religion (C), custom (D), and advancements in technological change (B) dictate gender relationships in a culture, and agricultural advances (E) usually cause women to lose status and rewards in a society.

33. **B**—The British enacted the first effective settlement, and Jamestown was the first permanent English settlement (1607) to be followed by the Plymouth Colony and a continuous dominant stream of settlement until after 1870. The French (A) had explored Canada's eastern seaboard but had not established any permanent settlements in the United States Russian (C), Chinese (D), and Swiss (E) migrated to the United States in lesser, and much later, streams and headed west.

34. **C**—Mining copper is a primary economic activity that deals with extracting minerals and resources from the Earth. Assembling automotive parts (A), sewing shirts (B), binding books (D), and stamping out toy soldiers (E) are all secondary economic activities that involve turning raw materials into usable products.

35. **D**—Folklore is composed of all the superstitions, beliefs, legends, customs, and ways of interacting that are shared by a group. Folklore is oral and not part of the written tradition (A). Folklore encourage preserving the old ways and not changing them (B) or blending them (C) into one culture. Also, folklore is part of the identity of a particular culture group and is not shared by other groups who also have their own folklore.

36. **D**—French and Spanish settlement patterns are based on long-lot holdings generally ten times longer than wide. All the other settlement patterns (A), (B), (C), and (E) are based on block patterns of land survey used in their homelands in Europe.

37. **A**—The rate of natural increase is found by subtracting the crude death rates from the crude birth rate, not the other way around (B) and migrations are not included. The other answers will not give the natural rate of increase as the fertility rate has nothing to do with this statistic (D) and (E). The doubling time (C) and is not a factor in the rate of national increase.

38. **B**—Birth rates decline and population growth rate is less rapid during Stage 3 because people are beginning to take some control over the size of their families, the death rate stays low, and the population size starts to level off. The other choices (A), (C), (D), and (E) are not true of Stage 3 of the model.

39. **D**—Strict pollution regulations are not found in EPZs where regulations are lax in general. All the other conditions such as reduced tariffs on exports (A), duty-free imports (B), customs duties exemptions (C), and high-quality infrastructure (E) are all found in EPZs.

40. **C**—Transnational corporations spread their facilities and processes across several countries based on comparative advantage. They obviously will not produce goods where production costs are the highest (A) nor conduct accounting and research services in LDCs where skilled labor is in short supply (B). Most transnational companies have headquarters based in DCs near the markets for their products and not in LDCs (D) or MDCs (E).

41. **A**—Myrdal's theory of cumulative causation states that a prosperous dominant core (developed regions) exploits the depressed and much

poorer periphery (developing regions). His theory claims the core will always dominate the periphery (B) and thrive and grow at the periphery's expense (C). Regions with initial advantage will just keep growing and prospering (D) and economic improvement in one region will be at the expense of other regions (E).

42. **A**—The first zone of Burgess's concentric zone model is a zone of transition that contains the lowest-income populations, ethnic ghettos, slums, and deteriorating buildings. The second zone (B) contains workers' homes—smaller houses on small lots. The third zone (C) is comprised of better houses, higher-rent apartments, and single-family homes. The fourth zone (D) contains low-density suburban housing, and there is no fifth zone (E).

43. **C**—The third zone is comprised of better houses, higher-rent apartments and single-family homes. (A) The first zone of Burgess's concentric zone model is a zone of transition that contains the lowest-income populations, ethnic ghettos, slums, and deteriorating buildings. The second zone (B) contains workers' homes—smaller houses on small lots. The fourth zone (D) contains low-density suburban housing, and there is no fifth zone (E).

44. **D**—Transportation arteries are the basis of Hoyt's sector model of urban land use. As cities grow, they expand outward along the main streets and highways, and workers who can afford to live farther from the CBD build houses in new neighborhoods extending outward along these transportation lines. While areas of industrialization (A) and the size of the CBD (B) may contribute to the location of low-income housing, they are not the main theme of this model. Also, the proximity of rich to poor (C) is nonexistent as the rich live farthest away from the poor. In this model, the city expands in a radial fashion and not circular, as in Burgess's model (E).

45. **A**—National sports teams, flags, anthems, and holidays all serve to stimulate a sense of nationalism, while sectarianism (B), political unrest (C), functional disputes (D), and resource disputes (E), all serve to divide and splinter a state.

46. **C**—Irredentism results when the people living in one state want to annex a territory whose population contains the same ethnic group but under another state's government. Nationalism (A) is the identification with the state and the acceptance of that state's ideals. Disputes over resources (B), boundaries or positional disputes (D), or policies regarding borders, functional disputes (E) are centrifugal forces seeking to divide a state.

47. **D**—Sadly, one neighborhood's efforts to reduce pollution are rarely supported by neighboring communities. Duplication of efforts (A) and inefficiencies in provision of services (C) occur often and social problems often spill over from the central city into the neighboring suburban communities (B). Municipalities often face conflicts over land zoning issues for shopping malls (E) which are placed right up against residential neighborhoods.

48. **D**—Political party affiliation is one of the few reasons why migrants move to a new location. Migrants usually move for educational opportunities (A), in search of a more pleasant environment (B), changes in life cycle such as aging or starting a family (C), or looking for a retirement community (E).

49. **E**—Overcrowding is a push factor of migration, causing the migrant to want to move in search of more room. All the other factors—safety (A), better climate (B), better schools (C), and job opportunities (D)—are pull factors of migration.

50. **A**—The internet is actually a conductor that facilitates diffusion of culture and new ideas. Distance (B), cultural obstacles (C), government interference (D), and rough terrain such as deserts, mountains, and oceans (E) inhibit, or block, cultural diffusion from occurring.

51. **C**—Hasidic Judaism is a traditional sect of Judaism that has stayed true to its very old belief system for many years. Halloween (A) is a fusion of ancient Celtic paganism and the Christian religion. Tex Mex, Chinese food, and many other ethnic foods in the United States are a mixture of authentic ethnic cuisine and

the American taste buds (B). Catholicism, as practiced in Louisiana, is a syncretic mixture of voodoo from West Africa, French and Spanish Catholicism, Native American spiritual customs, and Masonic rituals and beliefs (D). Mahayana Buddhism is a syncretic mixture of the oldest pure form of Buddhism and many teachings absorbed along the way (E).

52. **B**—Distance decay is the concept that you will visit nearby friends more often than distant ones, travel the shortest distance to find groceries, and use the closest cafeteria for meals if a college student. The gravity concept (B) states that bigger places possess a stronger attraction to us than do smaller ones. Complementarity (C) is the idea that two places only interact if one place has the supply another place seeks. Transferability (D) is the concept that spatial interaction occurs only when acceptable costs and time needs are met. Movement bias (E) is any aggregate predictability of flow in spatial interactions.

53. **E**—Movement bias is shown in a large shopping mall because a large flow of shoppers is already visiting the mall, making it an attractive location for other stores. The gravity concept (A) states that bigger places possess a stronger attraction to us than do smaller ones. Distance decay (B) is the concept that you will visit nearby friends more often than distant ones, travel the shortest distance to find groceries, and use the closest cafeteria for meals if a college student. Complementarity (C) is the idea that two places only interact if one place has the supply another place seeks. Transferability (D) is the concept that spatial interaction occurs only when acceptable costs and time needs are met.

54. **D**—The rectangular land survey system was introduced after the United States gained independence and the rectangular township and range surveys began. Long lot (A) survey systems were introduced in areas settled by the French and Spanish in North America. The New England village (B) was established by English colonists on the Atlantic Seaboard and consisted of a central village surrounded by allocated farm lands. Metes and bounds (C) was used from Pennsylvania southward to allocate land grants based on natural features and boundaries. The agricultural village (E) is a communal farming village in utopian communities, Mormon settlements, and Canadian Mennonite communities.

55. **B**—A map projection displays a round earth on a flat map and always has distortions. A map scale (A) shows the relationship between the size of a unit on the map and the same unit on the Earth's surface. A map legend (C) tells what the symbols, colors, etc. of a map mean. Aggregation (D) and simplification (E) are terms used by cartographers when deciding what data to display on a map.

56. **C**—Adobe construction is a unique form of building that reflects the Native American and Spanish-American influences of the U.S. Southwest region. The other items—trees in the courtyard (A), lights (B), and cross (D) by the front door, and mountains in the background (E)—are reflective of other regions also.

57. **C**—Distance decay reflects the declining intensity of something as it increases in distance away from its point or origin. Push (A) and pull (B) factors of migration are factors or situations that compel a person to move. Migration selectivity (D) is the process involving the age, education, and life course changes that affect migration decisions. A migration stream (E) is a channel of migrants from a certain origin to a certain destination.

58. **B**—When a country has the number of new persons arriving through birth or migration equal to the number leaving through death or emigration, it has zero population growth. The other choices, (A), (C), (D), and (E), are not related to population growth rate.

59. **D**—Demographic momentum occurs when a population with a greater number of young people matures and progresses through the population pyramid. Zero population growth (A) occurs when a country has the same number of new persons arriving through birth or migration as leaving through death or emigration. Rapid growth rate (B) occurs in populations with large numbers of young people. The homeostatic pla-

teau (C) occurs when a population is equivalent to the carrying capacity of the land in which they live. Overpopulation (E) is a value judgment that a territory is unable to adequately support its present population.

60. **E**—A spread, or trickle-down effect, of development would result in less infrastructure in the core and more in the periphery as it slowly begins to benefit. Congestion (A), high labor costs (B), high density (C), and environmental decay (D) all occur as spread effects in the core of this model.

61. **B**—A Mercedes-Benz dealership can only be found in the largest urban centers where consumers go seeking specialized expensive goods and services. Ordinary goods and services such as those found at Winn-Dixie grocery stores (A), shoe stores (C), family doctors (D), and medical clinics (E) can be found in smaller urban centers.

62. **C**—Zoning protects homeowners from living next to sewage plants, noisy factories, and brightly lit gas stations. Malls (A), fences (B), tunnels (C), and rivers may help separate housing areas somewhat, but zoning is the legal means of protection.

63. **D**—Freeway construction increased the need for everyone to have a car to get around. Urban sprawl (A), increased traffic (B), traffic congestion (C), and the need for more freeways (E) are all by-products of the construction of freeways.

64. **B**—These terms all reflect a means of segregating people's living space. Only ethnic cleansing occurred in Nazi Germany during World War I (A), and these are certainly not ways to integrate the different ethnic populations (C) or bring about community bonding (E). These terms have different meanings although all are means of segregating the ethnic groups (D).

65. **C**—France, along with most states in the world, is a unitary state with a central government and containing a single core region and a single nation of people. Canada (A), the United States (B), People's Republic of China (D), and Brazil (E) are federal states.

66. **B**—A central government governs the country as a single unit in a unitary state—not a federal state, which has a two-tiered system of governing (A). Federal states often have a written constitution (C), and lower-levels of government have unique power (D) and their own government and budget (E).

67. **C**—Ethnonationalism in Canada is exhibited in Quebec with its dominant French-speaking population. Irredentism (A) is when a nation's homeland is partially contained within another state, and secession (B) occurs when a strong separatist movement splits away from the state. A colony (D) is any people or territory separated from but subject to a ruling power. A nation-state (E) is a state whose territorial extent coincides with that occupied by a distinct nation or people.

68. **E**—A state does not have a national language, but it DOES have an independent territory (A), internationally recognized (B), has boundaries (C), and possesses full sovereignty over the land in which the inhabitants live (D).

69. **B**—Mary is trading proximity to shopping and restaurants for privacy. A win-win (A) is a solution that does not require a trade-off. An infill (C) is the creation of a small-scale housing development in a vacant urban area. Leapfrog development (D) occurs when homeowners jump over more expensive land on the edges of urban areas to build on cheaper abundant land farther out from the city. Ecologically sensitive space (E) is fragile, rare, or valuable natural areas that can be made into parks, wilderness, or open space.

70. **C**—Locations with strong labor unions are avoided by high-tech companies because union contracts hinder innovation and hamper workforce flexibility. Proximity to major universities (A), research facilities (B) locally available venture capital (D), and excellent available communication and transportation networks (E) are all positive motivators for high-tech to locate in the area.

71. **E**—A tolerant populace who do not mind change would not be a barrier to the diffusion of a cultural trait. Cultural barriers to change such

as language (A) and religion (B) and economic factors (D) can slow a new cultural trait from diffusing into a group. Physical barriers such as mountains, deserts, and oceans (E) also slow the diffusion of cultural traits.

72. **C**—A functional region has spatially-based interactions so the market area of Winn-Dixie denotes the customers who shop and interact there. Dixie (A), and the Pacific Northwest (D) are perceptual or vernacular regions which reflect how people view their spatial world. Pennsylvania (B) is a formal region with firm boundaries wherein certain laws and regulations apply uniformly and the Bible Belt (E) is a formal region that reflects uniformity in religious characteristics.

73. **E**—Our mental map is the information and images about our location that are stored in our brain to help us get around in our world. We usually would not need a Rand-McNally Road Atlas (A), world globe (B), road map (C), or GIS (D) to get to school in the morning!

74. **B**—The country's actual population in numbers is not found in the population pyramid—it is found in census data. The population pyramid is a predictive tool that displays a visual picture of a country's future social spending needs for the very old and the very young (A). It also displays the impact of wars (C), the age-sex information (D), and the impact of baby booms and external migrations on a population (E).

75. **C**—China is among the top 10 producers of several major industrial products and has many natural resources, a huge labor force, and an enormous market for goods (B). Japan lacks natural resources for industry (A), and Taiwan (D) and Singapore (E) are two of the "four tigers"—rapidly industrializing countries of East Asia.

Explanations for Section II (Free-Response Questions)

Question 1 (8 points total)

1A. (2 points)
- Popular culture—acceptable way of life for majority of population, mass production and consumption of goods and services, constantly changing, diffuses rapidly and is globalized, widespread dissemination of common tastes, preferences, and items.
- Folk culture—traditional, smaller groups who are geographically and/or socially isolated from larger society in which they live, slow to change, resistance to change, individuality, and distinctiveness.

1B. (2 points)
Examples in "built" environment:
- Popular culture—waste that is not biodegradable (Styrofoam, plastics). Pollution of air, water, soil.
- Folk culture—erosion, overuse of soil, overhunting of some species, pollution of water by animal waste.

1C. (4 points)

Question 2 (6 points total)

2A. (1 point)
Spatially variable costs influence locational cost and are the extra costs to overcome distance, attract labor, buy a plant site, etc.

2B. (4 points)
Examples include:

- Transportation of raw materials
- Transportation of finished products
- Labor costs
- Real estate prices of land for plant site
- Power supplies

2C. (1 points)
The least total cost location is likely to lead to profit maximization because the lower your costs of production, the greater your profits will be.

Question 3 (7 points total)

3A. (1 point)
Land survey is a way of claiming and allocating land by a charter group.

3B. (4 points)
The answers below are correct—any two of these are required for full credit.
- Nucleated villages and fragmented farms—New England—English settlers
- Metes-and-bounds—Pennsylvania southward, based on landscape features
- Township-and-range rectangular—rectangular divisions of land into townships, Land Ordinance of 1785
- Long lots—French and Spanish, closely spaced, long narrow lots fronting the river or water body, St Lawrence River Valley first

3C. (2 points)
The answers below are correct—any one of these are required for full credit. Must be specific in location and refer to original settlement group.
- New England villages like villages in England where settlers originated
- Agricultural villages—Mormon settlements, utopian and early religious communities in CA, NY, IN, Spanish American Southwest, Mennonites in Manitoba, Canada brought village concept from homeland Ukraine and Russia
- French long lots introduced first into St. Lawrence River Valley by French settlers, then into Mississippi River Valley, Detroit, Louisiana, French Quebec, etc.
- Spanish long lots—Rio Grande Valley of Texas and New Mexico
- Metes-and-bounds—Pennsylvania and south—royal land grants—England

5 Minutes to a 5

180 Activities and Questions in

5 Minutes a Day

Check off each activity as it is completed.

1. ☐	46. ☐	91. ☐	136. ☐
2. ☐	47. ☐	92. ☐	137. ☐
3. ☐	48. ☐	93. ☐	138. ☐
4. ☐	49. ☐	94. ☐	139. ☐
5. ☐	50. ☐	95. ☐	140. ☐
6. ☐	51. ☐	96. ☐	141. ☐
7. ☐	52. ☐	97. ☐	142. ☐
8. ☐	53. ☐	98. ☐	143. ☐
9. ☐	54. ☐	99. ☐	144. ☐
10. ☐	55. ☐	100. ☐	145. ☐
11. ☐	56. ☐	101. ☐	146. ☐
12. ☐	57. ☐	102. ☐	147. ☐
13. ☐	58. ☐	103. ☐	148. ☐
14. ☐	59. ☐	104. ☐	149. ☐
15. ☐	60. ☐	105. ☐	150. ☐
16. ☐	61. ☐	106. ☐	151. ☐
17. ☐	62. ☐	107. ☐	152. ☐
18. ☐	63. ☐	108. ☐	153. ☐
19. ☐	64. ☐	109. ☐	154. ☐
20. ☐	65. ☐	110. ☐	155. ☐
21. ☐	66. ☐	111. ☐	156. ☐
22. ☐	67. ☐	112. ☐	157. ☐
23. ☐	68. ☐	113. ☐	158. ☐
24. ☐	69. ☐	114. ☐	159. ☐
25. ☐	70. ☐	115. ☐	160. ☐
26. ☐	71. ☐	116. ☐	161. ☐
27. ☐	72. ☐	117. ☐	162. ☐
28. ☐	73. ☐	118. ☐	163. ☐
29. ☐	74. ☐	119. ☐	164. ☐
30. ☐	75. ☐	120. ☐	165. ☐
31. ☐	76. ☐	121. ☐	166. ☐
32. ☐	77. ☐	122. ☐	167. ☐
33. ☐	78. ☐	123. ☐	168. ☐
34. ☐	79. ☐	124. ☐	169. ☐
35. ☐	80. ☐	125. ☐	170. ☐
36. ☐	81. ☐	126. ☐	171. ☐
37. ☐	82. ☐	127. ☐	172. ☐
38. ☐	83. ☐	128. ☐	173. ☐
39. ☐	84. ☐	129. ☐	174. ☐
40. ☐	85. ☐	130. ☐	175. ☐
41. ☐	86. ☐	131. ☐	176. ☐
42. ☐	87. ☐	132. ☐	177. ☐
43. ☐	88. ☐	133. ☐	178. ☐
44. ☐	89. ☐	134. ☐	179. ☐
45. ☐	90. ☐	135. ☐	180. ☐

Day 1

Draw a line from each concept to its brief description.

Space   An area that displays a common trait

Place   The degree of generalization on a map

Scale   The extent of area that is occupied by something

Regions   Another word for location.

Day 2

1:500,00 is an example of a(n) _____ when referring to scale.

Day 3

Draw a line from each example of a region to the type of region.

Winn-Dixie grocery store   Formal region

Bible Belt   Functional region

French-speaking region of Canada   Perceptual (vernacular) region

Day 4

Which of the following three choices make up a cultural landscape?

(A)   Houses

(B)   Bridges

(C)   Rivers

(D)   Climate

(E)   Mountains

(F)   Highways

Day 5

Most demographers agree that future world population growth will occur in
_____ countries.

(A) developed

(B) developing

(C) undeveloped

The crude birth rate (CBR) of a country refers to the number of live births

(A)   per 100,000 population.

(B)   per 10,000 population.

(C)   per 1,000 population.

(D)   per 500,000 population.

Day 7

The key result of neo-Malthusianism has been

(A)   increased spending in food stamp programs.

(B)   increased total fertility rates.

(C)   famine relief.

(D)   government programs for birth control and planning.

In the demographic transition model, Stages 4 and 5 are characterized by the following demographic factor:

(A) high birth rates.

(B) high mortality rates.

(C) zero population growth.

(D) high sex ratios.

Day 9

Population pressure on agricultural land is typically expressed as

(A) physiological density.

(B) crude density.

(C) arithmetic density.

(D) rate of natural increase.

The population statistic that tells us the level of fertility at which a population will have just enough births to replace parents and compensate for early deaths is the

(A)   crude birth rate.

(B)   crude death rate.

(C)   total fertility rate.

(D)   replacement level.

Day 11

Which three of the following place characteristics would probably produce low population densities?

(A) Very remote

(B) Infertile land

(C) Moderate climate

(D) Coastlines

(E) Water scarcity

(F) Mineral resources

A population with large amounts of reproduction would have a _____ fertility rate, but might still have a low crude birth rate if most of the population were male or very young or very old.

Day 13

The changes in healthcare availability have had the greatest impact on this age group: _____.

As a rule, developing countries tend to have _____ rates of natural increase than more developed countries, generating a faster population growth in the developing countries.

Day 15

The rate of natural increase is found by subtracting the crude death rate from the
_____.

Day 16

The first stage of the demographic transition is marked by

(A)   low birth rates, low death rates.

(B)   declining birth rate, declining death rate.

(C)   high birth rates, high but fluctuating death rates.

(D)   high birth rates, declining death rates.

Day 17

Rapid increases in life expectancy are characteristic of which stage of the demographic transition?

(A) First
(B) Second
(C) Third
(D) Fourth

Day 18

Which of the following can be considered the chief cause for "missing females" in the world today?

(A) Poverty

(B) Underdevelopment

(C) Poor nutrition

(D) Cultural norms and practices

Day 19

Check out the United States and world population in real time. Look at the births, deaths, and migration statistics as they change in seconds. Note the top ten most populous countries at https://www.census.gov/popclock/.

Day 20

Which three of the following statements are E. G. Ravenstein's migration principles? Most migrants

(A)   move long distances.

(B)   move in steps or stages.

(C)   move from cities to rural areas.

(D)   move from rural areas to cities.

(E)   are adults.

(F)   settle in rural farmlands.

Draw a line from each type of migrant to its matching description.

Immigrant

A person forced out of the home region but does not cross any international boundaries

Emigrant

A person who resides outside the country of origin because of fear of persecution due to religion, political beliefs, ethnicity, or race

Refugee

A person who enters another country to make a new home there

Internally displaced person

A person who leaves one country intending to live in a different country

Migrants who enter a country to fill a need for labor are called _____
_____.

The theory that educated workers often migrate from poor countries to wealthy countries seeking better-paying jobs is called the _____.

Marriage, having children, and divorce are examples of decisions that affect migration according to the _____ theory of migration.

Day 25

The smallest distinctive item of culture is called a culture

(A) sociofact.

(B) complex.

(C) barrier.

(D) trait.

When one culture group undergoes a major change by adopting the characteristics of another dominant group, it has experienced

(A)   globalization.

(B)   assimilation.

(C)   transculturation.

(D)   acculturation.

Day 27

Which of the following is the most important medium for transmitting culture?

(A)   Legislation
(B)   Innovation
(C)   Language
(D)   Elementary school

Day 28

Check out your own community by typing in your zip code in the box on this United States Census Bureau "American FactFinder" website. Look at the total population, ethnic composition, housing characteristics by age, sex, race, etc., and many more interesting and fun facts at https://factfinder.census.gov/faces/nav/jsf/pages/index.xhtml.

Native American development of writing because of exposure to European American settlers making marks on a piece of paper in early American history is an example of

(A)   relocation diffusion.

(B)   expansion diffusion.

(C)   stimulus diffusion.

(D)   independent invention.

Day 30

The process of merging the cultural traits of two or more cultures in religion, foods, etc., is called

(A) syncretism.

(B) sociofact.

(C) diffusion.

(D) innovation.

Day 31

The world's oldest religion is

(A) Buddhism.
(B) Islam.
(C) Hinduism.
(D) Christianity.

Day 32

Visit this website: http://nativelands.org

This website deals with biological and cultural diversity in Latin America.

Draw a line from the term to its correct definition.

Assimilation   Increasing interconnection of all world regions

Acculturation   An equal exchange of traits between two cultures occurs

Globalization   A process in which immigrants become completely absorbed
                      and immersed in the host culture

Syncretism   Two or more culture traits blending to create a new culture trait

Transculturation   The process of adopting some of the cultural traits, values, and
                      behaviors of the host culture

Day 34

The dietary restriction of eating pork for a Muslim is an example of a cultural barrier called a(n) _____.

Which three of the following statements about culture hearths is true?

(A)   They were rural based.

(B)   They were urban-centered.

(C)   They were a place where innovations began and diffused outward to other regions.

(D)   The Mississippi River Valley is an example of a culture hearth.

(E)   Agriculture and trade were important factors in every culture hearth.

(F)   New ideas from surrounding hearths diffused inward to most culture hearths.

Watch the 15-minute PBS video "India: The Missing Girls: A Society out of Balance" at http://www.pbs.org/frontlineworld/rough/2007/04/the_missing_gir.html.

This video is about northern India's preference for sons, female feticide, and dowry. Think about the possible effects of gender preference practices on India's society.

In a country with many different spoken languages, a language that is agreed upon as a "language of business and trade" is called a(n) _____ _____.

Day 38

Put on your tourist hat and grab your camera! Browse Geobeats at http://www .geobeats.com and check out the video tours of places all over the world.

Day 39

Draw a line from each religion to a fact about that religion.

Christianity   A religion where one special person is believed to have special powers

Shamanism   The rejection of all religious beliefs

Secularism   The belief that spirits live insides rocks, trees, and other similar objects

Animism   A universalizing religion

Day 40

_____ is the oldest religion of the three monotheistic religions.

Day 41

Draw a line from each term to its best matching statement.

Hinduism   On the rapid rise in Europe today

Judaism   A religion that does not believe in worshipping gods but
                  instead in seeking truth

Secularism   A monotheistic religion with two main branches and a creed
                  of Five Pillars

Islam   A polytheistic religion that spread worldwide through
                  relocation diffusion

Buddhism   An ethnic religion and the oldest of the three monotheistic
                  world religions

Day 42

Visit this website at https://tud09156.files.wordpress.com/2013/06/p1030925.jpg

Check out the photo of an ethnic enclave in Cleveland, Ohio. Its toponym is a hint at the minority cultural group that settled there.

Day 43

Which two of the following statements describe a folk culture?

(A)   Watch lots of TV

(B)   Embrace mass media

(C)   Very influenced by cultural change

(D)   Independent of cultural mainstream

(E)   Self-sufficient in many ways and very family-centered

Day 44

The concept that successive societies leave their cultural imprints on a place is called
_____ _____.

The land survey method brought to the United States by English settlers that used natural boundaries such as rivers, trees, and large rocks as boundary markers is called _____.

A group of people with a common history and culture who occupy an area is called a(n)

    (A)   state.

    (B)   nation.

    (C)   country.

    (D)   nation-state.

Day 47

Which of the following is NOT an example of a compact state?

(A) Uruguay
(B) Philippines
(C) Laos
(D) Zimbabwe

Which of the following political state shapes might be the most efficient for communication and transportation?

(A)   Compact

(B)   Elongated

(C)   Prorupt

(D)   Fragmented

Which of the following state capitals is NOT a forward-thrust capital?

(A)   Brasilia, Brazil

(B)   Astana, Kazakhstan

(C)   Abuja, Nigeria

(D)   Berlin, Germany

Day 50

Match the term with the best descriptive statement below.

Relic boundary   A boundary forced upon existing boundaries as in Africa by European powers

Superimposed boundary   The Great Wall of China is an example of this boundary

Antecedent boundary   Boundaries imposed after cultural landscape is in place

Subsequent boundary   Boundaries imposed very early in settlement before cultural landscape developed

Day 51

A group of people with a common culture who occupy a territory and are linked by shared customs and beliefs is called a

- (A) country.
- (B) colony.
- (C) nation.
- (D) state.

Day 52

The part of a country that is located within another country's territory is called that country's

(A) enclave.
(B) colony.
(C) exclave.
(D) CBD.

Pledging allegiance to the U.S. flag is an example of

(A) centrifugal force.

(B) centripetal force.

(C) terrorism.

(D) unpatriotic behavior.

A minority group within a state that seeks to govern itself partially or totally is called a(n) _____ group.

    (A)   supranational

    (B)   nationalist

    (C)   terrorist

    (D)   separatist

Day 55

View this interactive website of maps of the world at https://www.mapsofworld.com/
thematic-maps/types-of-governments.html. As you hover your "mouse" over each
country, you can see its type of government, head of state, and head of government.

Day 56

The process of redrawing territorial district boundaries to benefit a particular political party is called _____.

Day 57

According to the von Thunen model, the most important determinant of the location of agricultural production is the

(A)   demand at the consuming center.

(B)   soil fertility of the production zone.

(C)   distance between the consuming center and the production site.

(D)   development of intervening opportunity.

Source: http://cultivatinghealthyplaces.files.wordpress.com/2012/08/dsc_00362.jpg

In the photo of urban subsistence farming above, which three processes are probably occurring?

(A)   Waste and garbage recycled as fertilizer

(B)   Help farmers feed families

(C)   Increasing need for waste disposal

(D)   Formerly unused land is being cultivated

Day 59

Which of the following situations is NOT usually a part of agribusiness or contract farming?

- (A) Wheat with a minimum protein content
- (B) Broiler chickens of a specified age and weight
- (C) Cattle fed to an exact weight
- (D) Certainty of growing season

When farmers cut down natural vegetation, burn it, and plant crops in the soil, choose three names for this practice below.

- (A) Intensive subsistence
- (B) Swidden
- (C) Plantation
- (D) Shifting cultivation
- (E) Slash-and-burn

The wandering but controlled movement of flocks and herds is called

(A)   slash-and-burn.
(B)   intensive subsistence.
(C)   shifting cultivation.
(D)   nomadic herding.

The most important factor in producing a plantation crop is

(A) time.
(B) money.
(C) climate.
(D) connections.

Draw a line to best connect each form of agriculture with the statement that applies.

Intensive subsistence agriculture   Small city gardens that supply the poor with food

Subsistence agriculture   Animal herding in a seasonal migratory pattern

Pastoralism   Heavy inputs of fertilizer and human labor producing generous crops on small acreage

Urban subsistence farming   The consumption of everything that is grown

Day 64

The evolution from a single farm to the integrated production and marketing partner-ship model is called _____.

Intensive subsistence agriculture is depicted by

(A)   high yields per unit of cultivated land.

(B)   high first-year yields, followed by production declines and land abandonment.

(C)   equal emphasis on crops and animals.

(D)   farms that specialize in producing a single crop.

Day 66

The Green Revolution

(A)   has made traditional peasant agricultural practices more secure and scientific.

(B)   has initiated a reverse flow of population from urban slums to newly productive lands.

(C)   refers to rebellions by developing world peasants angry about globalization.

(D)   increases output using high-yielding crop varieties and altered management practices.

Source: http://designpublic.in/blogs/wp-content/uploads/2013/07/BL16_01_
PEPSICO_1300228f.jpg

Regarding the above photo depicting contract farming in India, which of the following statements is probably true?

(A)   Contract farming sponsors provide material input, give technical advice, and buy all produce.

(B)   Contract farming provides farmers with access to reliable markets.

(C)   Contract farming gives farmers equal power in the relationship.

(D)   Contract farming gives farmers access to credit.

Day 68

Visit the website "The Good, The Bad, and The Ugly!" at http://carrington.edu/blog/student-tips/health/genetically-modified-food-pros-and-cons/ to learn more about GMOs (genetically modified foods).

Source: https://www.nrcs.usda.gov/Internet/FSE_MEDIA/nrcs144p2_021116.jpg

Which of the following conservation agricultural practices is shown in the photo above?

(A) Desertification

(B) Crop rotation

(C) Swidden

(D) Overgrazing

Day 70

Visit Urban Observatory at http://www.urbanobservatory.org/. It is interactive and allows you to compare and contrast maps of cities all over the world.

Which three of the following are considered primary economic activities?

(A)   Financial consulting

(B)   Agriculture

(C)   Hunting

(D)   Mining

Day 72

_____ economic activities are those that add value to materials by changing them into more useful products.

(A) Primary

(B) Secondary

(C) Tertiary

(D) Quaternary

(E) Quinary

Day 73

Which three of the following activities are tertiary economic activities?

(A) Fishing
(B) Banking
(C) Retail
(D) Mining
(E) Accounting

Day 74

Check out Google Maps at https://www.google.com/maps/about/treks/#/grid to see street views of remote and exotic places like Mt. Everest, the Great Barrier Reef, Amazon Basin, and many more!

Day 75

The most developed economies, also known as the industrial economies, remain the core in the core-periphery model of economic development and produce _____ of world export.

(A)   10%

(B)   30%

(C)   50%

(D)   75%

(E)   90%

Which three factors are partially responsible for reducing the core-periphery contrasts in productivity since the 1950s?

(A) Industrialization

(B) Neocolonialism

(C) Expanding world trade

(D) Technology transfers

(E) Shortage of raw materials on world markets

Day 77

Write the stages of development below for a traditional society over time using Rostow's Model of Economic Development. The first stage has been done for you.

Traditional society _____

_____

_____

_____

_____

Day 78

In the activity for day 77, which of the stages involves the development of a transportation system? _____

In the activity for day 77, which of the stages shows rapid urbanization as transportation systems and manufacturing growth? _____

Match the theory or model below with its *basic* belief.

Wallerstein's world systems theory   The core depends on the periphery to exist.

Rostow's model of economic development   Dynamic flow between core, semi-periphery, and periphery economies

Andre Frank's dependency theory   Modernization is the key to economic development

Complete the following chart of the three main expenses that must be minimized in locating an industry below based on Alfred Weber's least-cost theory. Place the MOST important expense at the top of the chart.

Assembly line production of like goods by a specialized labor force is called

   (A)   multiplier.

   (B)   footloose.

   (C)   deglomeration effect.

   (D)   fordism.

Day 83

Watch this short interactive video by Gapminder World to see if the U.N.'s Millennium Development Goal 4—a reduction of child mortality—has occurred at https://www.gapminder.org/videos/reducing-child-mortality-a-moral-and-environmental-imperative/.

Day 84

Check out the YouTube video series *Geography Now* at https://www.youtube.com/watch?v=868K4Iq8Z-g to learn about countries of the world in entertaining presentations with maps, photos, and a young and interesting narrator!

Match each world region with the best statement that applies.

Western Europe Early emphasis on water power freed region from dependence on England

Eastern Europe The "4 Tigers" have led this region to become one of the most productive in world

Eastern Asia Undergoing a deindustrialization with massive layoffs in iron and coal mining

Anglo America Centralized industrial planning led to a disconnect from market realities

Women's increased participation in the workforce globally has resulted from

- (A) strict attitudes toward lending women money for business start-ups.
- (B) public policies are more favorable for child care, etc.
- (C) increased opportunities for education and employment.
- (D) greater control over their fertility.
- (E) lack of economic growth.

Day 87

Check out this interactive map and collection of short articles by the nonprofit organization, The Fund for Peace at http://fundforpeace.org/fsi/. Learn what countries are the most fragile in terms of their political stability, global connections and alliances, and how this all relates to world peace.

The world's first cities relied most heavily on the formation of

(A) fortified city walls.

(B) agricultural surpluses.

(C) fearless armies.

(D) religion.

The earliest cities shared which four of the following characteristics?

(A)   Close to factories and worker housing

(B)   Focused on the marketplace

(C)   Surrounded by walls

(D)   Located on waterways

(E)   Centered on the temple or palace

The relative location of a settlement in relation to the cultural and physical geography of its surroundings is called its

(A) hinterland.

(B) site.

(C) situation.

(D) sense of place.

Day 91

Watch this YouTube video at https://www.youtube.com/watch?t=23&v=XvfeOD 46M0w about the gentrification process in Cincinnati, Ohio and see how it challenges the old mantra of the rich buying out the poor.

_____ migration is the movement of people from the countryside to the city to find better jobs and a better life.

Draw a line from each term to its correct definition.

Megalopolis   Self-sufficient suburban cities that contain industry, offices, and residential communities

Supercity   A city more than twice as large as the next largest city and far more important

Gateway city   A metropolitan area with a total population of over 10 million people

Primate city   A city established as a control center for colonial powers

Edge city   A very large city

Day 94

An almost unbroken succession of urban development stretching north from Boston to south of Washington, D.C., is called the

- (A) central place.
- (B) megalopolis.
- (C) hamlet.
- (D) megacity.

The theory that the second-largest city in a national urban system will be half the size of the largest is called the

(A)   central place theory.

(B)   multiple-nuclei model.

(C)   Latin American city model.

(D)   rank-size rule.

Day 96

Goods and services produced by city employees for export outside the city are part of the

(A) urban hierarchy.

(B) basic economic sector.

(C) hinterlands.

(D) nonbasic economic sector.

The opening of a new bank within a city adds both basic and nonbasic jobs to the economy through the

(A) central place theory.

(B) rank-size rule.

(C) urban hierarchy.

(D) multiplier effect.

Day 98

Visit this website, https://www.purposegames.com/games?t=484&so=mp, to play free map review games. Remember—good map knowledge is essential to doing well on the exam.

The idea that cities exist for economic reasons and people collect in them to share goods and services is called

(A)   central place theory.

(B)   urban hierarchy theory.

(C)   rank-size rule.

(D)   multiple-nuclei model.

Day 100

Which two of the following statements is true per Christaller's central place theory?

(A) Smaller central places serve people from far-off places generally.

(B) People will be willing to travel farther to obtain luxury goods than basic goods.

(C) The system of towns is interdependent.

(D) Many more large towns than small towns exist.

Day 101

View the website *Visualizing Density*, "Building Blocks: A Density Game" from the Lincoln Institute of Land Policy at http://www.lincolninst.edu/subcenters/visualizing -density/blockgame/index.aspx.

Do you have a future as an urban planner? Let's see! (You will need to create a free profile on this website before you can access the items in the index on the left of the home page.) Before you play the Density Game, you need to click on and read "The Density Problem," "Bird's-eye View," and take the quiz "How Dense Are You?" Then build your neighborhood according to the game. Let's see if urban planning is a possible future career for you!

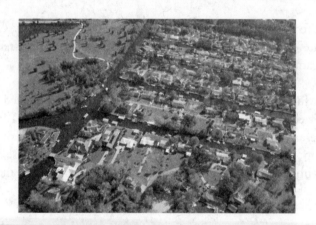

The main theme of human geography depicted in this photograph is

(A)   cultural diversity.

(B)   agriculture.

(C)   urban sprawl.

(D)   migration.

(E)   linguistic diversity.

Day 103

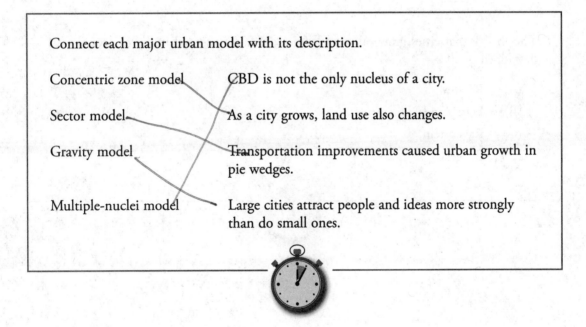

Connect each major urban model with its description.

Concentric zone model   CBD is not the only nucleus of a city.

Sector model   As a city grows, land use also changes.

Gravity model   Transportation improvements caused urban growth in pie wedges.

Multiple-nuclei model   Large cities attract people and ideas more strongly than do small ones.

5 Minutes to a 5

The theory that cities grow outward from a core using several nodes of growth was developed by

(A)   Rostow.

(B)   Harris and Ullmann.

(C)   Ravenstein.

(D)   Burgess.

Which geographer viewed the U.S. urban community of the 1920s as a set of concentric rings radiating outward from a central core?

(A)   Burgess

(B)   Rostow

(C)   Harris and Ullmann

(D)   Ravenstein

The amount of urban growth is

(A)   the same on every continent.

(B)   less than the amount of rural growth.

(C)   rising in most countries.

(D)   mostly occurring in highly developed regions.

Which three of the following are problems often encountered by many urban multi-cultural migrants?

(A)   Poverty

(B)   Minority segregation

(C)   Growing labor pool

(D)   Isolation

The greatest growth in urban areas will occur in

(A)　North America.

(B)　Sub-Saharan Africa.

(C)　Western Europe.

(D)　Australia.

Which three of the following occur in developing countries because of rapid urban expansion?

(A)   Deterioration of environment

(B)   Inadequate transportation

(C)   Housing shortages

(D)   High employment

The productive area surrounding a population center is called its

(A)   metropolis.

(B)   inner city.

(C)   central place.

(D)   hinterland.

Day 111

Latin American cities focus heavily on the (central/outer) _____ part of the city with transportation systems leading to (center city/outer) _____.

Slums and squatter settlements are called _____ or _____ and are found in the outer edges of the Latin American city.

East European cities, land use and architecture are heavily influenced by the
_____ era.

Day 114

Match the city type with its corresponding characteristic.

East European   Lack urban sprawl and suburbs

West European   Large central square with government and cultural
                       buildings

United States   Lack even basic sanitation and clean water

Sub-Saharan African   Low-income inhabitants in inner-city slums

Day 115

Check out this website, http://theplaceswelive.com/, for a look at the places we live!

Day 116

Which four of the following are problems for the rapidly growing cities of LDCs?

- (A) Lack of enough jobs
- (B) Shortage of clean drinking water
- (C) Housing shortages
- (D) Inadequate sanitation services
- (E) Too many aid workers

Day 117

Cities in developing countries that were built as religious centers are heavily influenced by _____.

Day 118

Visit this website, http://metrocosm.com/global-migration-map.html, to see a neat interactive real-time migration map of the world. Notice the speed, size, and composition of the migration paths. Hover your mouse over the colored circles to see the net migration number for that country.

Day 119

Modernized cities in the developing world usually take on _____ (Eastern or Western) characteristics. Circle the correct answer in parentheses.

Day 120

Land use in cities in the developing world is based on the chief purpose of the city.

True

False

Cities in the developing world produce a small amount of their country's gross domestic income (GDI).

True

False

Workers who produce goods and services for people outside the city are part of the
_____ (basic/non-basic) sector of the economy. They produce an income
flow of new money _____ (into/out of) the city.

5 Minutes to a 5

348 ›

Day 123

Workers who produce goods and services for people employed in the city (do/do not) generate an income flow into the city.

Basic jobs generate a healthier and more prosperous economic base for the city.

True

False

Visit http://agtr.ilri.cgiar.org/index.php?option=com_content&view=article&id=46&Itemid=66 to see the world density and distribution of livestock. Cows, pigs, chickens, goats, sheep, and even buffalo! Which animals are most widely distributed? Think about the food they eat and the climate where they are found and draw some conclusions. What religious food taboos are practiced in regions where certain animals are prevalent? Scarce?

The rehabilitation of old, run-down inner-city neighborhoods by middle and high-income people is called

- (A) suburbanization.
- (B) gentrification.
- (C) multiplier effect.
- (D) urbanization.
- (E) urban influence zones.

Which of the following is NOT a characteristic of a city in the developing world?

(A)   Modern centers of commerce

(B)   Surrounded by high-density squatter settlements

(C)   Experiencing large in-migrations of rural people into the city

(D)   Well-developed infrastructure

(E)   Produce a large share of their country's GDI

(F)   Possess modern, vibrant city centers and elite residential housing

Day 128

_____ _____ is an urban design movement in the United States that emphasizes creation of a sense of community.

New Urbanism promotes less dependence on _____ for transportation and seeks to reduce environmental pollution.

Urban renewal describes the process of locating and clearing run-down inner-city properties so private investors or public entities can rebuild the neighborhoods.

True
False

Day 131

_____ _____ is government-built and regulated low-income housing.

_____ refers to the concentration of a group of residents in a certain residential area of a city by social discrimination or legal means.

A large complex of office and commercial land use with more jobs than residents is a(n)

- (A) gated community.
- (B) primate city.
- (C) suburb.
- (D) edge city.
- (E) town.

Which urban model posits that high-rent residential areas grow outward from the center of the city along major highways with lower-rent inhabitants taking over successively?

(A)   Sector model

(B)   Central place model

(C)   Urban realms model

(D)   Concentric zone model

(E)   Multiple-nuclei model

The model where cities grow outward from a core utilizing several nodes of growth was developed by

(A)   Ravenstein.

(B)   Burgess.

(C)   von Thunen.

(D)   Hoyt.

(E)   Harris and Ullmann.

Day 136

Watch CityWorks (x)po 2011's video "Part 1: How Did We Get Here?" at https://vimeo .com/37039213.

Kennedy Smith gives us an overview of why CBDs in American cities declined over the past few decades.

Which category would this scene best fit? Folk culture or pop culture?

Rain gardens, green roofs, and active solar systems are associated with _____ _____ or sustainable building.

Day 139

The remainder of these items (139–180) are review for the exam, websites, videos, YouTubes, and questions based on graphics, maps, and photos.

---

http://www.purposegames.com/games (You can search for what you're looking for.)

Want to review for the AP Exam? Go to this website and search for any topic you want to practice. These are fun map-learning games that will help you learn places and locations. This will help in writing the FRQs!

Day 140

http://www.yourchildlearns.com/map-puzzles.htm

Check out this website for lots of map practice. You will learn your maps by playing with puzzles. Fun!

Day 141

http://www.lizardpoint.com/fun/geoquiz/

This is a great review website. You can make your own quizzes for review for the exam. There are also ready-made quizzes to check your knowledge. Remember—review, review, review!

http://freerice.com/category (choose the Geography category)

Try this game to review *and* help others. This review game gives 10 grains of rice to a needy child for each answer you get correct!

Day 143

http://www.cdc.gov/dhdsp/maps/gisx/resources/maps4.html

To review your knowledge of maps, go to this page at the Centers for Disease Control. This site gives description, uses, and examples of various thematic maps.

Day 144

http://www.indexmundi.com/map/?t=0&v=67&r=xx&l=en

Try out Index Mundi—a great site of human geography maps based on the CIA's *The World Fact Book*. You can create your own map, too!

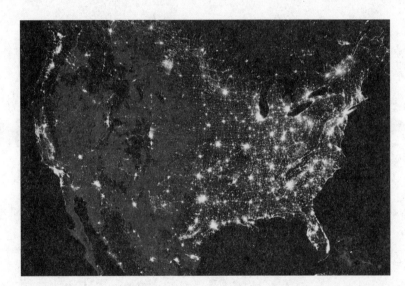

Source: http://www.publicdomainpictures.net/pictures/190000/velka/usa-city-lights.jpg

From analyzing the lights from various cities in the United States at night in this satellite image, which three of the following responses are correct?

(A) The Rocky Mountain region in the West is more sparsely populated than the East Coast.

(B) The U.S.–Mexico border region is heavily populated.

(C) There are many moderate-sized urban areas east of the Mississippi River.

(D) The Gulf Coastal region is sparsely populated and lacks any major urban areas.

(E) The Megalopolis is quite evident in this image.

A U S T R A L I A

Source: http://ian.macky.net/pat/map/au/au_blu4.gif

When analyzing the map of Australia above, what three facts are readily obvious to a geographer?

(A) The Tropic of Cancer bisects Australia.

(B) Railroads are an important part of Australia's transportation system.

(C) It is approximately 250 miles from Perth to Kalgoorlie.

(D) Australia is south of the equator.

A F R I C A · A F R I Q U E

Source: http://ian.macky.net/pat/map/afri/afri.html

When a geographer analyzes the map above, which of the following pairs is correct?

(A) Democratic Republic of the Congo—fragmented state

(B) South Africa—perforated state

(C) Namibia—land-locked state

(D) Somalia—compact state

(E) Zimbabwe—elongated state

Source: http://www.dkpblog.com/2012_10_01_archive.html

The neighborhood in the figure above represents a New Urbanism community. Which three of the following characteristics are accurate for this type of urban design?

(A) An emphasis on many streets and roads

(B) Mixed residential housing

(C) Squares and parks for maximized contact with neighbors

(D) Retail outlets and stores, restaurants, etc., are not permitted in the housing zones

(E) Sidewalks and closer placement of homes and shops to reduce dependency on cars

Watch Jeff Speck's TED Talk video on "The Walkable City" for more information about New Urbanism at https://www.ted.com/talks/jeff_speck_the_walkable_city.

"The Walkable City," Jeff Speck, TED, September 2013.

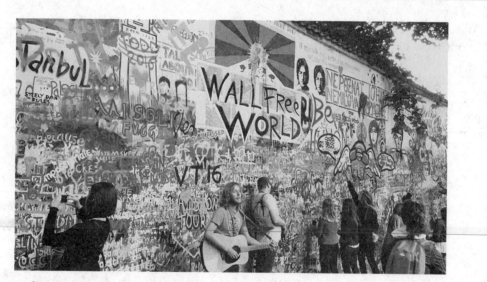

Source: https://pixabay.com/en/graffiti-popular-culture-lennon-wall-1634518/

The image above shows the Lennon Wall in Prague. This wall covered in colorful graffiti is an example of

- (A) traditional culture.
- (B) New Urbanism.
- (C) pop culture.
- (D) placelessness.

Source: https://www.dreamstime.com/stock-photos-meenakshi-hindu-temple-madu-rai-india-tamil-nadu-image31731623

The photo above depicts a place of worship in the _____ religion.

(A)   Roman Catholic

(B)   Muslim

(C)   Jewish

(D)   Hindu

(E)   Buddhist

Source: https://upload.wikimedia.org/wikipedia/commons/thumb/d/d1/Rok2.jpg/
375px-Rok2.jpg

Geographer D. W. Meinig believed there are three symbolic landscapes in the United
States. Which landscape does the photo above represent?

(A)   New England Village

(B)   Main Street

(C)   Southern California suburb

(D)   East Coast city

Source: https://upload.wikimedia.org/wikipedia/commons/d/d1/Serra_de_
Tramuntana_-_8.jpg

In the photo above, what three cultural features would a geographer find?

(A)   Land use

(B)   Dietary restrictions

(C)   Language spoken

(D)   Population and settlement

(D)   Transportation

Source: https://en.wikipedia.org/wiki/Romani_people_in_Croatia#/media/
File:Bundesarchiv_Bild_183-2004-0203-502,_Bei_Agram,_kroatische_Sinti_und_
Roma-Frauen_und_Kinder.jpg

The Romani (Roma, gypsy) people of Europe shown in the photo above are an example of a _____ without a state or political territory of their own.

   (A)   colony

   (B)   nation

   (C)   nation-state

   (D)   enclave

   (E)   exclave

5 Minutes to a 5

http://world-geography-games.com/

Go to the website to acquire good basic physical geography to complement and expand your knowledge of AP human geography.

Explore all the topics except "Earth," "Atmosphere," and "Flags." This knowledge is especially helpful in answering the FRQs on the AP exam. You will be asked to provide specific examples to support your answers, and your knowledge of world regions, countries, cultures will give you this specific knowledge to score high!

http://www.collegeboard.com/student/testing/ap/sub_humangeo.html?humangeo

The College Board site contains the previous exam FRQs and their rubrics. Study these to get a feel for the level of writing and explanation you will need for the actual exam!

Day 157

https://www.studystack.com/APHumanGeography

Check out this AP Human Geography flashcard website! It is divided into the main themes of AP Human Geography so you can choose a specific theme to review.

https://apgeographymhs.files.wordpress.com/2012/04/sbigideaspacket2012.pdf

For a very thorough overview of all the knowledge contained in the AP Human Geography class, check out this website!

Watch the YouTube video "Chapter 1 Key Issue 1—Basic Concepts—AP Human Geography" at https://www.youtube.com/watch?v=v2yuQ0Ljy-s.

This creative YouTube Video is a great refresher on key human geography concepts. It's a visual and quick-paced review of the basics!

Source: https://www.google.com/search?q=topographic+map&client=firefox-b-1-ab&
tbm=isch&tbo=u&source=univ&sa=X&ved=0ahUKEwilx76knOjaAhVpc98KHe7h
BrMQ7AkIfA&biw=1171&bih=571#imgrc=-ekTJlAAMSmK5M

All the following are uses of this topographic map EXCEPT

(A)   planning a hike or backpacking expedition.

(B)   finding good locations to hunt or fish.

(C)   locating potentially unstable landscapes when building and developing.

(D)   determining the population density of the nearest town.

(E)   locating springs, high points for cell phone signal pick up, nearby roads, and
ranger stations.

http://www.learner.org/courses/envsci/interactives/demographics/

Check out this website for a super great simulator of population momentum and the demographic transition.

This interactive demographics lab is part of Annenberg Learner's free resources in *The Habitable Planet*.

https://storymaps.geo.census.gov/arcgis/apps/MapSeries/index.html?appid=9e459da9
327b4c7e9a1248cb65ad942a&cid=16O104

The U.S. Census Bureau has created a short GIS presentation on "Rural America: A
Story Map." Manipulate the GIS layers to learn how the U.S. Census Bureau defines
"rural" and "urban."

Day 163

https://earthobservatory.nasa.gov/Features/ColorImage/

Discover NASA's top five tips and strategies to interpret a satellite image. And, yes, scale is one of them!

What items on the list below should you be sure to bring to the AP exam? Select all that apply.

(A)   Watch

(B)   Cell phone

(C)   Calculator

(D)   Pencils—several

(E)   Water bottle and snack

Day 165

What items below cannot be brought to the AP exam? Select all that apply.

(A) iPod

(B) Sweater

(C) Ruler

(D) Highlighter

(E) Blue ink pens

Day 166

For the multiple-choice section of the exam (Section I), you will have exactly _____ minutes to complete _____ multiple-choice questions.

Day 167

You will have _____ minutes to write the _____ free-response essays of Section II in the AP exam.

Day 168

For Section I of the exam (multiple-choice questions), what should you do if you do not know the answer?

(A)   Make a wild guess.

(B)   Eliminate obviously wrong answers and make your best guess of the remaining answers.

(C)   Ask a neighbor.

(D)   Skip and never come back to it.

Day 169

If you are unsure of the correct answer, leave it blank and move on.

True
False

Day 170

You can write in your test booklet.

    True
    False

You can fill in the ovals on the answer sheet in pen.

True

False

Read each answer choice carefully—some could look correct but have one word that makes them wrong.

True
False

Day 173

If you are not 100% sure, don't mark any answer.

True

False

Never leave a question blank.

   True

   False

There is a penalty for guessing.

   True

   False

Day 176

Count on having enough time to go back over your answers in the multiple-choice section.

True

False

Each multiple-choice question has four choices called distractors. Two distractors will be REALLY wrong.

    True

    False

Day 178

When answering a free-response question using the verb *analyze*, you should write about the relationship between two events by explaining the events and giving a conclusion based on facts.

True

False

When answering a free-response essay question, which of the following actions should you take? Choose all that are correct.

(A)   Find the verb (key action word) in the question.

(B)   If you draw a complete blank, find the geographic concept in the question and write a definition.

(C)   Write enough to answer the question using the vocabulary you learned in your class.

(D)   Limit yourself to 20 minutes per FRQ.

(E)   Answer the FRQ you know most about first.

Which of the following tips for writing exam FRQs are correct? Choose all that apply.

(A)   Pad your response with lots of words.

(B)   It's OK to skip a FRQ if you run out of time.

(C)   Label each part of your response to match the part of the question you are answering.

(D)   Always write an introductory and a concluding paragraph.

(E)   Write legibly and with an ink pen.

Answers

Day 1

Draw a line from each concept to its brief description.

Space — An area that displays a common trait

Place — The degree of generalization on a map

Scale — The extent of area that is occupied by something

Regions — Another word for location.

Day 2

Representative fraction   A representative fraction is the scale of a map stated as a ratio of a unit of distance on the map to distance measured in the same unit on the ground. In this example, 1 map unit is equal to 500,000 of the same units on the ground.

Day 3

Draw a line from each example of a region to the type of region.

Winn-Dixie grocery store — Formal region

Bible Belt — Functional region

French-speaking region of Canada — Perceptual (vernacular) region

A formal region displays a characteristic that can be generalized across the region such as speaking a language. A functional region is based on what occurs in the region. In this example, people who shop at Winn-Dixie. A perceptual region represents a mental map of most people's conception of a region. Most people think of the Bible Belt as a region where everyone attends church and prays.

Day 4

A, B, F The cultural landscape is made up of tangible changes to the earth's surface made by humans. Houses, bridges, and highways are part of the "built landscape" constructed by humans to modify the land to suit their needs. Rivers, climate, and mountains are part of the natural physical landscape.

Day 5

B Developing countries such as China and India as well as many in Sub-Saharan Africa and South America are projected to have rapid growth rates for the foreseeable future. Developed countries such as the United States, Russia, and most European countries are projected to maintain stable or declining rates of population growth.

Day 6

C The crude birth rate (CBR) of a country refers to the number of live births per 1,000 population. The CBR is called "crude" because it does not consider the age or sex structure of the population.

Day 7

D Neo-Malthusianism is based on the belief that reducing the country's number of births through government incentives and birth-control programs would raise all the residents' standards of living. (A) and (C) refer to increased government spending in social welfare programs, which do not directly impact population growth. (B) Increased fertility rates are in direct opposition to neo-Malthusianism's goal to reduce birth rates to raise everyone's standard of living.

Day 8

C Stage 4 of the demographic transition model is noted by low birth and death rates and a low rate of natural increase or even decrease. In Stage 5, the negative growth rates occurring in many European countries as well as the dwindling birth rates in other areas of the world contribute to zero population growth. (A) and (B) are incorrect because birth rates and death rates are falling in these stages—not increasing. (D) is incorrect because the demographic transition model does not take into consideration sex composition of the population.

Day 9

A Physiological density refers to total population divided by arable, or farmable, land. It assumes that all arable land is productive and used in a comparable fashion. (B) Crude density refers to the number of people per unit area of land and is used often; however, it can mask large differences in population density because it does not consider densely and sparsely populated areas. (C) Arithmetic density is the same as crude density and is wrong for the same reasons. (D) Rate of natural increase refers to the crude birth rate minus the crude death rate of a population without including immigration.

Day 10

D   The replacement level is the population needed for a population to continue to replace itself. (A) The crude birth rate is a measure of the number of babies born per 1,000 people and but does not tell us how many of these people are male or too young or too old to reproduce. (B) The crude death rate refers to the annual number of deaths per 1,000 people. (C) The total fertility rate is a measure of the number of babies born per woman of reproductive age in a population.

Day 11

A, B, E   (A) Very remote areas are too hard to access, so they usually have few inhabitants. (B) Infertile land that cannot produce food is also less densely populated. An example is the tropical rain forests of the world such as the Amazon River Basin and the Congo River Basin. (E) Scarcity of water as in desert regions produces lower population density, too. Moderate climate (C) and coastlines (D) attract human settlement and 60% of the world's inhabitants live within 60 miles of the ocean!

Day 12

high   This statement is true because even with a high rate of reproduction, the crude birth rate could be low if most of the population were not women of reproductive age (i.e., male, very young, very old).

Day 13

infants up to one year of age   This age cohort is most vulnerable to lack of healthcare, so increased availability of antibiotics and vaccinations, etc., improve the survival chances of the very young. Infant mortality rates reflect the level of a country's healthcare system as well as access to healthcare and nutrition.

Day 14

higher   This is not a universal rule but generally holds true, especially in the Southern Hemisphere (many countries in Sub-Saharan Africa and South America).

Day 15

crude birth rate

Day 16

C   The first stage of this model has high birth and high fluctuating death rates and is no longer found in any country. (A) A low birth rate combined with a low death rate tells us the country is in the fourth stage of demographic transition with a low rate of natural increase. (B) As both birth and death rates decline in a population, population growth slows. (D) High birth rates and declining death rates cause the population to increase rapidly and denote the second stage of the model.

Day 17

B   During Stage 2 of the model, improvements in healthcare reduce the death rate and lead to an increase in life expectancy.

Day 18

D In countries and regions where there is a history of traditional violence against women, there is a marked discrepancy in the male–female ratio. This is because females are culturally less desirable and possess lower status in the culture than males. (A), (B), and (C) poverty, underdevelopment, and poor nutrition play a role in infant mortality, but cultural norms and practices take the largest toll on females in some regions.

Day 19

Video   https://www.census.gov/popclock/

Day 20

B, D, E   Ravenstein's model suggests most people are adults who move in steps from rural to urban areas. (A) is incorrect because most people move short distances (C), (F) on a rural to urban migration.

Day 21

Draw a line from each type of migrant to its matching description.

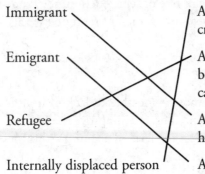

Immigrant

Emigrant

Refugee

Internally displaced person

A person forced out of the home region but does not cross any international boundaries

A person who resides outside the country of origin because of fear of persecution due to religion, political beliefs, ethnicity, or race

A person who enters another country to make a new home there

A person who leaves one country intending to live in a different country

Day 22

guest workers   Many countries in Europe welcome guest workers to supplement their labor force as their populations age out of the workforce.

Day 23

human capital theory of immigration   This migration usually benefits both countries as the worker brings valuable skills to the recipient country while also sending remittances (money) home to families.

Day 24

life course   Various events in a person's life affect both internal and international migrations. For example, research shows that families tend to move less for jobs and prefer to move from urban to suburban or rural areas once they have children.

Day 25

D   A trait is a single feature of a given culture. Examples of culture traits are the group's language, rite-of-passage (childhood to adulthood custom or ceremony), and eating utensils. (A) A sociofact is a cultural trait that deals with a culture's social organization—family, education, community. (B) A culture complex is a collection of individual cultural traits that are related. (C) A culture barrier is something that keep a cultural trait from spreading. An extreme form of this is a taboo such as a dietary restriction on eating pork for Jews and Muslims.

Day 26

D   Not all aspects of the host culture must be absorbed by the minority culture. For example, the immigrants may adopt the language and some of the social customs of the host culture, but also retain their own traditions and customs. (A) Globalization refers to growing connectivity between most areas of the world through transportation, communications, marketing, etc. (B) Assimilation is the process where a new immigrant becomes completely blended into the host culture while retaining their ethnic culture. (C) Transculturation is an even exchange of traits between two different culture groups.

Day 27

C   Language is the single most important way to transmit a culture. (A), (D) Legislation and elementary school are not the most important means of cultural transmission, although both play a role in the communication of culture within a society. (B) Innovation refers to changes within a culture that were created by the culture itself.

Day 28

Website   https://factfinder.census.gov/faces/nav/jsf/pages/index.xhtml

Day 29

C   Stimulus diffusion denotes the spread of an *idea* of something new but not the identical item itself. For example, Native Americans like the Cherokee saw early European settlers making marks on paper to record speeches and agreements and devised their own system of writing thereafter. (A) In relocation diffusion, an innovation is carried to a new location by humans migrating to that area. (B) Expansion diffusion involves the spread of an idea or item from one place to other places. (D) When innovations develop in more than one place without interaction or diffusion occurring (example of agriculture), we refer to this as independent, or parallel, invention.

Day 30

A   Syncretism involves the blending of two or more forms of a cultural trait into a new cultural trait. A good example of this is Roman Catholicism as practiced in Louisiana. Over time, voodoo practices from the West Indies merged with French and Spanish Catholicism, Native American spiritualism, and even Masonic traditions to form a syncretic religion practiced as Catholicism in that region. (B) A sociofact is an institution or accepted pattern of human interaction in a culture (family structure, school, religion). (C) Diffusion is the spread of a culture trait or new idea from an origin area to a new location. (D) Innovation is the origin of a new idea or practice in a culture group.

Day 31

C Hinduism is the oldest major religion in the world and is thought to date back over 4,000 years. (A) Buddhism is a universalizing religion (open to anyone who wants to join) that began as an offshoot of Hinduism in the 6th century BC. (B) Islam rose from Judeo-Christian roots to become a universalizing religion in AD 622 when the Prophet Mohammed declared the Muslim universal mission. (D) Christianity began in the first century AD and is a universalizing religion based on the life and teachings of Jesus Christ.

Day 32

Website   http://nativelands.org

Day 33

Draw a line from the term to its correct definition.

Assimilation   Increasing interconnection of all world regions

Acculturation   An equal exchange of traits between two cultures occurs

Globalization   A process in which immigrants become completely absorbed and immersed in the host culture

Syncretism   Two or more culture traits blending to create a new culture trait

Transculturation   The process of adopting some of the cultural traits, values, and behaviors of the host culture

Day 34

taboo   A taboo is a strong cultural barrier that prevents certain habits or new ideas from getting rooted in a culture or society. Food taboos are very strong in certain religions and many prevent eating special kinds of meat.

Day 35

B, C, E   All culture hearths were urban-centered, served as the origin of many innovations which spread outward, and were agricultural societies that traded with surrounding areas. (A) No culture hearth arose in a rural area. (D) The Mississippi River Valley was not a culture hearth. Examples of culture hearths include Egypt, Mesopotamia, West Africa, the Indus River Valley, China, and Meso-America. (F) New ideas diffused outward from culture hearths where they originated.

Day 36

Video   http://www.pbs.org/frontlineworld/rough/2007/04/the_missing_gir.html

Day 37

lingua franca   An example of a lingua franca would be Swahili in Sub-Saharan Africa or Mandarin Chinese in China. A lingua franca serves as a commonly understood language in a country with several spoken languages.

Day 38

Video   http://www.geobeats.com

Day 39

Draw a line from each religion to a fact about that religion.

Christianity   A religion where one special person is believed to have special powers

Shamanism   The rejection of all religious beliefs

Secularism   The belief that spirits live insides rocks, trees, and other similar objects

Animism   A universalizing religion

Day 40

Judaism   Of the three monotheistic religions that arose in Southwest Asia (the Middle East), Judaism originated first (a little later than Hinduism).

Day 41

Draw a line from each term to its best matching statement.

Hinduism   On the rapid rise in Europe today

Judaism   A religion that does not believe in worshipping gods but instead ing seeking truth

Secularism   A monotheistic religion with two main branches and a creed of Five Pillars

Islam   A polytheistic religion that spread worldwide through relocation diffusion

Buddhism   An ethnic religion and the oldest of the three monotheistic world religions

Day 42

Photo study—the answer is Italian.

Day 43

D, E A folk culture is a homogenous group of people with a strong family structure who live independent of the mainstream culture. (A), (B), (C) The members of a folk culture such as the Old Order Amish avoid the use of modern appliances, electricity, or innovations, and have their own newspapers and ways of communication that differ from those of the mainstream culture.

Day 44

sequent occupance   Sequent occupance is the concept that each society that occupies a region leaves behind traces of its culture in the cultural landscape. An example of this is the Native American, Spanish, and colonial influences still found in Santa Fe, New Mexico.

Day 45

metes-and-bounds   Metes-and-bounds is a land survey system brought to the United States by early English settlers. It used natural elements such as large rocks, trees, and streams as boundary markers and was used in Pennsylvania and areas south and east.

Day 46

B A nation is the people of a state or country. (A) A state is the political area with a definite boundary and population. (C) A country is also called a "state." (D) A nation-state is a state, or country, with over 90% of its people sharing a common culture and/or ethnicity. An example of a nation-state would be Japan.

Day 47

B The Philippines Islands are a fragmented state because water separates the islands. (A), (C), (D) Uruguay, Laos, and Zimbabwe are all compact states that are roughly round-shaped and easy to defend.

Day 48

A A compact state is easy to devise transportation and communication systems for because it is the same distance from the center to every border. A communications or transportation headquarters in the middle of the country could reach out to all areas easily. (B), (C), (D) Elongated, prorupt, and fragmented states all have distance issues to contend with as their borders are far apart and spread out.

Day 49

D Berlin, Germany is not a forward-thrust capital. (A), (B), (C) Forward-thrust capitals are often new capital cities that make a political statement by being located near contested borders (Islamabad, Pakistan) or near undeveloped areas to draw capital investment (Brasilia, Brazil.).

Day 50

Match the term with the best descriptive statement below.

Relic boundary — A boundary forced upon existing boundaries as in Africa by European powers

Superimposed boundary — The Great Wall of China is an example of this boundary

Antecedent boundary — Boundaries imposed after cultural landscape is in place

Subsequent boundary — Boundaries imposed very early in settlement before cultural landscape developed

Day 51

C Some nations do not have states, or countries, of their own. Examples of these nations are the Navajo, the Kurds, and the Roma (gypsies). (A), (D) Country and state both refer to a defined area with borders and a population. Examples are almost every country in the world, i.e., France, Italy, South Korea, Argentina, etc. (B) A colony is a country under full or partial control of another country.

Day 52

C An exclave is a piece of a country that is totally enclosed within the boundaries of another country. Nagorno-Karabakh is a piece of Armenia totally within the country of Azerbaijan. (A) Enclaves are pieces of a country surrounded by another country. To those living in Nagorno-Karabakh, they live in an enclave. (B) A colony is a country under full or partial control of another country. (D) A CBD is a city's Central Business District.

Day 53

B Centripetal forces are those that bind together and unify a country. Other centripetal forces are national anthems, national holidays, and a strong leader. (A) Centrifugal forces such as religious differences or political unrest divide and tear apart a country. (C) Terrorism is the use of violence to instill fear and intimidate a population. (D) Unpatriotic behavior would be doing something that would disrespect one's country such as burning the American flag or refusing to pledge allegiance.

Day 54

D A separatist group is a minority group within a country who seek self-governance. Examples are the Moros in the Philippines, the Sikhs in India, the Basques of Spain, and the Bretons of France. (A) Supranational refers to an association of three or more countries for mutual benefit. (B) Nationalist refers to a movement of patriotism and loyalty towards one's country. (C) While some separatist groups use radical means to gain attention for their cause, they do not come under the category of "terrorists."

Day 55

Website   https://www.mapsofworld.com/thematic-maps/types-of-governments.html

Day 56

gerrymandering   Gerrymandering involves the redrawing of voting districts to ensure fair and equal representation.

Day 57

C   As distance from the market increases, the value of land decreases and von Thunen's land-use model shows this quite nicely. Perishable products such as dairy are produced closest to the market in the inner ring. (A), (B), and (D) are all important factors in the production of a product, but they are not the most important in determining where the product is grown or produced.

Day 58

A, B, D   Waste and/or garbage may be used to fertilize crops and the crops will supplement the farmers' family menu. This land is probably brown fields or former industrial sites where raised bed urban gardening can be a useful addition to the landscape. (C) This urban garden will not lead to increased waste disposal as unused vegetables and weeds, etc., can be composted.

Day 59

D   The length and favorability of a growing season are never predictable! (A), (B), (C) These specifications are always a part of agribusiness or contract farming for various food processing industries. Agricultural products must meet certain criteria as stated in the contract.

Day 60

B, D, E   Swidden, shifting agriculture, and slash-and-burn all rely on cutting down and burning natural vegetation before planting crops in the soil. (A) Intensive subsistence agriculture relies on heavy applications of fertilizer and human labor to raise crops. (C) Plantation agriculture is the production of a large amount of a single crop, usually in tropical climates.

Day 61

D   Nomadic herders follow a carefully planned route to feed their herds. (A) and (C) Slash-and-burn and shifting cultivation are forms of farming used in tropical lands. (B) Intensive subsistence agriculture is used by poor urban farmers who invest large amounts of natural fertilizers and labor to produce large crops on small amounts of land.

Day 62

C   Climate is the single most important factor in growing plantation crops. (A), (B), (D) Time, investment monies, and business connections to market the crop are all important but without the best climate for growth, the single plantation crop will fail.

Day 63

Draw a line to best connect each form of agriculture given below with the statement below that applies.

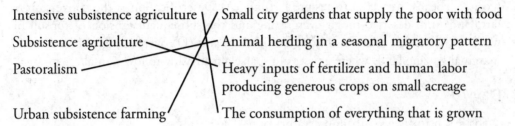

Intensive subsistence agriculture — Small city gardens that supply the poor with food

Subsistence agriculture — Animal herding in a seasonal migratory pattern

Pastoralism — Heavy inputs of fertilizer and human labor producing generous crops on small acreage

Urban subsistence farming — The consumption of everything that is grown

Day 64

agribusiness   Agribusiness is very efficient and is driven by the fast-food industry.

Day 65

A Many of these farmers live in the fertile river valleys and deltas of Asia where they can grow rice, which produces high yields per acre of land. (B) High first-year yields with declining production and finally abandonment describes nomadic farming in tropical regions. (C) Equal emphasis on crops and animals describes intensive subsistence farming as practiced in East and South Asia. (D) Farms that specialize in producing a single crop are plantation (examples: pineapples, coffee, cotton.)

Day 66

D The Green Revolution used a mix of hybrid seeds and improved farming practices to improve harvests in certain regions of the world. (A) Most poor farmers have not been able to benefit from the expensive seeds and fertilizers needed to benefit from the Green Revolution. (B) The Green Revolution did not draw people back to rural lands nor did it refer to rebellion by peasants in the Third World.

Day 67

A, B, D Contract farming gives farmers access to seeds, fertilizers, and credit, agricultural support and advice, and a market for the product. (C) Farmers do not have equal power in the relationship, however, and often lose direct control over their land.

Day 68

Website   http://carrington.edu/blog/student-tips/health/genetically-modified-food-pros-and-cons/

Day 69

B Crop rotation is a conservation measure where low-residue crops are planted in alternating rows with high-residue crops. The ground is planted in alternating crops (corn, soybeans, hay, etc.) to restore fertility. (A) Desertification is the conversion of farmlands into desert through overgrazing and the subsequent erosion of topsoil by wind. (C) Swidden refers to shifting cultivation, and (D) overgrazing often occurs in marginal grazing lands where grasses are sparse already due to low rainfall.

Day 70

Website   http://www.urbanobservatory.org/

Day 71

B, C, D Agriculture, hunting, and mining are all primary economic activities that extract natural resources from the Earth. (A) Financial consulting is a quinary activity representing special and highly paid skills in the postindustrial economy.

Day 72

B Secondary economic activities occur as manufacturing firms take raw materials and specialized labor and transform them into useful products. (A) Primary economic activities extract natural resources from the physical environment. (C) Tertiary activities are involved with providing service—retail, wholesale, insurance, banking, and restaurants, for example. (D) Quaternary activities involve specialized skills and knowledge such as software development, tax consulting, and statisticians. (E) Quinary activities represent the skills of top business executives, research scientists, and financial consultants.

Day 73

B, C, E Banking, retail, and accounting are tertiary activities because they provide consumer services. (A), (D) Fishing and mining are primary activities because they involve the extraction of a natural resource.

Day 74

Website   https://www.google.com/maps/about/treks/#/grid

Day 75

D Most developed countries produce 75% of the world's exports. (A), (B), (C), and (E) are incorrect figures.

Day 76

A, C, D All of these factors have helped reduce the dependency of periphery countries on most developed countries since the 1950s. (B), (E) Neocolonialism has only served to reinforce the old colonial dependencies of the past, while there is no shortage of raw materials on the world markets.

Day 77

Traditional society	Stage 1
Pre-conditions for take-off	Stage 2
Drive to maturity	Stage 3
The age of mass consumption	Stage 4

Day 78

Pre-conditions for take-off	Stage 2

Day 79

Drive to maturity	Stage 4

Day 80

Match the theory or model below with its basic belief.

Wallerstein's world systems theory — The core depends on the periphery to exist.

Rostow's model of economic development — Dynamic flow between core, semi-periphery, and periphery economies.

Andre Frank's dependency theory — Modernization is the key to economic development.

Day 81

Complete the following chart of the three main expenses that must be minimized in locating an industry below based on Alfred Weber's least-cost theory. Place the most important expense at the top of the chart.

Transportation Costs

Labor Costs

Agglomeration Costs

Day 82

D Fordism was invented when Henry Ford pioneered assembly line production.

Day 83

Video https://www.gapminder.org/videos/reducing-child-mortality-a-moral-and -environmental-imperative/

Day 84

Video https://www.youtube.com/watch?v=868K4Iq8Z-g

Day 85

Match the world region with the best statement that applies.

Western Europe — Early emphasis on water power freed region from dependence on England

Eastern Europe — The "4 Tigers" have led this region to become one of the most productive in world

Eastern Asia — Undergoing a deindustrialization with massive layoffs in iron and coal mining

Anglo America — Centralized industrial planning led to a disconnect from market realities

Day 86

B, C, D Women's role in the workforce has expanded over the years due to government policies to provide childcare, increased opportunities for education and employment, and greater control over their fertility. (A) Increased lending to women through microcredit has helped women own small businesses and (E) lack of economic growth has not hampered women's increased role in the global economy.

Day 87

Video http://fundforpeace.org/fsi/

Day 88

B Agricultural surpluses allowed the earliest cities to develop trade relationships with neighboring cities. (A), (C), (D) Fortified city walls, fearless armies, and religion all played an important role in early cities, but the most important single factor in their success is agricultural surpluses.

Day 89

B, C, D, E The earliest cities were often surrounded by walls for defense and had a place of worship in their center. Most were also located on a river, seacoast, or other waterway for transportation purposes. Early cities were centered on the marketplace, but now they depend on their industries to drive the urban economy. (A) Factories were not part of the earliest urban societies.

Day 90

C Situation describes the relative location of a city or town based on its relation to other places. (A) A hinterland is a productive area surrounding a city or town. (B) Site refers to the physical location of a place. (D) Sense of place refers to the special perception we have of a place based on our feelings and emotions related to that place.

Day 91

Video   https://www.youtube.com/watch?t=23&v=XvfeOD46M0w

Day 92

Rural-to-urban   This type of migration is widespread and is occurring in most countries of the world.

Day 93

Draw a line from each term to its correct definition.

Megalopolis — Self-sufficient suburban cities that contain industry, offices, and residential communities

Supercity — A city more than twice as large as the next largest city and far more important

Gateway city — A metropolitan area with a total population of over 10 million people

Primate city — A city established as a control center for colonial powers

Edge city — A very large city

Day 94

B Megalopolis refers to the long string of urban sites on the U.S. eastern Seaboard. A central place refers to Christaller's theory that cities are gathering places where people share goods and ideas for economic purposes and from which goods and services flow into their hinterlands. (C) A hamlet is a very small village in a rural area. (D) A megacity is a metropolitan area with a population of over 10 million people according the United Nations.

Day 95

D The rank-size rule says that the second-largest city in a country will be half the size of the largest city and so on. (A) Central place refers to Christaller's theory that cities are gathering places where people share goods and ideas for economic purposes and from which goods and services flow into their hinterlands. (B) The multiple-nuclei model developed by Harris and Ullman contend that cities spread from several centers of growth outward. (C) The Latin American city model has a central area of traditional marketplace, modern CBD, and important government buildings and churches with an exclusive corridor of commerce and wealthy residential buildings extending outward.

Day 96

B   This basic economic sector produces an inflow of new money into the city. (A) Urban hierarchy refers to a ranking of cities based on their size and intricacy of functions. (C) Hinterlands refers to the region served by an urban area. (D) The non-basic economic sector is the group of workers who produce goods and services for the residents of the city itself.

Day 97

D   The multiplier effect is the economic reality that at least two non-basic jobs are created for every new basic job in a city or region. (A) Central place refers to Christaller's theory that cities are gathering places where people share goods and ideas for economic purposes. (B) The rank-size rule says that the second-largest city in a country will be half the size of the largest city and so on. (C) Urban hierarchy refers to a ranking of cities based on their size and intricacy of functions.

Day 98

Website   https://www.purposegames.com/games?t=484&so=mp

Day 99

A   Central place is thought to exist mainly to provide goods and services to its surrounding region. (B) Urban hierarchy refers to a ranking of cities based on their size and intricacy of functions. (C) The rank-size rule says that the second-largest city in a country will be ½ the size of the largest city and so on. (D) The multiple-nuclei model developed by Harris and Ullman contend that cities spread from several centers of growth outward.

Day 100

B, C   These are two assumptions of Christaller's model. (A) Larger places attract people from far-off places because they generally have luxury goods for sale. (D) Christaller's theory assumes there are more smaller places than larger ones.

Day 101

Website   http://www.lincolninst.edu/subcenters/visualizing-density/blockgame/index.aspx

Day 102

C   The photo, taken by the U.S. Fish and Wildlife Service, shows population density along waterways in a community. Is the population especially dense in this community? Why or why not?

Day 103

Connect each major urban model with its description.

Concentric zone model — CBD is not the only nucleus of a city.

Sector model — As a city grows, land use also changes.

Gravity model — Transportation improvements caused urban growth in pie wedges.

Multiple-nuclei model — Large cities attract people and ideas more strongly than small ones do.

Day 104

B This theory represents the multiple-nuclei model developed by Harris and Ullman. (A) Rostow's theory on developing economies states that they pass through a successive series of stages. (C) Ravenstein theorized that there are seven laws of migration that summarize migration flows. (D) Burgess developed one of the first urban models called the concentric zone model.

Day 105

A Burgess developed one of the first urban models, called the concentric zone model. (B) Rostow's theory on developing economies states that they pass through a successive series of stages. (C) Harris and Ullman developed the multiple-nuclei model where cities develop from several specialized nodes. (D) Ravenstein theorized that there are seven laws of migration that summarize migration flow.

Day 106

C Urban growth is on the rise in most countries of the world. (A) Every continent is seeing urban growth but not at the same rate. (B) Cities are growing more rapidly than rural areas. (D) Developing countries are experiencing high rates of growth due to increasing rural-to-urban migration by job seekers and those looking for better benefits for their families.

Day 107

A, B, D Poverty, involuntary segregation, and isolation are just a few of the problems faced by immigrants in cities today. (C) Immigrants find work easily in most cities and do not have a problem due to a growing labor pool. European countries are especially in need of workers due to their decreasing or even negative population growth rates.

Day 108

B Sadly, these cities are growing far faster in population than in economic wealth. (A), (C), (D) These areas also have growing urban populations, but the greatest growth will be in the region least able to provide the residents with amenities—Sub-Saharan Africa.

Day 109

A, B, C Developing countries cannot keep up with their growing urban populations as their transportation systems are overwhelmed, their physical environments polluted, and inadequate housing and clean water shortages plague their governments. (D) High employment due to rapid expansion of cities is not a problem in developing countries.

Day 110

D The hinterland is a productive area surrounding a city or town. (A) A metropolis is a large busy city. (B) An inner city is the older, central part of a city that is often characterized by crowded low-income neighborhoods. (C) Central place refers to a market center for the exchange of goods and services by people in the surrounding area.

Day 111

central, center city—see page 137

Day 112

favelas barrios—see page 137

Day 113

communist—see page 137

Day 114

Match the city type with its corresponding characteristic.

East European — Lack urban sprawl and suburbs

West European — Large central square with government and cultural buildings

U.S. — Lack even basic sanitation and clean water

Sub-Saharan African — Low-income inhabitants in inner-city slum

Day 115

Website   http://theplaceswelive.com/

Day 116

A, B, C, D Housing and job shortages along with lack of clean water and sanitation services plague most cities in less developed countries. Too many aid workers would not be a problem, and they are welcome if they can alleviate the extreme poverty of the urban poor.

Day 117

religion   Typically, a cathedral, temple, or mosque can be found in or near the center of these cities where religious worship and ceremony served as the main function when the city began.

Day 118

Website   http://metrocosm.com/global-migration-map.html

Day 119

Western—see page 139. The Western influence is very heavy in developing countries because global communications and transportation linkages bring Western pop culture to these regions quickly.

Day 120

True   If the city was developed as a port facility to export raw materials, for example, the land use will reflect the importance of the waterfront. Warehouses, rooming houses and small bars and cafes located close to the waterfront will service the workers.

Day 121

False   Cities in developing countries produce a considerable share of their country's gross domestic income (GDI). For example, Mumbai creates one-sixth of the GDI of India!

Day 122

basic, into   The basic economic sector produces goods and services for "export" out of the city. In other words, the basic sector brings a fresh inflow of money into the city's economy. A hospital that serves people from other cities is part of the basic sector, but when it serves someone who lives within the city, its function becomes a nonbasic economic function.

Day 123

do not   These nonbasic jobs provide services for people who live and work in the city. An example would be a bus driver or policeman.

Day 124

True   The influx of new money into the city's economy generates improvements in infrastructure and services. At the same time, other industries are attracted to the city thus increasing the basic sector of the economy while the new workers require the goods and services of the nonbasic sector.

Day 125

Website   http://agtr.ilri.cgiar.org/index.php?option=com_content&view=article&id =46&Itemid=66

Day 126

B Gentrification involves the restoration of housing in older, run-down inner-city neighborhoods by middle-and-high income groups. (A) Suburbanization is the expansion of suburban populations. (C) The multiplier effect refers to the relationship between basic and non-basic jobs and their effects in a city's economy. (D) Urbanization is the process of city growth and expansion. (E) Urban influence zones are the areas outside the city that are still influenced by the city.

Day 127

D Cities in developing countries struggle unsuccessfully to provide even the most basic services such as clean drinking water and sanitation to their rapidly growing populations. (A), (B) Cities in the developing world are centers of business and trade surrounded by rings of squatter settlements. (C) Rural migrants flock to these cities hoping for good jobs and a better life. (E), (F) Cities in developing countries produce a significant amount of the country's GDI and have a lively central city with high-end shopping and residential areas.

Day 128

New Urbanism New Urbanism emphasizes the sense of community and social engagement that used to be so prevalent in neighborhoods of yesteryear. Sidewalks and mixed housing and retail sectors create a sense of small-town living that people long for today.

Day 129

cars The emphasis on sidewalks and pedestrian-friendly right-of-ways promote cleaner air and a healthier lifestyle.

Day 130

True Urban renewal allows private or public investors to purchase run-down urban inner-city properties to create parks, schools, or new housing. It effectively also reduces the amount of affordable housing for low-income residents, however.

Day 131

Public housing Public housing is no longer being built because it is not maintained and quickly becomes a haven for criminals and drug lords.

Day 132

Ghettoization This process can be voluntary or forced segregation of a group because of their religion, race, or ethnicity.

Day 133

D An edge city is usually situated on the outer fringes of an older city and is often located along a major highway intersection. (A) A gated community is a planned community with access restricted to residents and their guests. (B) A primate city is a country's leading city and is far larger than the other cities and far more complex in function. (C) A suburb is a residential area outside the city limits. (E) A town is a smaller version of a city possessing a small CBD and performing fewer functions.

Day 134

A The sector model is an urban land use model that has pie-shaped wedges of land coming outward from the CBD along major highways. (B) The central place model explains central place theory using settlement sizes and spacing regularities. (C) The urban realms model shows the various areas of a city as spatial components called "realms." (D) The concentric zone model depicts the city spatially as a series of zones, or rings expanding outward per land use. (E) The multiple-nuclei model describes urban land use as developing from several nodes of growth and not just one.

Day 135

E Harris and Ullman developed the multiple-nuclei model of urban land use, which countered (B) Burgess's concentric zone model and (D) Hoyt's sector model. (A) Ravenstein developed several laws of migration to explain why migrants move from one place to another. (C) Von Thunen developed a model of agricultural land use.

Day 136

Video   ttps://vimeo.com/37039213

Day 137

Folk culture because it shows an old barn in Appalachia.

Day 138

green building   Green building refers to the practice of building structures using environmentally safe materials and renewable resources to be healthier for humans and the environment.

Day 139

Website   http://www.purposegames.com/games

Day 140

Website   http://www.yourchildlearns.com/map-puzzles.htm

Day 141

Website   http://www.lizardpoint.com/fun/geoquiz/

Day 142

Website   http://freerice.com/category

Day 143

Website   http://www.cdc.gov/dhdsp/maps/gisx/resources/maps4.html

Day 144

Website   http://www.indexmundi.com/map/?t=0&v=67&r=xx&l=en

Day 145

A, C, E   These responses are correct and easily found upon examination of this satellite image. Some basic geography of the United States needs to be shown in locating the Rocky Mountains and Mississippi River. Also, the term "Megalopolis" is an AP Human Geography term that refers to the Eastern Seaboard region of the U.S. is useful in this exercise. (B) While there are areas of greater population density along the U.S–Mexico border (Tijuana/San Diego and Ciudad Juarez/El Paso), the border is lightly populated for the most part. (D) The Gulf Coast has a fairly high population density as noted by the almost continuous light band along the Gulf of Mexico.

Day 146

B, C, D   These answers are correct and can be found by using the map scale and map key and by noting the location of the important elements of the global grid such as the equator and meridians. (A) The Tropic of Capricorn (not Cancer) bisects Australia.

Day 147

B   South Africa is perforated by the small countries of Lesotho and Swaziland. (A), (E) The Democratic Republic of the Congo (DRC) and Zimbabwe are compact states. (C) Namibia is not a land-locked state, since it has a long water border. (D) Somalia is an elongated state that has a very long water border.

Day 148

B, C, E   New Urbanism communities maximize human social contact and interaction by mixing residential housing in with retail shops, creating parks and squares for increased contact, and making it safer and more enticing for individuals to walk around the community. (A) Streets and roads are deemphasized to create less pollution and confusion in the community. (D) Retail stores and cafes, restaurants, etc. are sprinkled throughout the community to encourage a friendly, small-town atmosphere.

Day 149

Video   https://www.ted.com/talks/jeff_speck_the_walkable_city

Day 150

C   Graffiti made up of popular culture photos, slogans, images, and the like makes the Lennon Wall an example of pop culture. (A) Prague's traditional culture would not condone graffiti. (B) New Urbanism is more about a concept of creating communities that create the home town way of life and graffiti does not reflect that lifestyle. (D) Placelessness is the loss of a place's unique characteristics and flavor that make it distinctive.

Day 151

D   This temple or shrine of the Hindu religion exemplifies the many gods of the religion and is probably located near water in a favorable location so the gods will visit. (A) Roman Catholics worship at churches and cathedrals and (B) Muslims worship at mosques. (C),(E) Jewish and Buddhist worshipers worship at temples, but they do not worship multiple gods as depicted on this structure.

Day 152

B   Meinig's Main Street symbolic landscape is represented above. You can see the emphasis on trade and commerce from the stores and businesses that line the street. (A) The New England Village Meinig identified would have a central green or commons, Protestant church, and meeting house to show its American values of democracy and the role of religion in the community and nation. (C) In the Southern California suburb, Meinig identified the single-family house on a small lot, an automobile-centered society of nuclear families in a non-urban environment. (D) An East Coast city would be an urban cultural landscape of waterfront areas perhaps and was not a construct used by Meinig to define the cultural landscape.

Day 153

A, D, E   The cultural landscape in this photo would tell a geographer much about the land use, population and settlement patterns, and transportation methods used by the residents of the area. Terracing and use of stone in architecture as well as dirt lanes hint at this seaside villa's human geography. Proximity to the sea hint at the water as an important factor in the community's economy as well as transportation. (B), (C) Cultural traits such as languages and dietary restrictions are not evident from this cultural landscape.

Day 154

B   The Roma, or gypsies, are a people, or nation, without a political territory or country to call "home." (A) A colony is a country under full or partial control of another country. (C) A nation-state is a state, or country, with over 90% of its people sharing a common culture and/or ethnicity. (D) An enclave is a piece of a country surrounded by another country. (E) An exclave is a piece of a country that is totally enclosed within the boundaries of another country. Nagorno-Karabakh is a piece of Armenia totally within the country of Azerbaijan.

Day 155

Website   http://world-geography-games.com/

Day 156

Website   http://www.collegeboard.com/student/testing/ap/sub_humangeo.htm?humangeo

Day 157

Website   https://www.studystack.com/APHumanGeography

Day 158

Website   https://apgeographymhs.files.wordpress.com/2012/04/sbigideapacket2012.pdf

Day 159

Video   https://www.youtube.com/watch?v=v2yuQ0Ljy-s

Day 160

D   Topographic maps are detailed, accurate graphic representations of features that appear on the Earth's surface. They show relief, water features, vegetation, and cultural features of the landscape but they do not show population densities. They would be very useful for (A), (B), (C), or (E), however, and could be used for planning hikes, locations for fishing, building, or other useful locations.

Day 161

Website   http://www.learner.org/courses/envsci/interactives/demographics/

Day 162

Website   https://storymaps.geo.census.gov/arcgis/apps/MapSeries/index.html?appid=9e459da9327b4c7e9a1248cb65ad942a&cid=16O104

Day 163

Website   https://earthobservatory.nasa.gov/Features/ColorImage/

Day 164

A, D, E   Be sure and bring a watch so you can keep track of time during the exam, several pencils with erasers, a water bottle, and some snacks for break time. (B), (C) You are not allowed to bring a calculator or cell phone into the exam room with you.

Day 165

A, C, D   Do not bring an iPod, ruler, or highlighter into the exam room—this is not permitted. (B), (E) You may bring a sweater or jacket and some black or blue ink pens to the exam.

Day 166

60, 75   You will have exactly 60 minutes to answer 75 multiple choice questions during the exam. Never leave a question blank as there is no penalty for guessing!

Day 167

75, 3   You will have 75 minutes to write the three free-response short essay answers. Make sure and give yourself enough time to write all three by using your watch!

Day 168

B   It is a good strategy to eliminate the most obvious wrong answers and then make an educated guess from the remaining answers. (A) Making wild guesses is only OK if you are totally clueless as to the correct answer! (C) NEVER ask a neighbor for an answer! (D) Don't skip any multiple-choice questions because there is no penalty for guessing. You may get lucky and guess the right answer!

Day 169

False   There is no penalty for guessing and your score is based on the total number of multiple-choice questions you answer correctly!

Day 170

True   Yes, you can write in your test booklet!

Day 171

False   You must use a pencil to fill in the ovals on your answer sheet.

Day 172

True   Read each answer choice slowly and be on the lookout for one word that will make that choice wrong.

Day 173

False   Make your best guess and don't leave any blanks. There is no penalty for guessing!

Day 174

True   Don't leave any blanks! Make a good guess using the strategies found in this book. Then move on.

Day 175

False   There is no longer a penalty for guessing.

Day 176

False   You will have less than one minute to answer each multiple-choice question, so eliminate answer choices until you can make a "best" guess and then move on. Do not expect to have time to go back and review or think more about answers.

Day 177

True   Two distractors will be very obviously wrong, so cross them off and look for the word that makes two of the remaining choices incorrect. Eliminate these two and make the right choice!

Day 178

True *Analyze* is a power verb, so you need to give details about the relationship you are describing. Write at least two fact-filled sentences that explain, arrive at a conclusion, and justify that conclusion.

Day 179

A, B, C, D, E ALL of these actions should be taken when writing a free-response essay question response!

Day 180

C, E Always label each part of your response to match the part of the question you are answering. Example: 1A, 3C, etc. Always use a black or blue ink pen and never write with pencil, because it smears. Write large enough to be easily read and use your best handwriting. Readers are NOT handwriting experts, although they try very, very hard to decipher students' handwriting!

Appendixes

absolute location—The actual space a place occupies on the Earth's surface.

acculturation—The change that occurs within a culture when it adopts a practice from another culture.

agglomeration effects—The cost advantages (external economies) for an individual company gained by locating near similar functional industries or companies.

agribusiness—Commercial agriculture in which large corporations own and operate various steps in the production process with an emphasis on profit.

agricultural density—The number of people living in rural areas per unit of agricultural land.

alliance—An association among countries for the purpose of mutual defense or trade.

animism—The belief that spirits (including ancestral) live within objects such as animals, rivers, rocks, trees, and mountains.

antecedent boundary—A boundary placed before the cultural landscape was developed.

artifact—Tangible pieces of material culture.

assimilation—The process in which immigrants become totally integrated into the host culture.

backwash effect—The negative impact to the peripheral region sometimes caused by increased flows of labor and capital into a nearby high-growth region.

basic sector—Goods and services produced for individuals outside the urban work area.

bid-rent curve—The concept that the concentric circles in Burgess's concentric zone model are based on the amount people are willing to pay for land in each zone.

biotechnology—The application of scientific techniques to modify and improve plants, animals, and microorganisms to enhance their value.

built environment—The material culture of an environment.

carrying capacity—The number of people an area can support on a sustained basis.

central business district (CBD)—The business area found at the center of every older central city and urban area.

central place theory—A theory developed by Walter Christaller that states that cities exist for economic reasons and that people gather in cities to share goods and ideas.

centrifugal force—A strong, divisive force, such as religious differences or a weak communication systems, at work in a country.

centripetal force—A strong, unifying force, such as a charismatic leader or nationalism, at work in a country.

chain migration—That part of a migrant flow (usually relatives and friends) that follows former migrants to an area.

channelized migration—Repetitive pattern of migration not linked to family or ethnicity (senior citizens moving to the Sun Belt).

charter group—The first group of settlers to establish a new and lasting culture and society in an area.

compact state—A state that is basically round in shape, such as Poland or Bhutan.

colonialism—A system in which a country declares control over a territory or people outside its own boundaries, usually for economic purposes.

commodity chain—A chain of activities from the manufacturing to the distribution of a product.

concentric zone model—The model of urban land use developed by Burgess which demonstrates the invasion and succession processes that occur as the city grows and expands outward.

confederation—A loose association of states organized for the purpose of retaining cohesion, such as the former republics of the USSR.

congregation—An ethnic group's grouping together in a specific part of the city to support each other and minimize conflicts with those in the non-ethnic group.

consequent boundary—A type of subsequent boundary that is drawn to accommodate existing linguistic, cultural, or religious boundaries.

conservation agriculture—A modern method of farming that balances maximum crop yield with sustainable farming methods and protection of the environment.

creative destruction—The reinvestment of funds in new, profitable ventures and regions that were once used to fund ventures and regions that are now not as profitable.

creole—A simplified mixture of two or more languages that is adopted in areas of cultural diversity.

crude birth rate (CBR)—The number of babies born per 1000 people per year.

crude death rate (CDR)—The number of deaths per 1000 people per year.

crude density—The number of people per unit of land (also called arithmetic density).

cultural barrier—hindrances to cultural diffusion that occur in a society and keep cultural traits from spreading.

cultural diffusion—The process in which culture is spread from one region to another.

cultural landscape—The unique landscape made up of all parts of a culture—both material and nonmaterial.

culture—The cluster of traits that make a group of people special and unique.

culture region—A portion of the Earth's surface occupied by populations sharing recognizable and distinctive cultural characteristics.

culture hearth—A place where innovations and new ideas originate and spread outward (diffuse) to other regions.

culture trait—A single feature of a culture, such as religion or language.

decolonization—The process by which former colonies gain their independence from the mother country.

deindustrialization—The reduction in industrial activity that occurs when decreased profits and declining business cause a reduction in industrial employment.

demographic transition model—A model that shows the link between population growth and economic development using four or five stages of economic development.

demography—The study of the characteristics of a human population.

density—The number of an item within a unit of area.

dependency ratio—The ratio of people under age 15 and those 65 and older to those age 15 to 65.

dependency theory—A theory of economic development proposed by Andre Gunder Frank based on the periphery's dependence on the core.

desertification—The transformation of agricultural lands into deserts because of overgrazing and soil erosion.

developed countries (DCs)—Countries such as the United States, Germany, and Australia who have the highest levels of economic development.

developmentalism—The idea that every country and region will eventually make economic progress toward a high level of mass consumption if they only compete to the best of their ability within the world economy.

devolution—The breakdown of central authority in a country.

distance decay—The principle that says migrants try to minimize the friction of distance by moving to locations closer to them rather than farther away.

distribution—The array of items on the Earth's surface. All spatial distributions have density, dispersion, and some type of pattern.

domino theory—The theory prevalent during the Cold War Era that once a country became communist, its neighbors were likely to soon become communist also.

doubling time—The length of time it takes for a country's population to double in size if the growth rate stays the same.

dialect—A speech variant of a language, which reflects the local region in which it is spoken.

ecumene—The part of the Earth that is fit for humans to live.

edge city—A new urban complex that consists of a large node of office buildings and commercial operations with more workers than residents.

elongated state—A state that is long and narrow, such as Vietnam or Chile.

enclave—A piece of territory completely surrounded by another territory of which it is not a part.

environmental determinism—The theory that human behavior is controlled by the physical environment.

ethnic enclave—A residential community where the residents either voluntarily live, or are forced to live, in a segregated (separated) fashion due to race, religion, or ethnicity.

ethnic island—A small ethnic settlement centered in the middle of a larger group of the population.

ethnic religion—A religion that is a part of a particular ethnic or political group (Judaism, for example).

ethnocentrism—The belief that one's own ethnic group is superior to all others.

exclave—An outlier, or piece of a territory, that is completely enclosed within the borders of another country.

exclusive economic zone (EEZ)—An expanse of water up to 200 nautical miles off a country's coast that is designated for that country's natural resource exploration and exploitation.

export-processing zones (EPZs)—Small areas of a country with exceptional investment and trading conditions that are created by its government to stimulate and attract foreign investors and business.

federal state—A type of government that gives local political units such as states or provinces within a country a measure of power.

First Agricultural Revolution—The domestication of plants and animals and the resulting start of a sedentary society (also called the Neolithic Agricultural Revolution).

first effective settlement—The first group (charter group) of settlers who establish a new and lasting culture and society in an area.

fixed cost—The cost of land, plant, and machinery that is not variable.

folk culture—A homogenous group of people with a strong family structure who follow a simple, traditional lifestyle of self-sufficiency and independence from the society's cultural mainstream.

footloose firms—Firms that produce something that requires minimal transport costs.

Fordism—The process (named after Henry Ford, its founder) of using assembly-line techniques and scientific management in manufacturing.

formal region—A region with a high level of consistency in a certain cultural or physical attribute.

forward capital—A capital city that is located away from the core region for economic or political reasons in a symbolic gesture.

fragmented state—A state that has two or more areas of territory separated by another country.

functional region—A region with a node, or center hub, surrounded by interconnecting linkages. Usually connections relate to trade, communications, transportation, etc.

gateway city—A city that served as the control center for a former colonial power.

gentrification—The process of renovating an older, run-down neighborhood near the center city by middle-class and high-income families.

geographic information system (GIS)—The marriage of mapping software with a database for the purpose of overlaying various data layers on a basic locational map grid.

gerrymandering—The process of redrawing territorial district boundaries to favor a certain political party.

ghetto—An ethnic enclave where the residents live segregated (separated) by race, religion, or ethnicity in a voluntary or sometimes, forced, manner.

ghettoization—The concentration of a certain group of residents in a certain residential area against their will through legal means or social discrimination.

globalization—The increasing interconnection of all regions in the world through politics, communication, transportation, marketing, manufacturing, and social and cultural processes.

GMO (genetically modified organism)—An organism that is created when scientists take one or more specific genes from one organism and introduce them into another organism thus creating a new version.

gravity model—A law of spatial interaction that states that larger places attract people, ideas, and goods more strongly than smaller places.

Green Revolution—The development and transfer from the developed world to the developing world, of higher-yield and fast-growing crops through new and improved technology, pesticides, and fertilizers, for the purpose of alleviating world hunger.

gross domestic product (GDP)—The approximate value of all final goods and services produced in a country per year.

gross national product (GNP)—The gross domestic product (GDP) plus the value of income from abroad such as earnings from a US company based abroad.

growth pole—An urban center deliberately placed by a country's government to stimulate economic growth in the hinterland.

heartland–rimland theory—Halford Mackinder's theory that the country that dominated the landmass of Eurasia (heartland) would eventually rule the world (rimland).

hierarchical diffusion—The adoption of an official language by the ruler or administration, a language diffused downward into the society.

hinterlands—The surrounding trade area of an urban area.

host society—The dominant culture group in an area receiving a minority group.

human capital theory of migration—The migration theory that states that educated workers often migrate from poor countries to wealthy countries seeking better-paying jobs.

imperialism—The use of military threat, cultural domination, and economic sanctions to gain control of a country and its resources.

import substitution—The production of goods and services internally by the periphery country that were once supplied by the core.

Industrial Revolution—The movement from home-based cottage industries to factory industries with several workers under one roof that the use of machines facilitated in England in the late 1700s.

innovation—A new invention.

intensive subsistence agriculture—A form of agriculture that depends on heavy inputs of fertilizer and human labor on a small piece of land for substantial crop yield.

internally displaced person—A person who is forced out of the home region due to war, political or social unrest, environmental problems, etc., but who does not cross any international boundary.

intervening opportunity—The idea that migrants will choose a location closer rather than farther if all other factors are roughly the same.

irredentism—The destabilizing situation that arises when an ethnic group supports and seeks to unite with its ethnic population in another country.

land survey—A method for parceling out land to its occupants (differs according to the charter group's ethnicity in the United States and Canada).

language family—A group of languages that are related and derived from a single earlier language.

latitude—The degrees north or south from the equator for a location on the surface of the Earth. Measured in parallels.

least-cost theory—A theory, developed by Alfred Weber, that states that three main expenses—labor, transportation, and agglomeration—must be minimized when locating an industry.

less-developed countries (LDCs)—Countries located on the edge of the world core that are seeking improved conditions for their residents through economic growth.

life course theory of migration—A theory that states that the interaction effects of family life course events (became married, had a child, became divorced) with migration have important repercussions on a society.

lingua franca—A language that is not part of the culture of the country but is one that is informally agreed upon as the language of business and trade.

localization economies—The cost savings for individual industries as a result of grouping together in a certain location.

locational interdependence theory—A theory developed by Harold Hotelling that suggests that competitors, in their effort to maximize sales, will try to limit each other's territory by locating close to each other in the middle of their combined customer base.

longitude—The distance east or west from the Prime Meridian, measured in degrees, minutes, and seconds using lines of identical longitude, called meridians.

long-lots system of land survey—A land survey method used by French and Spanish charter groups in North America in which long lots of land extended outward from river frontage.

maquiladora—A foreign-owned assembly company located in the United States–Mexico border region in order to take advantage of cheaper labor, favorable tax breaks, and lax environmental regulations.

material culture—The artifacts (tangible things) of a culture such as tools, weapons, and furniture.

Mediterranean agriculture—A form of specialized agriculture in which crops grown in a Mediterranean climate of warm year-round temperatures and sunny summers (grapes, olives, figs, dates, citrus fruits, etc.) are grown.

megacity—A metropolitan area with a total population of over 10 million people according to the United Nations.

megalopolis—A group of supercities that have merged together into one large urban area.

mentifact—Nonmaterial parts of a culture such as language, religion, artistic pursuits, folk stories, myths, etc.

mental map—A map in one's mind.

metes-and-bounds land survey system—A land survey system used in North America where natural boundaries such as rivers, trees, and large rocks were used to mark land boundaries.

meridian—A line of identical longitude.

migration—The movement of humans from one place to another.

Millennium Development Goals—The United Nations mandate of eight development goals designed to eliminate poverty by the year 2015.

model—A simplified generalization of something in real life.

modern commercial agriculture—Large-scale agricultural production for profit using specialized methods, technologies, and genetically engineered seeds.

monoculture—The production of a single crop for commercial markets (corn, wheat, rice, etc.).

monotheism—A religion that worships one god.

more developed countries (MDCs)—Countries such as the United States, Germany, and Australia who have the highest levels of economic development.

multiple-nuclei model—A model of urban land use developed by Harris and Ullman based on separated and specialized multiple nuclei.

multiplier effect—The ratio of non-basic jobs to basic jobs that shows the effect basic job creation has on the creation of non-basic jobs.

nation—A unified group of people with a common culture.

nationalism—A strong love of, and loyalty to, one's country.

nation-state—A state in which over 90 percent of the population is comprised of a specific culture or group of people.

neo-colonialism—The periphery's continued exploitation by, and dependency on, the core in modern times even though they are no longer colonies.

neo-Fordism—The evolution of mass production into a more responsive system geared to the nuances of mass consumption by using flexible production systems that allow production processes to shift quickly between various products.

Neo-Malthusianism—the belief that population growth has a tendency to exceed food supply but that government policies can successfully rein this growth in.

New Urbanism—An urban design movement that emphasizes the pedestrian-friendly return to earlier close-knit neighborhoods and a sense of community.

non-basic sector—Goods and services produced by urban workers for people employed within the urban area.

nonmaterial culture—Mentifacts (language, religion, artistic pursuits, folk stories, myths, etc.) and sociofacts (educational and political institutions, religious organizations, family structure, etc.) that comprise a culture.

offshoring—The practice of contracting with a third-party service provider in another country to take over or supervise part of the business operations.

organic farming—The process of producing food naturally without the use of synthetic fertilizers, pesticides, and other inputs.

outsourcing—The production of goods and parts abroad for sale in one's own country.

pastoralism—A form of subsistence agriculture in which animals are herded in a seasonal migratory pattern.

pidgin—A simplified language created by merging two other languages.

perceptual region—A region defined by feelings and prejudices that may or may not be true. A region derived from one's mental map.

perforated state—A state that totally surrounds another country, such as South Africa (which surrounds Lesotho) or Italy (which surrounds San Marino).

physiologic density—The number of persons per unit of agricultural land.

place—Another word for location.

place utility—A person's satisfaction or dissatisfaction with a place.

placelessness—The loss of a place's unique flavor and identity due to the standardizing influence of popular culture and globalization.

plantation agriculture—Monocropping, or planting a single crop for profit, is a specialized form of agriculture and is usually located near the former colonial markets.

polyculture—The production of several crops.

population density—The number of persons per unit of land area.

population diagram—A model that shows the composition of a population by age and sex. Also called an age-sex pyramid.

population momentum—The propensity for a growing population to continue growing even though fertility is declining because of their young age distribution.

polytheism—A religion that worships more than one god.

popular culture—The ever-changing cultural norms associated with a large, diverse group of people who are very influenced by mass media, mass production, and mass merchandising.

possibilism—The theory that the physical environment merely establishes limits of what is possible on the human population.

primate city—A city that is at least twice as large as the next largest city and more than twice as significant (not just the largest city in a country).

primary economic activity—An economic activity that takes something from the ground (farming, mining, forestry, etc.).

projection—A type of map based on representing a round Earth on a flat piece of paper with the resulting inaccuracies determining the best use of the particular type.

prorupt state or **protruded state**—A state, such as Thailand or Myanmar (Burma), that is round in shape with a large extension.

protolanguage—A reconstructed ancestral language that forms the basis for a language family.

public housing—Government-constructed and regulated low-income housing in urban areas.

pull factor of migration—Factors such as better job opportunities or a more pleasant climate that "pull" or attract a migrant to a new area.

push factor of migration—Factors such as war, high crime, or overcrowding that "push" a migrant to a new region.

quaternary economic activities—Economic activities that deal with information and knowledge processing.

quinary economic activities—The economic activities that deal with the highest level of decision-making in both the government and private sectors of the economy.

race—A group of people with a common biological ancestor.

rank-size rule—The rule proposed by Zipf that states that if all cities in a country are placed in order from the largest to the smallest, the second largest city would have about ½ the population of the largest city, the third largest city would have about ⅓ the population of the largest city, the fourth largest city about ¼ the population of the largest city, etc.

rate of natural increase (NIR)—the crude birth rate minus the crude death rate.

rectangular land survey system—A system using rectangular grid divisions to divide new land settlements after the United States won independence from England.

region—An area that displays a common trait such as culture, government, language, landform, etc.

relative location—The location of a place in relation to the location of other places.

relict boundary—An old boundary between countries that is no longer used.

remote sensing—The process of detecting the nature of an area from a distance.

replacement level—The population level necessary to assure the population continues to replace itself.

representative fraction—The scale of a map represented as a ratio or a fraction, such as 1:25,000.

Rostow's model of economic development—A model of development for countries based on stages of economic growth and modernization. Also called modernization theory.

rural-to-urban migration—The movement of people from the countryside to the city usually in search of economic opportunities (jobs) and a better life (both "pull" factors of migration).

scale—The degree of generalization on a map. Scale can also mean the size of a unit on a map as a ratio of its size on the map to the same units on the Earth's surface.

secondary economic activities—Economic activities that involve the processing of raw materials into finished goods by manufacturing.

sector model—The model of urban land use developed by Hoyt that shows urban growth in pie-shaped wedges, or sectors, based on transportation improvements.

secularism—The rejection of all religious beliefs and is spreading rapidly in certain areas of the world such as Europe.

segregation—The physical separation of two groups of a population (in the United States this is usually based on race).

sense of place—The special perception we have of a certain place based on our feelings, emotions, and associations with that place.

separatism—The striving to become separate from a larger group.

Second Agricultural Revolution—An agricultural revolution starting in the seventeenth century that increased efficiency of crop production and distribution through use of new machinery.

sedentary—The condition where a group of humans is able to live in one location and grow crops and raise animals.

sequent occupance—The concept that successive societies leave their cultural imprints on a place, each contributing to the cumulative cultural landscape.

shamanism—A form of tribal, or traditional, religion that reveres a particular person, the shaman, as one with special healing or magic powers.

shifting agriculture—The form of subsistence agriculture in which crops are grown in different fields on a rotating basis.

site—The physical location of a place.

situation—The location of a place based on its relation to other places.

specialty farming—Farming that grows crops to provide small upscale niche markets with fresh produce.

sociofacts—The educational and political institutions, religious organizations, family structure, etc. that make up the nonmaterial aspects of a culture.

sovereignty—The internationally recognized exercise of a country's power over its people and territory.

space—The extent of area that is occupied by something.

spatial diffusion—The spread of something over time or space.

spread effects—Benefits to the peripheral region that accrue because of economic development in the nearby core region.

state—A country, or a political unit in to which the Earth is divided.

step migration—The series of small moves of a migrant to reach a destination.

subsequent boundary—A boundary drawn after a cultural landscape is already in place.

subsistence agriculture—A form of agriculture in which everything that is produced is consumed by that population. Forms of subsistence agriculture include shifting, swidden/slash-and-burn, and intensive subsistence.

suburbanization—The movement of people from urban core areas to the surrounding outer edges of the cities.

supercity—A very large city.

superimposed boundary—A boundary forced on a territory after existing boundaries are already in place.

supranationalism—The association of three or more states for mutual benefit.

sustainability—The principle that we must meet our present needs without compromising the ability of future generations to meet their needs.

sustainable development—The concept that it is possible to balance economic growth without jeopardizing the environment and equitable human access.

swidden agriculture—The form of subsistence agriculture in which crops are grown in different fields on a rotating basis. Also called shifting agriculture or slash-and-burn agriculture.

syncretism—The birth of a new culture trait from blending two or more cultural traits.

taboo—A potent form of cultural barrier that prevents certain habits or new ideas from establishing themselves in a society due to already-established prohibitions, customs, and rules.

terrorism—The use of violence in a controlled and intentional way to force attention onto issues.

tertiary economic activities—Economic activities that provide services.

tipping point—The point at which a critical number of minority inhabitants is reached and triggers an outmigration of charter group.

transculturation—An equal exchange of traits or influence between two culture groups.

transhumance—The constant movement of herds in a set seasonal pattern of grazing.

transnational corporations (TNCs)—Global corporations that have facilities and processes spread among several companies in a global assembly line.

truck farming—Commercial gardening and fruit farming in the United States.

uneven development—The huge contrast of wealthy neighborhoods and poor neighborhoods found within urban areas and the continuing uneven allocation of funds to foster this condition.

uniform region—A region with a high level of consistency in a certain cultural or physical attribute (also a formal region).

unitary state—A state with a strong central government that retains most of the political power.

universalizing religion—A religion in which anyone can become a member.

urbanization—The rapid growth of, and migration to, large cities.

urban renewal—The process of identifying properties in inner city neighborhoods that are then acquired, cleared of residents and structures, and handed over to private investors or public agencies for construction of parks, schools, or new housing.

urban sprawl—A separate-use system of residential housing neighborhoods on the outskirts of urban areas that do not contain retail activities. Also called conventional suburban development (CSD).

urban subsistence farming—The cultivation of small city gardens for food in the cities of the developing world.

vernacular region—A popular region that is named for the way people perceive it.

vertical integration—Contracts between farmer and producer in the agricultural industry.

von Thünen's agricultural land use model—A model of agricultural land use that illustrates the relationship between the cost of land and transportation costs involved in getting a product to market.

world city—A global city that serves as an important linkage or connection point in the global economic system.

world-systems theory—The theory, developed by Immanual Wallerstein, that there is only one world system in which all nation-states historically compete for capital and labor.

zero population growth (ZPG)—A condition in which births plus immigration equals deaths plus emigration for individual countries.

KEY GEOGRAPHIC MODELS AND THEIR CREATORS

GEOGRAPHER	AP HUMAN GEOGRAPHY TOPIC	MODEL/THEORY
Carl Sauer	Cultural Geography	Cultural Landscapes
H. Carey	Economic Geography	Gravity Model
Manuel Castells	Economic Geography	Technopoles
Peter Hall	Economic Geography	Technopoles
August Losch	Economic Geography	Agglomeration/Spatial Influence
W. W. Rostow	Economic Geography	Economic Development
Immanuel Wallerstein	Economic Geography	Core-Periphery Model
Immanual Wallerstein	Economic Geography	World Systems Model
Alfred Weber	Economic Geography	Location of Industry Theory/ Least Cost/Agglomeration
Vidal de la Blache	Nature/Environment	Possibilism
Friedrich Ratzel	Nature/Environment	Environmental Determinism
Alfred Wegener	Nature/Environment	Plate Tectonic Theory
Halford MacKinder	Political Geography	Heartland Theory
Alfred Mahan	Political Geography	Sea Power Theory
Friedrich Ratzel	Political Geography	Organic Theory of Nations
Nicholas Spykman	Political Geography	Rimland Theory
Paul Ehrlich and Lester Brown	Population	Neo-Malthusianism
Thomas Malthus	Population	Malthusian Theory
E. G. Ravenstein	Population	Laws of Migration
Warren Thompson	Population	Demographic Transition Model
Esther Boserup	Population/Agriculture	Boserup Thesis
Ernest Burgess	Rural Geography	Concentric Zone Model
J. H. von Thünen	Rural Geography	Agriculture Model
John Borchert	Urban Geography	Stages of Evolution of American Metropolis
Walter Christaller	Urban Geography	Central Place Theory
Homer Hoyt	Urban Geography	Urban Sector Model
E. L. Ullman and Chauncey Harris	Urban Geography	Multiple Nuclei Model

RECOMMENDED READING

The Power of Place by Harm de Blij. How geography determines destiny.

Why Geography Matters by Harm de Blij. The title says it all. *Read it!*

The Geography of Bliss by Eric Weiner. A travelogue about where to live a happy life.

Confucius Lives Next Door by T. R. Reid. How Confucius still impacts Asian societies today.

The Fortune Cookie Chronicles—Adventures in the World of Chinese Food by Jennifer 8 Lee (check out that middle name). Chinese immigration experience through food.

A Walk in the Woods: Rediscovering America on the Appalachian Trail by Bill Bryson. A humorous but fascinating hike up the Appalachian Mountains. Laugh out loud!

Fast Food Nation by Eric Schlosser. As McDonald's says, "Have it your way." Very revealing!

Maphead by Ken Jennings. A must "read" for map lovers. Written as a travelogue of sorts.

Isaac's Storm by Erik Larson. The deadliest storm in U.S. history changes weather predicting forever.

What Every American Should Know About the Rest of the World by M. L. Rossi. Your snapshot of the world! Excellent "read."

Behind the Beautiful Forevers: Life, Death, and Hope in a Mumbai Undercity by Katherine Boo. This book has won soooo many awards and is a "must-read." You won't be sorry!

Jihad vs. McWorld by Benjamin Barber. Global capitalism and transnational corporations.

Nine Parts of Desire by Geraldine Brooks. The hidden life of Muslim women.

Prisoners of Geography: Ten Maps That Explain Everything About the World by Tim Marshall. How geography shapes international relations and the motivations of the world's governments. A quick read.

Where the Bluebird Sings to the Lemonade Springs by Wallace Stegner. Essays on the American West—the power of place demonstrated by one of my favorite authors ever.

Them by Nathan McCall. A quick read that reveals how gentrification really works.

Cadillac Desert: The American West and Its Disappearing Water by Marc Reisner. The definitive history of water resources in the American West—a lesson in the political economy of limited resources anywhere.

Infidel by Ayaan Hirsi Ali. A riveting biography of a Somalian woman on life as a Muslim girl and woman.

City of Joy by Dominique Lapierre. A description of daily life in an Indian city.

Geopolitics and Empire: The Legacy of Halford Mackinder by Gerry Kearns. International relations.

Geography of Nowhere: The Rise and Decline of America's Man-Made Landscape by James Howard Kunstler. Learn about suburbanization and urban development in the U.S. Have we lost our sense of place?

States of Mind by Brad Herzog. A trip to Small Town, USA: Wisdom, Faith, Freedom, Harmony, Love, Justice, Glory, Friendship—all towns full of history and life. Learn about life and what is really important.

Turn Here for Sweet Corn: Organic Farming Works by Atina Diffley. A fun account of organic farming.

Worlds Apart: Poverty and Politics in Rural America by Cynthia Duncan. Case studies of rural poverty in Appalachia, New England, and the Mississippi Delta.

Factory Girls: From Village to City in a Changing China by Leslie Chang. Demonstrates how the mass movement from rural villages to cities is transforming Chinese society.

Population
US Census Bureau (census information and data)
www.census.gov
Population Reference Bureau (population information)
www.prb.org

Urban Geography
Lincoln Institute of Land Policy
www.lincolninst.edu

Culture
Peace Corps (information on countries where it works)
www.peacecorps.gov/home/html

Agriculture, Economic Geography
CTI Centre for Geography, Geology, & Meteorology
(links to human geography topics including agriculture, development geography, economic geography)
http://www2.le.ac.uk/departments/geography

Geospatial
National Geographic Society at
http://www.nationalgeographic.org/encyclopedia/geographic-information-system-gis/

Global Geography
UN Environment Programme (UNEP) (links to global issues and resource databases)
www.unep.ch

Physical Geography
US Geological Survey (maps, data, and resources for geographers)
www.usgs.gov

General
ThoughtCo. Geography (hyperlinks to specific areas of geography)
https://www.thoughtco.com/geography-4133035
National Geographic Society (archive of maps, articles, videos, etc.)
www.nationalgeographic.com

Map Practice, Games, Quizzes, Review Activities
Lizard Point (test your geography knowledge)
www.lizardpoint.com/fun/geoquiz
Shepard Software (geography games)
www.sheppardsoftware.com/web_games.htm
Maps.com (map games)
www.maps.com/FunFacts.aspx?nav=FF#
Quia Web (learning activities, quizzes)
www.quia.com

CIA World Factbook, 2010
The Green Editor, Wikimedia Commons, 2008
United States Geological Survey
US Census Bureau
US Department of Agriculture
World Bank

The Cross-Platform Prep Course

McGraw-Hill Education's multi-platform course gives you a variety of tools to help you raise your test scores. Whether you're studying at home, in the library, or on-the-go, you can find practice content in the format you need—print, online, or mobile.

Print Book

This print book gives you the tools you need to ace the test. In its pages you'll find smart test-taking strategies, in-depth reviews of key topics, and ample practice questions and tests. See the Welcome section of your book for a step-by-step guide to its features.

Online Platform

The Cross-Platform Prep Course gives you additional study and practice content that you can access *anytime, anywhere*. You can create a personalized study plan based on your test date that sets daily goals to keep you on track. Integrated lessons provide important review of key topics. Practice questions, exams, and flashcards give you the practice you need to build test-taking confidence. The game center is filled with challenging games that allow you to practice your new skills in a fun and engaging way. And, you can even interact with other test-takers in the discussion section and gain valuable peer support.

Getting Started

To get started, open your account on the online platform:

Go to www.xplatform.mhprofessional.com

↓

Enter your access code, which you can find on the inside back cover of your book

↓

Provide your name and e-mail address to open your account and create a password

↓

Click "Start Studying" to enter the platform

It's as simple as that. You're ready to start studying online.

Your Personalized Study Plan

First, select your test date on the calendar, and you'll be on your way to creating your personalized study plan. Your study plan will help you stay organized and on track and will guide you through the course in the most efficient way. It is tailored to *your* schedule and features daily tasks that are broken down into manageable goals. You can adjust your test date at any time and your daily tasks will be reorganized into an updated plan.

You can track your progress in real time on the Study Plan Dashboard. The "Today's Knowledge Goal" progress bar gives you up-to-the-minute feedback on your daily goal. Fulfilling this every time you log on is the most efficient way to work through the entire course. You always get an instant view of where you stand in the entire course with the Study Plan Progress bar.

If you need to exit the program before completing a task, you can return to the Study Plan Dashboard at any time. Just click the Study Task icon and you can automatically pick up where you left off.

Practice Tests

One of the first tasks in your personalized study plan is to take the Diagnostic Test. At the end of the test, a detailed evaluation of your strengths and weaknesses shows the areas where you need the most focus. You can review your practice test results either by the question category to see broad trends or question-by-question for a more in-depth look.

The full-length tests are designed to simulate the real thing. Try to simulate actual testing conditions and be sure you set aside enough time to complete the full-length test. You'll learn to pace yourself so that you can work toward the best possible score on test day.

Tests	📋 Dashboard	🎚 Confidence Levels	✏ Notes	🔖 Bookmarks				

SAT Diagnostic Test: Reading

	Question Review Category Scores						Review All
	# ▾	**✔ ⇕**	**Preview (Click question preview to expand)**	**Time ⇕**	**Difficulty ⇕**	
	1	✓	In the first paragraph, Karl Smith's work is presented primarily as a controversial sociological hypothesis. a warning about potentially dangerous...	0 min 19 sec	Moderate	Review
	2	✗	The author suggests that promising research in the social sciences is sometimes ignored because it is not presented by authorities with the proper ...	0 min 2 sec	Easy	Review
	3	✓	The author suggests that promising research in the social sciences is sometimes ignored because it is not presented by authorities with the pro...	0 min 3 sec	Easy	Review
	4	✓	According to the graph, which of the following is closest to the percent increase in violent crime in America from 1963 to 1993? 600% 400% 75% 2...	0 min 1 sec	Expert	Review
	5	✓	According to the graph, which decade of violent crime statistics provides the LEAST support to Rick Nevin's hypothesis? 1963–1973 1980–1990 1983–...	0 min 2 sec	Difficult	Review
	6	✗	The author mentions "sales of vinyl LPs" (line 74) primarily as an example of another economic factor that may explain a social trend. how harmful...	0 min 1 sec	Easy	Review

66%
Correct

• • •

Questions Taken
52 of 52

Avg. Answer Time
0 min 59 sec

Avg. Correct Answer Time
0 min 48 sec

Avg. Incorrect Answer Time
1 min 2 sec

Lessons

The lessons in the online platform are divided into manageable pieces that let you build knowledge and confidence in a progressive way. They cover the full range of topics that you're likely to see on your test.

After you complete a lesson, mark your confidence level. (You must indicate a confidence level in order to count your progress and move on to the next task.) You can also filter the lessons by confidence levels to see the areas you have mastered and those that you might need to revisit.

> *Use the bookmark feature to easily refer back to a concept or leave a note to remember your thoughts or questions about a particular topic.*

Lessons   Table of Contents   Confidence Levels   Notes   Bookmarks

Browse

◀   ▶   What's new in the redesigned SAT?

What's new in the redesigned SAT?

Beginning in spring 2016, the redesigned SAT features ten major changes.

1. More time per question

The redesigned SAT gives you more time per question, making it less likely that you will underperform due to time restrictions.

Section	Old SAT Time Per Question	New SAT Time Per Question
Writing and Language	43 seconds (49 questions, 35 mins)	48 seconds (44 questions, 35 mins)
Mathematics	78 seconds (54 questions, 70 mins)	84 seconds (57 questions, 80 mins)
Reading	63 seconds (67 questions in 70 mins)	75 seconds (52 questions, 65 mins)

Rate Your Confidence

High

Medium

Low

Continue »

Category :
Attacking the New SAT: Twelve FAQs

Practice Questions

All of the practice questions are reflective of actual exams and simulate the test-taking experience. The "Review Answer" button gives you immediate feedback on your answer. Each question includes a rationale that explains why the correct answer is right and the others are wrong. To explore any topic further, you can find detailed explanations by clicking the "Help me learn about this topic" link.

Quantitative-Data Sufficiency

⏱ This question: 00:17   ⏱ Total: 00:17   Done practicing

Question 1 of 24

Review Answer ON

Direction :The following data sufficiency problem consist of a question and two statements, labeled (1) and (2), in which certain data are given. You have to decide whether the data given in the statements are *sufficient* for answering the question.
A. Statement (1) ALONE is sufficient, but statement (2) alone is not sufficient.
B. Statement (2) ALONE is sufficient, but statement (1) alone is not sufficient.
C. BOTH statements TOGETHER are sufficient, but NEITHER statement ALONE is sufficient.
D. EACH statement ALONE is sufficient.
E. Statements (1) and (2) TOGETHER are NOT sufficient.

Q. Is x an integer?

(1) x is evenly divisible by $\frac{1}{2}$

(2) x is evenly divisible by 2.

Solution:
The correct answer is B.
A reminder: The question stem starts with *is*, so this is a *yes* or *no* problem. The first step is to determine whether statement (1) is sufficient, which we can do by trying out some real numbers. If x is 2, which is evenly divisible by $\frac{1}{2}$ then the answer would be *yes*. But if x were 1.5, which is also evenly divisible by $\frac{1}{2}$ then the answer would be *no*. Since you can get either *yes* or *no*, statement (1) is not sufficient and you should cross off A and D. Now let's move on to statement (2). There are no non-integer numbers that are divisible by 2, so *yes* is the only possibility. Statement (2) is sufficient, so we can eliminate C and E. Thus the answer is **B**.

❌ Incorrect

Help me learn about this topic

Correct answer   Your answer

A
B
C
D   ✕
E

Continue

Difficulty Level: Unrated

You can go to the Practice Dashboard to find an overview of your performance in the different categories and sub-categories.

Question Categories		
Category Name	**Completion**	**% Correct**
Quantitative-Problem Solving	94 of 297	72%
Arithmetic	75 of 75	84%
Elementary Algebra	35 of 189	60%
Geometry	0 of 49	--
Quantitative-Data Sufficiency	49 of 49	81%
Arithmetic	6 of 6	75%
Elementary Algebra	30 of 30	86%
Geometry	13 of 13	82%
Verbal	0 of 129	--
Reading Comprehension	0 of 46	--
Critical Reasoning	0 of 64	--
Sentence Correction	0 of 19	--

Dashboard

77% Correct

Questions Taken
159 of 491

Avg. Answer Time
2 min 52 sec

Avg. Correct Answer Time
2 min 20 sec

Avg. Incorrect Answer Time
3 min 6 sec

Avg. Session Duration
18 min 41 sec

Practice   Dashboard   Confidence Levels   Notes   Bookmarks

Reset All Questions

Dashboard

The dashboard is constantly updating to reflect your progress and performance. The Percentile Rank icon shows your position relative to all the other students enrolled in the course. You can also find information on your average scores in practice questions and exams.

A detailed overview of your strengths and weaknesses shows your proficiency in a category based on your answers and difficulty of the questions. By viewing your strengths and weaknesses, you can focus your study on areas where you need the most help.

Strengths & Weaknesses ℹ

Writing and Language

Beginner   Basic   Intermediate   Proficient   Advanced   Expert

Reading

Beginner   Basic   Intermediate   Proficient   Advanced   Expert

Math

Beginner   Basic   Intermediate   Proficient   Advanced   Expert

The Heart of Algebra	N/A	Beginner	Basic	Intermediate	Proficient	Advanced	Expert
Advanced Mathematics	N/A	Beginner	Basic	Intermediate	Proficient	Advanced	Expert
Additional Topics	N/A	Beginner	Basic	Intermediate	Proficient	Advanced	Expert

🔒 Riding dolphins
🔒 What doesn't kill yo...
🔒 Good Karma
🔒 Stenographer

Top Performers

David Flores
Jenny
Elle
Shadaj L
Grant Foray
Coco Ma
Angela Jeon
Sarah Kim
Madison McClane
Gabi Kreuscher
...
Tenant Admin

Flashcards

The hundreds of flashcards are perfect for learning key terms quickly, and the interactive format gives you immediate feedback. You can filter the cards by category and confidence level for a more organized approach. Or, you can shuffle them up for a more general challenge.

All th

includ

all fra

Real Numbers

1 of 14

Did you get it right?

| No | Kinda | Yes |

Another way to customize the flashcards is to create your own sets. You can either keep these private or share or them with the public. Subscribe to Community Sets to access sets from other students preparing for the same exam.

Flashcards   Study   Community Sets   My Sets

Create Set

Title

Math review

Description

Topic – Select one of our topics from the dropdown or add your own

Math equations

Access
- Public
- Private

Create Set   Cancel

Game Center

Play a game in the Game Center to test your knowledge of key concepts in a challenging but fun environment. Increase the difficulty level and complete the games quickly to build your highest score. Be sure to check the leaderboard to see who's on top!

Game Center ⊞ Dashboard ▣ Card Picker ◎ Card Hunter I ◎ Card Hunter II ♥ Card Coupler ▣ Card Sweeper

Card Picker

Your highest score: 0
Your rank: Not yet determined

Start playing

Leaderboard
Top 1: Alyssa - 232001
Top 2: Fatima - 188598
Top 3: Sheena Lu - 80160

Card Hunter I

Your highest score: 0
Your rank: Not yet determined

Start playing

Leaderboard
Top 1: Siddh - 1997
Top 2: Siddh - 1997
Top 3: Eileen - 1915

Card Hunter II

Your highest score: 0
Your rank: Not yet determined

Start playing

Leaderboard
Top 1: Siddh - 23990
Top 2: Eileen - 9037
Top 3: Ira - 8927

Card Coupler

Your highest score: 0
Your rank: Not yet determined

Start playing

Leaderboard
Top 1: Toni - 1398
Top 2: Siddh - 1062
Top 3: Ri - 1051

Social Community

Interact with other students who are preparing for the same test. Start a discussion, reply to a post, or even upload files to share. You can search the archives for common topics or start your own private discussion with friends.

Discussions Public Private

Public Discussions ❶   Filter ▾

What do you want to discuss...

PA Hey, I have to take the SAT Exam in 55 days and i'm just starting to study now. Is it possible or should I take the exam at a later date?

Created 4 days ago by Prosperity Antoine | 0 replies | Last activity: 4 days ago
Reply to this Comment

RJ Is it possible to practice a full day exam as i would when walking into to take the SAT???

Created 2 months ago by River Jones | 0 replies | Last activity: 2 months ago
Reply to this Comment

Mobile App

The companion mobile app lets you toggle between the online platform and your mobile device without missing a beat. Whether you access the course online or from your smartphone or tablet, you'll pick up exactly where you left off.

Go to the iTunes or Google Play stores and search "McGraw-Hill Education Cross-Platform App" to download the companion iOS or Android app. Enter your e-mail address and the same password you created for the online platform to open your account.

Now, let's get started!